# THE NEW MAJORITY

A Look at What the Preponderance of Women in Journalism Education Means to the Schools and to the Professions

The Women's Project
College of Journalism
University of Maryland
Funded by the Gannett Foundation

Maurine H. Beasley
Kathryn T. Theus

UNIVERSITY
PRESS OF
AMERICA

Lanham • New York • London

Copyright © 1988 by

University Press of America,® Inc.

4720 Boston Way
Lanham, MD 20706

3 Henrietta Street
London WC2E 8LU England

All rights reserved

Printed in the United States of America

British Cataloging in Publication Information Available

**Library of Congress Cataloging-in-Publication Data**

Beasley, Maurine Hoffman.
The new majority : a look at what the preponderance of women in
journalism education means to the schools and to the professions /
Maurine H. Beasley, Kathryn T. Theus. p. cm.
"The Women's Project, College of Journalism, University of Maryland."
Bibliography: p. Includes index.
1. Women in the press—United States—History—20th century.
2. Journalism—United States—Study and teaching—Case studies.
3. University of Maryland, College Park. College of Journalism.
Women's Project—Case studies. 4. Women journalists—Training of,—
United States—Case studies. I. Theus, Kathryn T., 1945– .
II. University of Maryland, College Park. College of Journalism. Women's Project. III. Title.
PN4888.W65B4    1988
302.2'34'0973—dc 19    88–2456 CIP
ISBN 0–8191–6914–5 (alk. paper)
ISBN 0–8191–6915–3 (pbk. ; alk. paper)

All University Press of America books are produced on acid-free
paper which exceeds the minimum standards set by the National
Historical Publications and Records Commission.

# TABLE OF CONTENTS

### Part I:

### From Nellie Bly and Jennie June to Journalism School

Chapter 1. Sob Sisters and a Few Footholds: 1908-1930 .......... 5
Chapter 2. The Numbers Grow, and a War Helps: 1931-1960 .... 21
Chapter 3. A New Majority, With Little Change in the Schools: 1961-1985 ............................. 38

### Part II:

### One School Looks at Itself: The University of Maryland Study

Chapter 4. Alumni, Employers and Students Respond .......... 53
Chapter 5. Statistical Summary of Three Surveys ............... 60
Chapter 6. Women in the Field Offer Their Views ............. 87
Chapter 7. Four Challenges That Were Identified, and What May Be Done About Them ...................... 116
           Acquiring Better Writing Skills ................... 116
           Finding Suitable Role Models .................... 119
           Persuading Employers, and Not Settling for Less .... 125
           Reconciling Career and Family Life ................ 131

### Epilogue:

### Next Steps for Professionals and Educators

### Appendices:

A. Chronology of "Firsts" by Women in Journalism Education .. 145
B. Selected Previous Research on Women Journalism Students and Graduates ........................................... 147
C. Survey Instruments ....................................... 148

### Selected Bibliography

### Index

# About This Study

The College of Journalism at the University of Maryland wanted to explore the ramifications of the change from a male majority to a female majority among journalism students nationally. Should the schools be doing anything differently? How will the professions served by journalism education be affected, and what will (or should) change there? We requested and were given a grant from the Gannett Foundation to conduct this two-year study.

It does not purport to explore the issues in the depth ultimately required. It does, however, establish an important historical and contemporary framework, identify and briefly examine significant issues for future analysis, summarize past studies of parts of this subject, and offer recommendations for action and future study.

The book is the work of women faculty members in the College of Journalism. Maurine H. Beasley, professor, was project director. Kathryn T. Theus, then assistant dean of the College and director of undergraduate studies, was associate director of the project. Theus is now associate director of the National Center on Postsecondary Governance and Finance, University of Maryland. The initial employer survey was the work of Barbara Hines, now at Howard University. Graduate students who assisted were Kathy Lemke, Laurie Evans and Roz Tartaglione.

The book is based on a report originally issued in a limited number of copies in October 1985.

We would like to acknowledge the assistance and encouragement of colleagues at other universities: Marion Marzolf, University of Michigan; Jean Gaddy Wilson, University of Missouri; and Katherine C. McAdams, formerly of the University of North Carolina and now at the University of Maryland.

> Reese Cleghorn
> Dean
> College of Journalism
> University of Maryland
> College Park, Md.

October 1987

# PART I:

# From Nellie Bly and Jennie June to Journalism School

# Chapter 1

# Sob Sisters and a Few Footholds: 1908–1930

At its beginnings a century ago, journalism education was an inhospitable, if not actually hostile, field for women. Yet in spite of prejudice in hiring and widespread fears that they would lose their femininity by emulating male journalists, women were not deterred from enrolling in journalism schools. Over the years so many have flocked to colleges offering journalism training that by 1977 the percentage of women students enrolled in journalism nationally had surpassed that of men students. Since then the percentage of women has continued to increase, giving rise to concern that the field is becoming "feminized," and may become a "pink-collar" ghetto comparable to nursing.[1]

Until now almost no attempt has been made to study the historical factors that have resulted in this trend. Why have journalism schools drawn women students even though these students traditionally have had more difficulty than their male counterparts in moving into the job market? What social and cultural factors have operated within these schools themselves to address women students? To what degree has journalism education reinforced social stereotypes regarding a restricted role for women and to what degree has it broadened women's role? And, most important of all, what can be learned from an historical examination of women's participation in journalism education that will enhance understanding of the present enrollment patterns?

The goal of traditional historical research in this book is to increase understanding of the current gender shift by tracing the experience of women within journalism education during its formative period. The following research questions have been asked: (1) Did early journalism education offer women the same kind of preparation offered men? (2) Were women graduates prepared to compete with men in the job market? (3) What factors led women to study at the first journalism schools? To investigate these questions this study has made use of general histories of journalism education, memoirs and biographies of pioneer journalism graduates and educators, manuscript collections and publications pertaining to the first journalism schools, early textbooks, and files of *The Matrix,* formerly the official publication of Women in Communications, which began as Theta Sigma Phi, a sorority for journalism students. These materials have been selected to provide an overview of the types of experiences afforded to the first women graduates.

When academic training in journalism first was proposed in the post-Civil War era, all references were to instruction for "young men." General Robert E. Lee is credited with having planned the first course of instruction in journalism at the college level. As president of the all-male Washington College (now Washington and Lee University), he proposed in 1869 that scholarships be established to allow students to prepare for newspaper careers by receiving instruction in printing at a commercial shop. The scholarships were never awarded. In line with Lee's idea, however, Kansas State College (now University) initiated a course in printing for journalists in 1873. In 1878, the University of Missouri began formal collegiate teaching of journalism by offering a course in the history of journalism in the English department.[2]

But it was a woman, Martha Louise Rayne, a figure usually omitted from the history of journalism, who deserves the credit for establishing the first actual school of journalism in the world. In 1886 she set up a private school in Detroit to give practical journalistic training to women. Rayne, a novelist and journalist who had written for the *Chicago Tribune* and the *Detroit Free Press,* proposed her school in the *Free Press* in 1885. Male journalists immediately scoffed. "The wicked American journalist, without exception, made fun of the proposal," one *Free Press* article stated. When she proceeded to open her school, another Detroit paper noted, "Many newspapers pooh-pooh the idea, but Mrs. Rayne is a thorough journalist, and may do the laughing herself later."[3]

The school, apparently called simply Mrs. Rayne's School of Journalism, continued until about 1900. Although it was not a formal academic institution, its course of study somewhat paralleled that given subsequently in colleges. A handbill advertising the school listed the course of study: "Preparation of manuscript. Words and how to use them. The art of saying things. Literary style. The art of taking pains. Reporting, essay writing, reviews, sketches, short stories, forms of poetry, novel-writing, etc." Creative writing was stressed in part because newspapers of the era published much literary content.[4]

Mrs. Rayne saw the potential for training women because at the end of the nineteenth century a small but growing number of women were beginning to seek careers in journalism. In 1872, Frederic Hudson of the *New York Herald* commented on this trend: "There are now quite a number of female managers and publishers of newspapers in the United States. They do not push themselves forward or make themselves very conspicuous in their profession. They are not propagandists; they are simply getting a living, and making what money they can without ostentation." To Hudson, as it would be to many later commentators, the question of proper behavior for women in newspaper offices would be of paramount interest. Men were expected to be aggressive. Women were not.[5]

A year before opening her school, Mrs. Rayne had counseled women in a popular book of advice titled *What Can a Woman Do; Or Her Position in the Business and Literary World.* One chapter explained local newspapers were willing to pay for "pleasant, readable sketches" and that some papers even had women reporters. In this category were listed Mrs. Sallie Van Pelt, a baseball reporter in Iowa, and a Mrs. Fitzgerald, a night police reporter for the *Chicago Inter-Ocean,* although Mrs. Rayne pointed out most women reporters covered meetings, weddings and social events.[6]

Her observations of women journalists were borne out by official statistics. In 1870, the first year the U.S. census contained a category of persons who described themselves as journalists, only 35 women so listed themselves, less than 0.6 percent of the total. By 1880 the number of women had increased to 288 out of a total of 12,308, or 2 percent of the total. Ten years later it had climbed again to 888, out of a total of 21,849, or 4 percent.[7]

Included in the statistics were a few notable women like Elizabeth Cochrane, who, as "Nellie Bly," attained fame by stunts such as feigning madness to investigate a mental hospital and racing around the world. But these figures in general reflected the women drawn into newspaper work by the addition of material aimed at women readers and shoppers. This included wedding and society notes, women's columns, and advice on fashion, housekeeping and cooking. The census figures, which presumably included only those with full-time paid positions, did not include an untold number of others who sold freelance contributions, including poetry and stories, aimed at women readers.[8]

Consequently journalism represented a new occupational area for American women in the Victorian era. One of the first to recognize its potential was Jane Cunningham Croly, who, as "Jennie June," pioneered the first syndicated women's column in the *New York Dispatch* in 1859. After women were barred from attending a banquet for Charles Dickens sponsored by the New York press corps, Mrs. Croly was determined to improve their status. She organized Sorosis, the nation's oldest women's club, in 1868. Subsequently she helped form the General Federation of Women's Clubs as well as the Women's Press Club of New York, of which she was president for life.[9]

Mrs. Croly also became the first known woman to teach journalism at the college level. In 1896 she was employed to teach a journalism course at the New Rutgers Institute for Young Ladies. This was a private school in New York, previously known as the Rutgers Female College. (It had no connection with Rutgers University at New Brunswick, New Jersey.)[10]

Women, nevertheless, were not considered as prospective journalism students when proposals to establish journalism courses in academic institutions sparked a controversy in the newspaper industry that continued for years. Distinguished journalists, all male, argued pro and con on the advisability of college instruction for men journalists, overlooking the possibility of women students. Joseph Pulitzer of *The New York World,* who eventually endowed the school of journalism at Columbia University, argued in favor: "I see no reason why a chair in journalism, filled by a man of real talent and character, could not be made beneficial." On the opposite side, J. C. Goldsmith of *Frank Leslie's Illustrated,* contended the apprentice-system, which he called the school of "hard knocks," was most likely to produce capable editors: "Give the boy a good academical education, not omitting Latin and the modern languages, put him to writing wrappers on a large daily journal, and let him work up to the city department."[11]

In spite of a preponderance of opposition from the profession, however, by the turn of the century it was plain that academic journalism education would be a reality. The Wharton School of Business at the University of Pennsylvania listed a series of five courses in journalism in its 1893-94 catalog, and at least seven other schools, mainly in the Middle West, established instruction in journalism before 1900. The list included the University of Kansas, Denver University, Iowa State College (now University), Indiana University, the University of Michigan, the University of Nebraska and Temple University.

The first recognized school of journalism was opened at the University of Missouri in Columbia, Missouri, in 1908. Not surprisingly, it admitted women, since the university itself had accepted women for three decades, after having graduated its first two in the liberal arts in 1876. Both of these women, Ella Dimmitt and Ida Minter, soon were married and did not pursue careers, like many of the first waves of women to be graduated from state universities. In general these pioneers in co-education did not work outside the home after marriage, although they frequently exercised community leadership. This was a phenomenon soon to become apparent also among women journalism graduates.[12]

Missouri's two-year curriculum was patterned after one suggested by Dr. Charles W. Eliot, president of Harvard University, in response to a question by Pulitzer. The Missouri dean, Walter Williams, spelled out the purpose of the school in its first bulletin: To supply "well-equipped men for leadership in journalism, with high ideals and special training." Women were not mentioned. Strongly endorsed by the Missouri Press Association, the curriculum of the new school aimed to prepare graduates mainly for newspaper work. Most of the course titles made this evident: History and Principles of Journalism, Newspaper Making, Newspaper Administration, Magazine and Class Journalism (a reference to early trade publications), Newspaper Publishing, Newspaper Jurisprudence, News-Gathering, Correspondence (which covered the handling of personal items sent to small papers by amateur writers) and Office Equipment.[13]

A total of 97 students, 84 men and 13 women, enrolled in the school during its first year, although only a fraction sought to graduate in the new discipline. Six women registered for journalism classes in the first semester. Later they were hailed as "coming society editors," in the official history of the school. The first class was graduated in 1910, when five men and one woman, Mary Paxton (later Keeley), who was elected class secretary, received bachelors' degrees in journalism. Keeley taught for years at Christian College (now Columbia College), a women's school in Columbia, Missouri. She also worked for two years on the *Kansas City Post,* which made her one of the first women to work on a newspaper in Kansas City.[14]

But, if rare on the metropolitan scene, women were no strangers to journalism in rural Missouri (or in other states). The same year the University of Missouri opened its journalism school, the Missouri Press Association elected its first woman officer, Mrs. Lily Herald Frost of the *Vandalia Leader,* who became third vice-president. It is likely she was the wife of a newspaper editor and assisted her husband in his business, according to common practice.[15]

In previous years editors' wives had addressed press association conventions on the joys of combining domestic responsibilities with acting as their husbands' assistants. As Mrs. R.M. White, whose husband published the *Mexico* (Missouri) *Ledger,* put it in a paper read in 1891 to the Northeast Missouri Press Association, the editor's wife, because of her position in the community, "has the same opportunity to lead that are (sic) offered to her liege lord." She proceeded to explain, "the editor's wife may have to take care of children, do her house work, cut the wood brought in by delinquent subscribers....even get up on cold mornings and make fires, as I do. But, nevertheless, wife being the noblest sphere of women, it's better to be an editor's wife than nobody's wife at all."[16]

Dean Williams made special efforts to invite women, often those from country papers, to address students during annual Journalism Week ceremonies that honored outstanding editors and prepared graduates for the current job market. Sometimes the advice to young women was simply to work at their husbands' sides. Mrs. Florence R. Boys, woman's page editor of the *Plymouth* (Indiana) *Pilot* and publisher of a syndicated woman's page, spoke plainly at an early Journalism Week: "My woman's page was begun for my husband's paper. Finding that it was copied by other papers over the state, it occurred to us that it would be a good scheme to make of it a (syndicated) service." However, she continued, the venture was not very profitable: "It would probably be difficult, if not impossible, for a woman to make a good living on it alone. It is a good sideline for the wife or daughter of an editor." Such advice made it obvious women graduates were expected to fill roles different from, and subordinate to, those of men within the journalistic field.[17]

At the same time the University of Missouri set up a separate journalism school, other universities developed departments of journalism. By 1910 departments were organized at the state Universities of Wisconsin and Washington, New York University, a private school, and Marquette University, a Catholic institution. Classes in journalism also were being offered at other state schools: Ohio, Nebraska, Michigan, Indiana, Illinois, Kansas State, Pennsylvania, North Dakota, Oklahoma and Colorado, as well as at Cornell University. In addition, Depauw University, Greencastle, Indiana, and Bessie Tift College, a women's school at Forsyth, Georgia, both announced journalism instruction (although apparently Tift did not actually offer classes before 1923).[18]

Within journalism education men and women students soon organized into different social worlds. In 1909 ten male students at Depauw University founded Sigma Delta Chi, an honorary fraternity restricted to "upperclassmen who expected to make journalism their work," according to the organization's official history. The constitution specified chapters could be established only in colleges where a newspaper was published and "attention was given to journalistic instruction." By 1912 when the fraternity held its first national convention at Greencastle, it had established chapters at ten universities. Although Depauw was a co-educational school, no consideration was given to admitting women to the fraternity.[19]

At the University of Washington in Seattle, the establishment of a Sigma Delta Chi chapter led a group of seven women to form their own journalism sorority called Theta Sigma Phi, complete with secret motto, badge and ritual similar to those of the male fraternity. "In our relations with the masculine majority, there existed a fine spirit of bon camaraderie not unmixed with rivalry," Helen Ross Lantz, one of the founders, recalled years later. "So when the lads on the *Daily* newspaper staff had tantalized us for weeks with some sophomoric secret, we impulsively retaliated one day by appearing wearing pledge ribbons of a significance so mysterious as to baffle even ourselves....From such a frivolous beginning grew spontaneously the idea of a permanent, worthwhile organization."[20]

Concerned with upholding the conventional image of womanhood within an occupation dominated by hard-boiled men, the women tried to emphasize their purity. "We had a lot of quaint ideas in those days," Lantz wrote. "Venturing into the newspaper world, dominated by the rougher sex, would very likely have a coarsening effect upon our manners to say nothing of our morals, so we chose for our flower the violet, 'symbol of womanly modesty'."[21]

The idea of a separate journalism sorority was greeted enthusiastically by some male journalism educators. Willard G. Bleyer, dean of the department of journalism of the University of Wisconsin, telegraphed the University of Washington to get a charter for coeds at his school. Merle Thorpe, organizer of the Washington journalism department and later editor of *The Nation's Business,* also endorsed the idea of the organization. Thorpe specifically mentioned women in an early Washington catalogue, referring to "men and women intending to enter newspaper work as a profession." He encouraged the organizational efforts of Lanz, the only one of the seven founders to own a typewriter, who exhausted herself "pecking out laborious and messy looking copies of the Constitution, By-Laws and Ritual for some incipient chapter." By 1915 there were chapters at eight universities: Washington, Wisconsin, Missouri, Indiana, Kansas, Oklahoma, Oregon and Ohio State.[22]

A comparison of the subsequent lives of the founders of the two organizations shows the diversity in the careers of early men and women journalism graduates. Of the ten men who founded Sigma Delta Chi, all except two initially went into newspaper work. One, Eugene C. Pulliam, formed his own publishing company and eventually acquired the *Indianapolis Star* and the *Arizona Republic* (Phoenix). Of the remaining two, one became a teacher and the other a lawyer.[23]

The seven Theta Sigma Phi founders, six of whom married, moved into more diverse paths than the men. Olive Mauerman Smith became a teacher and writer. Rachel Marshall became a Hollywood script writer and married a Polish nobleman, who agreed to be called Mr. Marshall. Helen Graves Wakefield went into San Francisco real estate. Irene Somerville Durham became a captain of women police officers and chief of the crime prevention bureau in the Seattle police department. Georgina MacDougall Davis combined raising a family, writing and dedicating herself to Theta Sigma Phi activities. Blanche Brace, who remained single, distinguished herself with the *New York Herald Tribune* and was a publicist and short story writer. Lantz, the first national president, later noted her own "writing career lasted only a few years," during which time she acted as club editor of the *Seattle Times* and a special writer for the *Seattle Post-Intelligencer*. Unlike the men, as a group the women did not find jobs within the field for which they had prepared.[24]

Journalism education received an enormous boost in prestige in 1912 when the Pulitzer School of Journalism finally opened at Columbia University. It was established after nearly a decade of contention between Columbia officials and Joseph Pulitzer, who originally had agreed to give a $2 million endowment for the school in 1903. One disagreement was over the qualifications of students. The university insisted students should have preliminary college training, but Pulitzer did not want to bar individuals who lacked academic preparation but were otherwise suitable. The school consequently was open to men and women of good moral character who had graduated from high school and passed an entrance examination. It began on a four-year basis but those entering with a bachelor's degree could complete their coursework in a fifth year, a significant point since the school eventually limited itself to a fifth-year professional program.[25]

Women were grudgingly accepted. Speaking in 1949, Carl W. Ackerman, a member of the first graduating class and later dean at Columbia, commented that "in early days of this school there was opposition to the admission of women students." Referring to the "strong prejudices of college professors," Ackerman told of a professor asked for advice on admitting women: "...his classic reply was that no teacher could teach mathematics to a boy if there was a girl in the room and that if a boy could learn mathematics with a girl in the room he would never grow up to be a man."[26]

Columbia did not follow the Missouri plan of teaching newspaper business operations since Pulitzer himself objected to exposing journalism students to business training, holding editorial and advertising functions should be totally divorced. But like Missouri, which operated its own community newspaper, Columbia stressed practical experience, providing fourth-year students with a simulated city room for the acquisition of reporting, interviewing and editing skills. A somewhat different approach to journalism education was taken by Bleyer at Wisconsin. His students took fewer courses in journalism than in the social sciences and had no laboratory newspaper, although they were encouraged to work on the university's daily. Bleyer was credited with being the father of the social science, as opposed to the techniques, approach to teaching journalism.

Neither plan led to wide opportunities for women students. Formal education in journalism evolved at a time when numerous occupational fields were developing into professions. These included business and public management, accounting, engineering and civil service. The new professions aimed to provide academic programs to train management for the giant institutions, including metropolitan newspapers, that marked America's transformation from an agricultural to an industrial society. Women as a group were excluded from serious consideration as managers in all of these areas including journalism.

Yet journalism instruction was available to the women who wanted it. From 1910 to 1920, journalism courses were started in 74 institutions, almost all of which admitted women. Showing the growing interest in the field, the American Association of Teachers of Journalism was started in 1912 and the American Association of Schools and Departments of Journalism five years later. Both were forerunners of the present Association for Education in Journalism and Mass Communication. By 1920 at least a few journalism classes were offered at 131 colleges, 10 of which, mainly co-educational state universities, offered intensive professional programs.[27]

To a degree World War I gave opportunities to women when newspapermen left their desks for the battlefields. The wartime experiences of Frances Stone Burns, a journalism graduate of the University of Washington, were typical. Mrs. Burns, the first editor of *The Matrix,* started in 1915 as the official publication of Theta Sigma

Phi, recalled the impact of the war years later: "From 1915 until the beginning of 1920 I worked on Tacoma, Washington, papers, the *News* and *Ledger,* and, because of my training, did courts and special assignments, work that men would have done if there had not been a war on." She was married to Alfred Burns before he was sent overseas in 1917 and "worked through his return in late summer of 1919," she continued. "Then in 1920 we came to Boston to live and I put newspaper work, as I thought, behind me forever. We had two sons, Alfred and Dugald...." To her surprise, however, during World War II, when another wartime shortage of men journalists existed, she was able to resume a newspaper career as a part-time food writer for the *Boston Globe*.[28]

Another early journalism school graduate who benefitted from expanded opportunities for women due to World War I was Minna Lewinson, one of 11 women and eight men to be graduated from Columbia University journalism school in 1918. The preponderance of women was due to men having left the university to go to war. Lewinson became the first woman to be hired by the *Wall Street Journal,* where she worked from her graduation until June 1923.[29]

According to a Columbia classmate, Liliane Refregier Davison, Lewinson was hired because the war had drawn off male reporters. Certainly she had an exceptional record. Along with another student, Henry Beetle Hough, Lewinson was awarded a Pulitzer Prize in 1918 for a paper written on the wartime services of the American press. It was an unusual honor never to be given again, classified as a "newspaper history award." It gave Lewinson the distinction of being the first woman to win a Pulitzer Prize.[30]

From 1920 to 1930 journalism programs continued to expand, being added in 175 schools. Women constituted a sizeable element of students. By 1928, for example, the University of Missouri had awarded 916 bachelor's degrees in journalism during its 20-year history, with 564 going to men and 352 going to women.[31]

On a national level the number of women employed in reporting and editing jobs doubled in the 1920s, according to census figures. They showed nearly 12,000 women, or 24 percent of the total in the reporting and editing category, an increase of 7.2 percent from 1920 to 1930. Many of these women worked for women's pages or women's magazines or in other areas considered appropriate for their sex. Even though women had been given the right to vote in 1920, the number of women who covered straight news or politics on newspapers remained small.[32]

Occasionally women made it to general assignment status if they were willing to be "sob sisters." This was the term given female writers who wrote lurid, adjective-laden stories that exploited women's presumed predisposition to emotional outbursts. A male graduate of the Columbia journalism school remembered fifty years later how amazed members of his class had been when one of their number, Frances Fink, landed a job as a "sob sister" with a tabloid, the *New York Graphic,* in 1930.[33]

"Sob sisters wrote lurid stories about the sex intrigues of the famous and the infamous.... The stories had sad endings—the wages of sin—so the reporters of these tear-jerkers were called sob sisters. The school's curriculum was not precisely geared to the training of sob sisters," Harry Winston commented ironically. "Reporting [to the professors] consisted of interviewing newsmakers rather than peering through windows from fire escapes." He remembered, nevertheless, that other students envied Fink the chance to write a "juicy saga."[34]

But for most women students the path ahead was clearly limited—leading to the women's pages or other special writing aimed at women readers. Women were not given the same choice of assignments in journalism schools as men, or if they were, they were not seen as performing the assignments on a par with male students. This point was borne out by a collection of assignments published by the University of Missouri in 1927. Of 16 editorials included, only one written by a woman appeared (and that was titled "Religion"). Of 14 news stories published in the collection, only two were written by women, and one of those had a society focus ("Renew Betrothal After 35 years") and the other a feature angle ("300 Students Go for Hike"). But of 28 feature stories in the group, nine were written by women and of five examples of fiction and special articles, three were done by women.[35]

The collection itself was edited by Sarah Lockwood Williams, one of the first women to teach journalism in a professional school. After receiving her bachelor's degree in journalism from the University of Missouri in 1913, she had worked for newspapers in St. Joseph, Missouri, Tulsa and Philadelphia before returning to the University of Missouri as an assistant professor in 1921. She resigned from her position after her marriage to Dean Walter Williams in 1927, although she came back to the faculty following his death.[36]

Other women teachers in journalism schools during the 1920s included Helen Patterson at the University of Wisconsin, Helen Hostetter at Kansas State and Frances Grinstead, who followed Lockwood at the University of Missouri. These women had experienced sex discrimination in their own careers, and they endeavored to teach their women students how to meet it. One solution seemed promising: Home economics journalism, which translated into writing articles for women's pages and magazines.

A leading exponent was Patterson, an early woman member of the American Teachers of Journalism, who taught journalism at the University of Wisconsin from 1923 to 1957. A graduate of the University of Kansas, she had experienced the customary discrimination against women journalists. She also had to overcome the skepticism shown by editors toward all journalism graduates.

"In the days when I was right out of college, we were warned not to tell we were journalism school graduates when job-hunting or we wouldn't get hired," Patterson told a reporter who interviewed her in 1961. After she was promoted from reporter to city editor of a Kansas daily, the publisher of the paper informed her, "If I'd had known you were from a journalism school, I'd never have hired you."[37]

But she filled that job and went on to other "firsts" in Kansas— first woman wire editor, first woman critic, first woman copy editor. In college she had been the first woman editor of the campus newspaper. "I changed jobs a lot and kept moving around," she said, "because in those days women in journalism were so looked down upon that in order to get a raise, you had to find a better job."[38]

At Wisconsin Patterson began a course called "Writing For Homemakers" and encouraged both journalism and home economics students to take it. "Speaking for myself," she told the reporter, "I have little interest in cooking and such, but I recognize the enormous market for articles on the home and think it offers a wide opportunity for women writers." As a specialist on the writing of feature articles and public relations for organizations, Patterson lectured all over the United States. She was an associate professor of journalism when she retired following her marriage to Grant M. Hyde, director of the journalism program at Wisconsin.[39]

Hostetter, who began her career as a high school English teacher, was inspired to obtain a journalism degree from Northwestern University after she was assigned a high school journalism class and discovered she loved journalism. Her first reporting job was on a newspaper in Sioux City, Iowa, where she was society editor, although she originally had vowed that she would "take in back stairs to scrub," before she would write society news. Next she worked at Mount Union College in Ohio, combining college public relations and the teaching of journalism.[40]

In 1926, she started teaching at Kansas State, where she developed a course, "Journalism for Women," to prepare women to write for women's pages. Soon it included "Home Page" training during which students prepared model women's pages for local newspapers. In 1941 she became editor of the *Journal of Home Economics,* but she returned to Kansas State in 1946 as the first woman in journalism education to hold a full professorship. Yet her salary, $3,600 annually, was lower than that paid male professors.[41]

Grinstead, too, experienced discrimination in both her professional and academic careers. She received a bachelor's degree in 1921 and a master's degree in 1928 from the University of Missouri. Before joining the Missouri faculty, she was city editor of the *Mexico* [Missouri] *Intelligencer* and women's editor of the *Spartanburg* [South Carolina] *Journal.* It soon became clear to her "that Red Cross news, music criticism, school news and other 'non-women news' I had been doing on top of a full day's work as women's feature editor gave me opportunity to do the general writing but not to get recognition for it," she remembered years later. When an opening came up in the city room, a man was hired even though she had been promised the job.[42]

She eventually retired in 1967 after 35 years of teaching on the university level, first at the University of Missouri and then at the University of Kansas. Yet she was never made a full professor, although she gained acclaim for the teaching of feature and magazine writing and published numerous articles and a novel. "In all modesty," she once commented, "I cannot accept this fact as a fair assessment of performance," but she was proud to have been a woman journalism faculty member at a time when these were rare.[43]

The problems facing women were outlined in detail in two early textbooks aimed at women journalism students. In 1926 Genevieve Jackson Boughner, former instructor in journalism at the University of Wisconsin and the University of Minnesota, wrote *Women in Journalism: A Guide to the Opportunities and a Manual of the Technique of Women's Work For Newspapers and Magazines.* A year later appeared *Writing and Editing for Women: A Bird's Eye View of the Widening Opportunities for Women in Newspaper, Magazine & Other Writing Work,* by Ethel M. Colson Brazelton, lecturer on journalism for women at the Medill School of Journalism at Northwestern University.

Both authors sought to tell women just how to establish themselves in spite of male bias. Boughner noted she had given at the University of Wisconsin the first course in "Features of Interest to Women in Magazine and Newspapers" ever offered in a journalism school. She urged women to "capitalize their tastes and instincts rather than oppose them, as they are called upon to do in many lines of newspaper writing in which they duplicate men's work." She declared the labor market demanded it:

> ...the increasing number of men and women taking courses in journalism, the constantly diminishing number of newspapers, and the difficulty experienced by heads of schools of journalism in finding work for women graduates, point unmistakably to the desirability of specialization on the part of the woman beginner in some branch of magazine or newspaper work, that demands the distinctly feminine background and experience.[44]

Both Boughner and Brazelton were quite precise on what these areas should be: Society, club news, homemaking, women's pages (including beauty and fashion news), children's activities and stories, shopping advice, feature stories and advice on personal problems. Boughner also suggested writing news about women in politics and women in sports, while Brazelton mentioned the new fields of motion picture criticism, house organs, trade papers and commercial publicity and advertising. But she urged women to avoid direct competition with men, even though this would mean limitation in their subject matter.

"'The woman's angle'—or attitude, or viewpoint—is necessary to the proper reflection of those human beings who, quite aside from any questions of choice or possible preference, have been born feminine," she advised dryly. "The fact of sex, the 'woman's angle' is the woman writer's tool, but it must never be her weapon." The line between a tool and a weapon, however, was a fine one, it seemed, as Brazelton went on to counsel women on clothing and deportment essential for success. She quoted a male editor who insisted, "30 percent of the newspaper woman's success, especially as a reporter" depended on making a good impression by dress and social skills.[45]

According to Brazelton, it was impossible to obtain exact statistics on the number of women in journalism "because of the amazing rapidity with which young women slip in and out of such jobs." She estimated the number between 20,000 and 25,000, of whom 2,106 were "busily engaged in the study of American journalism." She noted women were sometimes paid only one-third less than men doing the same work and cited reasons in defense of this discrimination, including "continual turn-over due to feminine restlessness." That the low pay itself might have led to the "restlessness" was not pointed out.[46]

In fact, she counseled women who wanted to be journalists that they must be prepared for heroic sacrifices. "If you desire to write more than you do to fall in love, get married, become rich and distinguished, or realize any other delightful prospects that you can imagine, don't rest until the coveted job is yours," she exhorted. For those who were not prepared to renounce love, fame or fortune, apparently there was little hope of employment.[47]

Male journalism instructors also offered negative advice. In a textbook of the 1930s women were told they were biologically unsuited for reporting: "The general tempo—with the deadline-fighting element always present—is such to bar many women because of nervous temperament." Further, the authors, a city editor and a journalism professor, stated, "Most women are incapable of covering police and court news."[48]

Yet in spite of discouragement, women continued to enroll in schools of journalism. Why? To answer the question, one has to look at the alternatives available. Aside from teaching and nursing, both of which paid relatively poorly, the professions in general were not hospitable to women in this period. Although the 1930 census showed nearly 11 million working women, many of them held low-skill jobs, with three of every ten employed as domestic servants. In the professional field, three-quarters were either teachers or nurses. The total number of workers represented only 24.3 percent of the women in the country, so obviously the majority of women remained at home.[49]

Therefore, journalism represented one of the few relatively interesting career fields available for women. Because of its heavy concentration on the liberal arts, journalism education offered an extension of English and other liberal arts programs, attractive to many women who attended college but did not wish to teach. Due to rapid turnover in the job market, journalism was an occupation women could pursue for a few years prior to marriage, in spite of discrimination and low salaries.

Journalism education provided a credential for women who, far more than men, were barred from the alternative route of on-the-job training. Men were hired as copy boys and moved up; women were not. In addition, journalism schools produced some women who stood out as role models for others. One was Genevieve Forbes Herrick, a graduate of Northwestern University and the top woman reporter for the *Chicago Tribune*. Herrick was repeatedly referred to in the Brazelton book. One of the assignments given there asked students to write an essay stating in 500 words what a comment by Herrick meant to them. The comment: "The good woman reporter must have a woman's view-point and a man's pen-point." She seemed to be saying journalism provided women a way to keep their femininity at the same time they mastered a skill monopolized by men.[50]

So journalism education meant something different to women than to men. On the surface, it might appear that men and women received the same education since they sat side-by-side in the same classrooms. An observer did not have to be keen, however, to determine that the two sexes were not treated equally. Women faced a set of expectations and barriers not presented to men.

## ENDNOTES

1. Paul V. Peterson, "Enrollment Surges Again, Increases 7 Percent to 70,601," *Journalism Educator* 34 (Jan. 1979), p. 3; see also "The Wage Gap: Myths and Facts" published by National Committee on Pay Equity, 1201 16th St. N.W., Washington, D.C., 20036.
2. De Forest O'Dell, *The History of Journalism Education in the United States* (New York: Columbia University Teachers College, 1935), pp. 16-45; Albert A. Sutton, *Education for Journalism in the United States From Its Beginning to 1940* (Evanston, Ill: Northwestern University, 1945), pp. 7-10.
3. "The School of Journalism," *Detroit Free Press,* April 21, 1887, p. 17, and "The City," *Detroit Tribune,* July 17, 1886, p. 4, as quoted in James S. Bradshaw, "Mrs. Rayne's School of Journalism," *Journalism Quarterly* 60 (Fall 1983), pp. 513-517.
4. Undated handbill, Lucy A. Leggett papers, Burston Historical Collections, Detroit, as quoted in Bradshaw, p. 517.
5. Frederic Hudson, *Journalism in America* (New York: Harper, 1873), p. 499.

6. M.S. Rayne, *What Can a Woman Do: Or Her Position in the Business and Literary World* (Detroit: F.B. Dickerson Co., 1886), as quoted in Bradshaw, pp. 515-16.
7. U.S. Census Office, *Compendium of the Eleventh Census* (Washington, D.C.: U.S. Government Printing Office, 1897), Part III, p. 516, as quoted in Bradshaw, p. 513.
8. Marion Marzolf, *Up From the Footnote: A History of Women Journalists* (New York: Hastings House, 1977), pp. 20-21.
9. Henry Ladd Smith, "The Beauteous Jennie June: Pioneer Woman Journalist," *Journalism Quarterly* 40 (Spring 1963), pp. 160-174.
10. Ibid., pp. 173-74.
11. Joseph Pulitzer and J. C. Goldsmith, as quoted in Sutton, *Education for Journalism in the United States From Its Beginning to 1940,* pp. 108-9.
12. Luella H. Goodson, "A Co-ed of the '70s Recalls Missouri University Life," undated clipping, *Kansas City Star,* in Ida Aldrich Minter scrapbook in possession of Maurine Hoffman Beasley. Beasley is the granddaughter of Ella Dimmit Hoffman, who also wrote in the scrapbook of her experiences at the University of Missouri and of her marriage to a man, Louis Hoffman, whom she had defeated in an essay contest. See also, Janet Wilson James, "Introduction," *Notable American Women, A Biographical Dictionary* (Cambridge, Mass.: Harvard University Press, 1971), p. xxviii.
13. Sara Lockwood Williams, *Twenty Years of Education for Journalism* (Columbia, Mo.: Stephens Publishing, 1929), pp. 53, 72.
14. Ibid., pp. 452-53, 147. See also Ishbel Ross, *Ladies of the Press* (New York: Harper's, 1936), p. 575.
15. Sara Lockwood Williams, "The Editor's Rib," *The Matrix* 27 (Dec. 1941), p. 10.
16. Williams, "The Editor's Rib," *The Matrix* 27 (Feb. 1942), p. 14.
17. "Women and the Newspaper," (Columbia, Mo.: University of Missouri Bulletin, Journalism Series No. 30, 1924), p. 13.
18. Sutton, *Education for Journalism in the United States From Its Beginning to 1940,* p. 16; Janice Ruth Wood, "The Foundation Years of American Journalism Education, 1908-1930," unpublished master's thesis in journalism, University of South Carolina, 1981, pp. 23-24, 35.
19. Charles C. Clayton, *Fifty Years for Freedom 1908-1959: The Story of Sigma Delta Chi's Service to American Journalism* (Carbondale, Ill.: Southern Illinois University Press, 1959), pp. 9, 18, 226-27.
20. Helen Ross Lantz, "Seven Sisters With Vision," *The Matrix* 29 (Aug. 1944), p. 5.
21. Ibid.
22. Ibid., pp. 6-13; Wood, "The Foundation Years of American Journalism Education," p. 45. See also Anne Hecker, "WICI Survives the Challenges of Time," *Pro/Comm* 4 (April 1984), pp. 2, 6.
23. Clayton, Fifty Years for Freedom, pp. 100-101.
24. Lantz, "Seven Sisters With Vision," pp. 6, 13; Ross, *Ladies of the Press,* p. 125.

25. Wood, "The Foundation Years of American Journalism Education," p. 39.
26. Text of speech, "The Inside of a Newspaper Should Be Like the Inside of the Home," given on June 6, 1949, Box 164, Carl W. Ackerman papers, Library of Congress.
27. Sutton, *Education for Journalism in the United States From Its Beginning to 1940*, p. 17.
28. As quoted in L.E.R. Kleinhenz, "'30' to Thirty Years," *The Matrix* 30 (Aug. 1945), p.9.
29. Kathleen K. Keeshen, "Journalism's Pulitzer Penwomen," unpublished paper prepared as part of Ph.D. coursework in American studies at University of Maryland, Feb. 1978, p. 12.
30. Ibid., pp. 10-16.
31. Sutton, *Education for Journalism in the United States From Its Beginning to 1940*, pp. 17-18; Williams, *Twenty Years of Education For Journalism*, p. 453.
32. Marzolf, *Up From the Footnote*, pp. 51-52.
33. "College Walk," *Columbia* 10 (Nov. 1984), p. 49.
34. Ibid.
35. Sarah Lockwood Williams, ed., "Written by Students in Journalism: Selected Articles Written by Students in the School of Journalism, University of Missouri as a Part of Their Class Work During 1926-27," (Columbia, Mo.: University of Missouri Bulletin No. 26, 1927).
36. Williams, *Twenty Years of Education for Journalism*, pp. 442-43.
37. Judy Donovan, "Wisconsin Author Recalls Colorful Journalism Career," *Tucson* (Ariz.) *Star*, Jan. 11, 1961.
38. Ibid.
39. Ibid. See also Marzolf, *Up From the Footnote*, pp. 252-253.
40. Marzolf, *Up From the Footnote*, p. 254.
41. Ibid., pp. 254-55.
42. Ibid., pp. 255-56.
43. Ibid., pp. 256-57.
44. Genevieve Jackson Boughner, *Women In Journalism: A Guide to the Opportunities and a Manual of the Technique of Women's Work for Newspapers and Magazines* (New York: D. Appleton & Co., 1926), p. viii.
45. Ethel M. Colson Brazelton, *Writing and Editing for Women: A Bird's Eye View of the Widening Opportunities for Women in Newspaper, Magazine & Other Writing Work* (New York: Funk & Wagnalls, 1927), pp. 3, 8, 190.
46. Ibid., pp. 199, 208.
47. Ibid., p. 208.
48. Philip W. Porter and Norval N. Luxon, *The Reporter and the News* (New York: D. Appleton-Century Co., 1935), p. 8.
49. Susan Ware: *Holding Their Own: American Women in the 1930s* (Boston: Twayne, 1982) p. 24.
50. Brazelton, *Writing and Editing for Women*, p. 10.

# Chapter 2

# The Numbers Grow, and a War Helps: 1931–1960

The Depression that engulfed the United States in the 1930s adversely affected higher education but journalism programs continued to expand. Between 1930 and 1940, an additional 144 schools began instruction in journalism, even though economic conditions forced cutbacks in other academic areas. Journalism education began to include preparation for the emerging fields of radio work and public relations.[1]

In some journalism schools, an increased emphasis on theory emerged also, with more direct application of social science theories to the study of communications. As Grant M. Hyde of the University of Wisconsin expressed it in 1936, "We began to realize that our job was to show the students how to correlate...social science courses with each other and with the problems of journalism. Hence, we set up courses in 'public opinion'—in 'the influence of the press'." These courses involved psychology, economics, sociology, political science and related subjects.[2]

But women students were not particularly encouraged to move in this direction. They still were viewed skeptically by journalism educators who feared that the women would take jobs away from males. The issue was addressed forthrightly by R.E. Wolseley, a male professor at Northwestern University, in an article in *The Matrix* in 1939, in which he estimated 8,000 women were employed on United States newspapers. Wolseley referred to a statement in *Editor and Publisher,* the newspaper trade publication, by the American Association of Schools and Departments of Journalism, the organization of accredited journalism schools. In it the organization attempted to reassure the newspaper industry that schools were not flooding the market but were weeding out unsuitable prospects. "The strategies used in this weeding out process were explained," Wolseley noted. "It is directed at two types of students: incompetents or misfits and women."[3]

According to Wolseley, the injustice to women was unfortunate, but the fault lay with women themselves. "The situation men fear is this: That many women will win high places in journalism and displace many men and that those men will receive only social opprobrium as a result," he stated. Wolseley contended women were not willing to support stay-at-home husbands, although men were quite willing to support stay-at-home wives. Through this convoluted reasoning, he concluded: "...women cannot become journalists. Men will not let them. And the men cannot be blamed."[4]

Faced with the depths of prejudice against them, women had to behave with extreme care if they did succeed in obtaining employment. In a 1936 history of women journalists, Ishbel Ross, who herself had been a *New York Herald-Tribune* "front-page girl" (as outstanding women reporters were called in that era) before her marriage to a *New York Times* rival, described the newspaperwoman's predicament. Ross wrote:

> The woman reporter really has to be a paradox. She must be ruthless at work...gentle in private life...not too beguiling to dazzle the men and disrupt the work...comradely with the male reporters...able to take the noise and pressure and rough language of the city room without showing disapproval or breaking into tears under the strain of rough criticism. She must do her own work, asking no help or pampering, and make no excuses.[5]

In contrast to the strain involved in a career, marriage offered a conventional alternative for women journalism graduates. It was one they chose at a great rate. In fact, the sizeable number of journalism graduates who left the field for marriage was one reason journalism schools did not have as conspicuous an effect on the profession as early educators had hoped.

A 1939 survey of the ten previous graduating classes of 16 accredited schools of journalism showed that 63.5 percent of the graduates were in journalistic work. Within that group, 33.6 percent were employed by newspapers, press services or syndicates. But 21 percent of the graduates represented women who had married and retired from the field. The percentage in this category was far higher than the percentage of graduates in the remaining categories: advertising (other than newspaper), 11.2 percent; business publications and magazines, 7.7 percent; public relations, 6.9 percent; radio, 3.4 percent; printing and graphic arts, 0.7 percent.[6]

Educators tried to solve the problem of women students in different ways. Some schools, like Columbia, limited the number of women admitted. "As the market for our students is selective, our plan of education in journalism is realistic," Dean Carl W. Ackerman reported in 1935. "The press expects this School to graduate men, and a limited number of women, who are prepared for immediate employment by a newspaper or press association...."[7]

Other universities set up courses especially for women, following the pioneer efforts of the previous decade. In the academic year of 1939–40, there were 3,668 women students enrolled in 67 schools of journalism, according to a survey taken by Jo Caldwell Meyer, national secretary of Theta Sigma Phi. She identified the following courses for them:

Columbia University—"Women in Journalism," which combined "graduate methods of independent research with the practicalities of future employment";

Iowa State College [now University]—"Magazine Writing and Editing for Home Economics Publications," "Radio Writing and Editing for Home Economics Publications" and "News Writing for Home Economics Women";

Kansas State College [now University]—"Journalism for Women," which prepared students for women's pages and women's magazines;

Northwestern University—"Women's Departments in Newspapers and Magazines," which surveyed columns devoted to clubs, society, fashion, beauty, home-making, foods and shopping;

University of Oklahoma—"Reporting Women's Interests," a laboratory course in women's page material;

University of Southern California—"Women's Departments in Newspapers and Magazines," required of all women journalism majors;

Stanford University—"Women's Departments," which allowed majors with high academic standing to do independent study in this area;

University of Wisconsin—"Women's Fields in Newspapers and Magazines," which covered writing and editing for women's pages, and publicity work for social and educational institutions;

Butler University—"Specialized Writing for Women";

Texas State College for Women [now Texas Women's University]—"Technical Writing," designed for women's publicity work;

Texas Technological College [now University]—"Home Economics Journalism."[8]

Caldwell did not criticize these courses as limiting the aspirations of women to the status quo. She heralded them as a step forward in adjusting the curriculum to the needs of women. "Some schools and departments of journalism, which do not yet have vocational courses for women, give careful advice to their students so that they will be equipped with a specialty," she reported.[9]

At Marquette University advertising and trade magazine courses were "slanted for women in particular," she noted, while other courses, "such as editing," were "adapted to use for women." Women students at the University of Minnesota were counseled into areas for which the director of the department considered women "particularly suited," including department store and agency advertising, public relations, radio writing, and magazine writing and editing.[10]

The special courses and advice offered preparation for a declining job market that continued to be hostile to women who sought work as newspaper reporters. A loss of advertising revenue in the early 1930s cut into newspaper profit margins, causing 145 suspensions of dailies during 1931-33, an additional 77 in the following two years, and another 167 in the years from 1937 to 1939. Women lost their jobs at a faster rate than men, a fact recognized by Eleanor Roosevelt, who initiated White House press conferences limited to women reporters when she became First Lady in 1933. She hoped to provide women with news that men reporters could not get as a way of helping women keep newspaper jobs.[11]

The move to provide specialized instruction for women encountered some objections from those who believed women should take the same coursework as men in journalism school. The issue was addressed in *The Matrix* in 1932 by a newspaperwoman, Jean James, who asked the question, "What should a school of journalism teach women?" Her general answer: "The same things that it teaches men." She pointed out, "One frequently hears the remark that since women do a different type of work from men on newspapers, it is foolish for them to take the same courses." James called this reasoning "fallacious" and cited instances of staff members from women's pages required to substitute for male reporters in times of illness, vacations, or "news crises."[12]

Similarly she disagreed with those who favored teaching women "classical studies" instead of the "mechanical side of the newspaper." James argued, "Teach the woman student the essential facts about the art of printing, the composing room, the process of engraving, stereotyping, make-up and the parlance of the news and composing room," but, she added, "not the expletives!" She supported giving women extra training in writing feature stories, nevertheless, since they were "frequently called upon to do features and in many cases develop a slant on them that is different from the type of story a man writes."[13]

The expansion of formal coursework in journalism for women marked a move within journalism education to establish a subspecialization of journalism akin to other feminine-serving professions. This kind of journalism centered around advising women how to improve their homemaking and consumer skills. Unlike general reporting, which emphasized the disclosure of conflict and controversy, home economics journalism emphasized a genteel idea of service. Its ideology was comparable with that of other feminine-dominated professions that expanded in the early twentieth century: teaching, social work, nursing, librarianship, and home economics itself.[14]

For some women these feminine professions became accepted alternatives to marriage and homemaking, but only a minority chose this course. For most women college graduates, including journalism students, the preferred option came to be: college, work in the labor force in a feminine profession, and then marriage and homemaking. This option helped protect women against the dire prospect of not attracting husbands by enabling them to support themselves if necessary.[15]

Courses aimed at women led to the employment of a few additional women in journalism schools. At Columbia University, for example, Eleanor Carroll was hired in 1936. She remained on the faculty for 11 years, moving from assistant to full professor and acting as associate dean. A graduate of Wellesley College, she also had obtained both bachelor's and master's degrees in journalism from Columbia and had been managing editor of the *Delineator,* a magazine for women, before joining the faculty. According to the official history of the Columbia journalism school, she was brought in "to add the woman's touch, teach a sequence of studies in the magazine, and lend wise counsel." In later years she recalled she had been hired when a faculty group decided "a woman on the faculty would be a natural development. No whoop-de-do."[16]

But even if a few women were accepted within journalism education, the field remained suffused with prejudice against women as newspaper reporters. A group of employers who addressed women journalism students at Ohio State University in 1940 made this quite plain. As *The Matrix* dryly reported, "There seemed to be a general agreement among the members of the employers' symposium that women don't have any more chance for jobs on newspapers than Jews have of surviving in Germany." The editors present, who represented the *Cleveland Plain Dealer, Ohio State Journal, Columbus Citizen* and *Columbus Evening Dispatch,* indicated "that no matter how good a woman is, a man would probably be given preference," the article continued.[17]

Still, there were determined women who succeeded even in direct competition with men. According to census figures, the number of women editors and reporters in the United States climbed from 7,105 in 1920 to 14,786 in 1930 and to 15,890 in 1940. It is not known how many of these women were journalism graduates. Many of the best known, such as Anne O'Hare McCormick, a foreign correspondent for the *New York Times,* who in 1937 became the second woman to receive a Pulitzer Prize, had not set foot in a journalism school. Her formal education had ended with graduation from a Catholic academy for young women.[18]

Yet role models such as McCormick and Dorothy Thompson, another preeminent woman foreign correspondent in the 1930s, were among factors that drew women students to journalism school. Hollywood also glamorized the occupation with films like "Mr. Deeds Goes to Town" (1936) and "His Girl Friday" (1940), which featured the "girl reporter." In addition, Eleanor Roosevelt's press conferences, covered by some journalism graduates, served to elevate women's interest in the field.[19]

Among the women reporters closest to the First Lady was Ruby

Black, who ran her own Washington news bureau. Black was a former national president of Theta Sigma Phi and a graduate of the University of Texas. A self-made woman who had worked her way through college, Black had studied journalism at the University of Texas and taught it at the University of Wisconsin. Both she and Genevieve Forbes Herrick, another member of Mrs. Roosevelt's inner circle of reporters, provided visible proof that a woman equipped with a journalism degree could overcome the obstacle of her sex.[20]

Graduates of schools of journalism constituted 57 percent of 881 women journalists included in a detailed study published in 1938. It showed that only 422, or 47.9 percent, were employed on newspapers, although the majority had obtained their first jobs there. Of the 422, about 16 percent were engaged in advertising, circulation and promotion instead of news. Other journalistic areas were listed and the percentage of women given in each: magazines, 8.9 percent; advertising and publicity, 10.8 percent; publishing, 1.8 percent; free lance writing, 8.6 percent; journalism teaching, 2.1 percent. Another 19.9 percent of the 881, or one in five of the women, were not actively engaged in journalism at the time of the survey, including 5.6 percent in other professions (mainly teaching), 4.5 percent in secretarial and other business occupations and 6.7 percent in full-time homemaking. No figures were given on broadcasting and no breakdown was given on journalism versus non-journalism graduates in the various categories.[21]

Journalism alumnae were quoted in the study on the need to give women a wide range of courses since they were unlikely to be hired as newspaper reporters: "Deliberately their attention should be brought to the attractive fields of sales promotion and merchandising—through the written appeal, of course,—and also to those in magazine writing and editing on the more progressive types of journals," one said. Radio offered additional opportunities, she continued. "Fortunately, some of the schools are now giving radio continuity-writing, a wise step forward in keeping up with the new vocational outlets which we must find—or create for ourselves."[22]

The perseverance of those determined to be reporters was lauded. One example described a journalism graduate who sent a letter of application to 175 newspapers after her pay had been cut from $25 per week in 1930 to $10 in 1934. At the same time she still was expected to function as society editor, news gatherer, headline writer and proofreader. Letter number 156 finally netted her a job on a larger paper, first as society editor at $18 a week, and after eight months as wire editor at $25 a week.[23]

The survey found that college, but not necessarily journalism school, training did pay off in dollars and cents. It determined that at the end of five to ten years of experience journalism graduates had median salaries above those of both liberal arts graduates and non-college women working on newspapers. But the survey also showed that liberal arts graduates with 11 to 15 years experience far outstripped both journalism graduates and non-college women in newspaper pay. Perhaps this reflected a tendency of capable journalism graduates to leave newspaper work after ten years. In addition, the survey found journalism graduates often stayed in smaller communities in the states where they had been educated instead of moving to metropolitan areas with higher pay scales.[24]

The 1938 survey formed the basis of a book on careers for women in journalism, which gathered information on sex discrimination and the combination of marriage and career. Sex discrimination was noted most frequently by newspaperwomen surveyed, although advertising women "also reported invulnerable opposition to admitting women into the upper salary brackets." Newspaperwomen found discrimination in salary more often than in assignments. Frequently the two areas were linked together—certain assignments led to higher pay than others.[25]

Four varieties of reaction to discrimination on newspapers surfaced in the study. Five percent of the women claimed to have encountered no personal discrimination, contending in general, "If women get poor salaries it is because they accept them supinely." Twenty percent displayed a passive attitude, agreeing, "on the whole, newspaperwomen are worth less than newspapermen." This group contended certain assignments were not suitable for women, including those related to industrial conditions, labor and politics. Another 20 percent admitted discrimination but claimed it was "no more severe than in other fields of work." The largest faction, 55 percent, however, affirmed the presence of unjustified discrimination.[26]

"With all the managing editors I have met, education and writing ability are not the essentials they seek in a woman reporter," a journalism graduate said. "In the very few women they do take on (for flashy feature work), what they look for is the bold front and the 'gift of the gab'."[27]

The survey showed women's chances of earning good salaries were decidedly better in promotional writing and magazines than in newspaper work. Salary figures cited showed that both men and women earned low salaries on newspapers when they started their careers. But men advanced upward and left the women far behind. The median disparity given between men and women's salaries on newspapers was 23 percent.[28]

The study pointed to a relatively high number of working wives in the sample: 257 out of 881, or 33.6 percent. It attributed this to the opportunity women journalists had to meet prospective husbands. In nursing and librarianship, it noted, women outnumbered men nine to one and in teaching four to one, according to the 1930 census. But men outnumbered women three to one among editors and reporters and eight to one in advertising. Since the census reported 28.9 percent of all women workers to be married, journalism contained a higher percentage of married women than the labor market as a whole.[29]

Surprisingly, the survey found married women were not discriminated against in salary. In advertising and publicity, for instance, the married workers' median was $37 a week, about $3 higher than the median for the whole advertising group.[30]

Perhaps it was because journalism appeared to offer the possibility of combining marriage and career that the field became increasingly popular with women in the 1930s. Iona Robertson Logie, a counselor at the Hunter College high school in New York and the survey director, discovered journalism was a conspicuous choice of vocation for young women along with the more traditional occupations of teacher, secretary and "business woman."[31]

Still formal education in journalism remained questionable in the opinion of experts. A book of career advice, titled *Lady Editor,* urged women journalism graduates to be modest about their college training. It insisted that editors who condemned journalism school did so because graduates acted "rigid and conceited." Women were warned, "Never, never, quote your professor to your editor." The authors urged graduates to "let the editor think that he is training you," partly as a way of letting him relive his own youth.[32]

Opportunities for women journalism graduates expanded with United States entry into World War II, following the Japanese attack on Pearl Harbor on December 7, 1941. Prior to Pearl Harbor men were drafted for military service, leaving women as their replacements in newsrooms. "The selective service act is giving women their long-sought opportunity to do general reporting," declared Abbie A. Amrine, a 1939 graduate of the University of Missouri. "We're going to be changed from the woman's department into the straight news room." Amrine offered her own example. She had been society editor of the *Pratt* (Kansas) *Daily Tribune* for a year and a half and a cub general reporter on *The Times* at Leavenworth, Kansas, before the act took effect in 1940.[33]

"Now, taking the place of a man who has been drafted, I am working with the more drastic complications of deaths, accidents, rains, and community speakers," she wrote in *The Matrix*. "My conclusion is that the men have been impressing us with a false importance of their jobs." She called for women "to go after more straight reporting jobs and prove that we can do them!"[34]

"Jobs, jobs, jobs! And no one to fill them. Odd, isn't it, how the job picture has changed in war months," Betty Hinckle Dunn, national secretary of Theta Sigma Phi, exclaimed in 1942. "Flippantly I tell my friends, 'The war means more opportunities for women and Negroes.'"[35]

The following year a study of newspapers in 43 states was undertaken by Dean Kenneth E. Olson of the Medill School of Journalism at Northwestern University. It revealed there were 2,187 current staff vacancies with an additional 4,169 expected within six months as men were called for induction. Statistics showed there were four jobs available on newspapers for every woman graduate from journalism schools.[36]

Editors of newspapers of all sizes pleaded with educators to "train more women." They suggested accelerated programs and short-term journalism courses to be offered those with college degrees in other areas. Women were urged to enter the mechanical as well as the news field. For instance, the *Daily Journal* at New Ulm, Minnesota, wanted journalism schools to direct women toward operation of typesetting machines.[37]

Northwestern University set up a special training program for women with three years of non-journalism coursework. It featured work in a typography laboratory and included printing press operation. The school also opened a class in reporting of public affairs, previously taken by men seeking masters' degrees, to women for background on covering courts, government and public offices.[38]

By 1943 women made up 50 percent of the staffs of many newspapers in smaller cities. Their opporunities in metropolitan journalism also increased. In Washington, D.C., women suddenly found themselves covering all kinds of beats, including the White House, State Department and Pentagon. There were nearly 100 women accredited to the Capitol press galleries, compared with 30 six years earlier. Women such as Inez Robb, a top writer for International News Service and a graduate of the University of Missouri School of Journalism, established themselves as war correspondents.[39]

Other women moved into broadcasting. In Detroit Fran Harris, a journalism graduate of Grinnell College, Grinnell, Iowa, switched from a shopping column of the air to newscasting. Until wartime shortages made her column impractical, Harris was "Nancy Dixon," leading listeners on a shopping tour of department stores. Harris "kept after the station to let me try newscasting until they finally gave in in desperation," she told an interviewer. She was hopeful the newscasting job would last "even after the war," and was trying to prove that a woman could attract advertisers. "We women all know we have to do twice as well as a man to go half as far," she said.[40]

The influx of women into journalism paralleled the general infusion of women into paid employment. After years of having been encouraged to see themselves as wives and mothers above all else, now women were told their civic duty included paid work to support the war effort. As an historian expressed it, "Although the popular ideology that women's primary role was in the home survived the war both in public discourse and in the beliefs of most women, the military crisis did create an ideological climate supportive of women's movement into the public realm."[41]

Between 1940 and 1945, the female labor force grew by more than 50 percent, from 11,970,000 women in 1940 to 18,610,000 in 1945. The proportion of women in the population who worked outside the home grew from 27.6 percent to 37 percent. By 1945 women were

36.1 percent of the entire labor force.[42]

While the war was going on, journalism educators were told women would have difficulty keeping their jobs when peace came. Results of a survey of 66 newspapers conducted by the Inland Daily Press Association were presented at a 1944 meeting of the American Association of Schools and Departments of Journalism. They showed 11 percent of the publishers queried planned to discharge their women employees after the war, while 48.4 percent intended to give first preference to returning servicemen but were willing to retain "any girl who wishes to continue and who can deliver in competition with men." An additional 19.7 percent were planning to eliminate women from positions on copy desks and from "tough" reporting assignments and some advertising accounts. Only 4.5 percent of the publishers hoped to employ all women who wished to stay.[43]

The wartime women journalists as a group were described as incompetent in a *Saturday Evening Post* article titled "Paper Dolls," which gave the number of female replacements nationally as 8,000. The article, overlooking those with formal journalism training, ridiculed the backgrounds of the replacements. In a patronizing "defense," the authors stated, "Editors are prone to forget that the majority of their new paper dolls were secretaries, file clerks, telephone operators, receptionists or copy girls a short time ago. They have been thrown into jobs demanding special training and knowhow without the basic training given men reporters in normal times."[44]

Regardless of their actual qualifications, some women may have seen themselves as unprofessional substitutes. One journalism graduate of the University of Oklahoma wrote in *The Matrix,* "I probably hold the distinction of being the only university coed to be graduated without ever having witnessed an athletic event, yet I became the first girl sports editor of a daily paper in Oklahoma." She explained she wound up with the job on the *Shawnee News-Star* because the "he-man ranks had been depleted by the call to arms." The managing editor felt "sorry enough for me and my struggles" that he covered the first high school games himself, she noted.[45]

But even women with sterling credentials faced demotion when the war ended in 1945. Dorothy Jurney, who had been acting city editor of the *Washington Daily News,* was told she would not be considered for the job permanently because she was a woman. She was asked to train her replacement, which she did, before moving to the *Miami Herald* as woman's editor. In Minneapolis Margaret Allison, who had written outstanding features for the city staff during the war, found herself moved back to the woman's page. And so it went across the country.[46]

Journalism educators looked forward to the return of men to the classroom. Speaking to the American Society of Journalism School Administrators in 1946, A.A. Applegate, head of the journalism program at Michigan State College (now University), predicted that the glut of women in the field would level off in two or three years. He foresaw no problem of too many women in journalism because he expected many, after brief careers, would desire to become homemakers. But he held out hope that "there will always be room for one or two excellent women on every newspaper."[47]

*The Matrix* reported that each woman journalism student throughout the nation confronted the question, "Just what kind of journalistic jobs are open to me now?" Joan Cameron, a graduate of the University of Wisconsin, offered an answer. She located a place in a journalistic field that holds "promise for women—war or no war," as *The Matrix* put it. Cameron was assistant editor of the *Wisconsin REA* (Rural Electric Association) *News.* She urged other women to seek jobs on specialized publications.[48]

In 1949 *Mademoiselle's* job editor surveyed 27 daily newspapers and 15 journalism schools, informing her readers, "Newspaper-bent? It's a bad year for it." Before the men came back, "you could have had a crack at a beginning job, even on a big-city daily, and it might have led into the metropolitan reporting most women aim for when they enter journalism," she continued. But now women who formerly handled straight news were back in women's departments. She quoted editors who justified their discrimination, as they had before the war, on grounds that women were too undependable and emotional for beats like sports, politics, business, labor, agriculture and finance or for copy editing and rewrite. Also, editors said women "get married and quit just about the time they're any good to you."[49]

Consequently women journalism graduates in the post-war period had a choice of three main options. They could go into specialized publications or the women's pages, trying to turn their sex into an asset instead of a liability. They could work twice as hard as their male competitors, trying to prove that they were twice as good. Or they could marry and devote themselves to being wives and mothers after a short-fling career. Many took the third option.

Those willing to confine themselves to the women's pages, writing about non-controversial topics, occasionally won praise from male educators. In 1949 Dean Ackerman of the Columbia journalism school honored women's page writers during a seminar of the American Press Institute, a program at Columbia University to train mid-career newspaper personnel. "In writing about health, schools, the church, food, child care, home living and other similar subjects, women as journalists contribute to the uplifting of our national life," Ackerman said. "There is as much wholesomeness in the inside of a newspaper as there is in the inside of a home."[50]

"Wholesomeness" as a steady news diet was scorned by those eager to tackle the same subjects as men. Marguerite Higgins provided one role model. A Columbia journalism graduate and war correspondent in World War II, Higgins won a Pulitzer Prize for her coverage of the Korean War for the *New York Herald-Tribune.* Her alma mater boasted of her achievements at the same time it pictured her as an oddity. "Marguerite Higgins, Girl Reporter, Covering War on the Korean Front Asks No Favors Because of Her Sex" read the headline on a Columbia journalism school publication in 1950. The story began, "There has not been a name like Marguerite Higgins in American journalism since the time of Nellie Bly. One of these days, songs will be written about her."[51]

It was the unsung women who were included in the first post-war survey of women journalism graduates. In 1952 Adelaide H. Jones, a journalism instructor at Drury College in Springfield, Missouri, mailed questionnaires to all women who had been graduated from thirteen journalism schools in 1941 to gather data on their professional and personal lives during the decade after graduation. The women came from these schools: the universities of Indiana, Louisiana, Montana, Iowa, Colorado, Georgia, Minnesota, Missouri, Oklahoma and Southern California and Iowa State College, Kansas State College and Texas State Collge for Women. Key findings were:

Women journalism graduates married as often as the average for United States women of the same age, 88 percent of the time, although women college graduates on the average married only 69 percent of the time; thus women journalism graduates married more often than women graduates in general.

The women journalism graduates had families averaging 3.56 persons, a higher average than the 2.64 persons attributed to women college graduates in general.

Of the entire group, 98 percent held one or more positions during the decade, with 77 percent, representing the greatest number of any one year, employed the first year after graduation. The 98 percent included 15 percent who went into non-journalistic work.[52]

In spite of wartime employment opportunities, the "proportion remaining in gainful employment decreased steadily to a low of 26 percent in 1949, which can be explained only by the high marriage rate of the group and subsequent interruption of employment for reasons due to marital status," Jones noted. After 1949 the employed group began to increase until it reached 34 percent by 1951, perhaps due to mothers returning to work after children were in school.[53]

Jones reported the graduates tended to take a first job on a newspaper and then to move into other areas. Public relations gained in popularity throughout the decade, with one in five of those employed in journalism at the end of 10 years in this field. Newspapers, although they lost graduates early in the period covered, ended up with one in four of those employed in journalism. About 10 percent of the employed graduates at the end of the decade were in agency advertising.[54]

The survey also found the women were not underpaid in relation to other women in the work force. The average earned more money than other college women in 1949—a period when comparative salary figures were available. Advertising was the most lucrative journalistic area.[55]

One conclusion seemed obvious to Jones. It was: "The journalism graduate...lived much more happily with her husband and family than with her profession." Jones called for "a better understanding of the needs of the woman journalism student and for more consideration of those needs in curricular planning, course counseling and job placement" as well as "a more realistic conception of the profession on the part of the student herself."[56]

Marriage as a prime aim of women journalism graduates in the 1950s was stressed in advice given Theta Sigma Phi members. "If you're playing with the idea of becoming a part-time mother—that is, combining your household with your pre-marital career—don't do it," concluded a panel of established career women and mothers, who spoke at a Los Angeles meeting in 1951. "You would be much happier to take the emotional warmth of your house and your family and forget your career. After seven years of trying to combine both, I realize now that I can have much more fun with my daughter's group of Brownies than with a radio script," a once-prominent radio comedy writer advised the group.[57]

Betty Angelo, who resigned from a general assignment reporting beat on the *Detroit News* to get married, urged women graduates to seek jobs on metropolitan newspapers, not to advance their careers but to hunt husbands. She said she had worked for a year and a half on a small-town paper but had met no eligible suitors. "I worked for a big city newspaper five years and met, among numerous other marriageable males, my husband—a newspaper editor on a rival paper," she wrote in *The Matrix*. "I could have saved myself a year and a half if I'd only come to the big city sooner!"[58]

Women who were brought to college campuses to advise students urged them to forget dreams of exciting journalistic pursuits. Winifred Jardine, who spoke at Iowa State in 1956, told how she managed to put her husband and three children first while employed as food editor of the *Deseret News* in Salt Lake City. She said she tested recipes she used on the food page in her own kitchen, wrote her stories at home and had her husband drop them off at the newspaper office.[59]

Discrimination against women was one factor that led to a serious shortage of qualified persons in the field as the 1950s ended. A 1958 survey by Alvin Austin, a journalism professor at the University of North Dakota, spelled out the situation. The survey showed a 30 percent drop in journalism school enrollment since 1948 and reported 67 percent of the editors responding listed a shortage of personnel as a major problem. According to the report, 3,500 new graduates were needed each year for newspapers, but journalism schools were turning out only 2,500, of whom about one-third were women. Austin cited low pay and negative advisement in high school as reasons for the enrollment decline. In 1957, for example, the average newspaper starting pay for men was only $76.96 weekly. It fell to $66 for women.[60]

Journalism schools, however, produced only a fraction of the women who held jobs in the field. Even with the revival of homemaking and the "baby boom" of the postwar period, an increase showed up in the total number of women classified as journalists by the United States census in 1960. The number of women employed as editors and reporters in newspaper, magazine and book publishing, which had increased by 7 percent from 1940 to 1950, continued to grow. By 1960 women represented about 37 percent of the total. In addition, according to the Women's Bureau of the United States Department of Labor, the percentage of women employed in public relations and publicity work increased an extraordinary 258 percent from 1950 to 1960.[61]

These figures reflected dramatic, but little-noticed changes, in the work force as a whole. After World War II the pace of female employment quickened rather than slowed, with twice as many women employed in 1960 as in 1940. The proportion of employed wives doubled from 15 percent in 1940 to 30 percent in 1960 and the number of working mothers leaped 400 percent.[62]

Journalism education, like higher education in general, did not recognize the significance of these trends. Women journalism students were counseled to settle for secondary status within the field. At the University of Missouri, for example, women news-editorial students routinely were steered into the "society" department of the *Columbia Missourian,* the daily newspaper produced by the school of journalism. There the kindly Queen Smith, a veteran society editor and assistant professor, drilled them in covering weddings and parties. The implications of the expanded number of working women, which would lead to the women's liberation movement of the 1960s, were far removed from what these women were taught.[63]

## ENDNOTES

1. Sutton, *Education for Journalism in the United States,* p. 18.
2. Grant M. Hyde, "The Next Steps in Schools of Journalism," *Journalism Quarterly* 14 (Winter 1937), pp. 35–41.
3. R.E. Wolseley, "Deadline for Women," *The Matrix* 24 (Feb. 1939), pp. 9–10.
4. Ibid., p. 11.
5. Ross, *Ladies of the Press,* pp. 3–13.
6. Carl W. Ackerman, *Report of the Dean of the Graduate School of Journalism for the Academic Year Ending June 30, 1940* (New York: Columbia University, 1940), p. 14.
7. Ackerman, *Report of the Dean of the Graduate School of Journalism for the Period Ending June 30, 1935,* p. 8.

8. Josephine Caldwell Meyer, "A B C for Jobs," *The Matrix* 25 (Aug. 1940), pp. 10-11.
9. Ibid., p. 12.
10. Ibid.
11. Edwin Emery and Michael Emery, *The Press and America: An Interpretative History of the Mass Media,* 4th edition (Englewood Cliffs, N.J.: Prentice-Hall, 1978), p. 436; Maurine Beasley, ed., *The White House Press Conferences of Eleanor Roosevelt* (New York: Garland, 1983), p. 1.
12. As quoted in Marzolf, *Up From the Footnote,* pp. 249-50.
13. Ibid., pp. 250-51.
14. Julie A. Matthaei, *An Economic History of Women in America: Women's Work, the Sexual Division of Labor, and the Development of Capitalism* (New York: Schocken, 1982), p. 257.
15. Ibid. p. 261.
16. Richard T. Baker, *A History of the Graduate School of Journalism, Columbia University* (New York: Columbia University Press, 1954), p. 107; Memo from Eleanor Carroll to Ramona R. Rush, as quoted in "Women in Academe: Journalism Education Viewed From the Literature and Other Memorabilia," unpublished paper presented at the Association for Education in Journalism convention at Ft. Collins, Colo., Aug. 1973, p. 51.
17. "Employers' Symposium," *The Matrix* 26 (Oct. 1940), pp. 7-8.
18. Ware, *Holding Their Own,* p. 74; Sandra G. Treadway, "Anne Elizabeth O'Hare McCormick," *Notable American Women: The Modern Period* IV (Cambridge, Mass.: Harvard University Press, 1980), p. 439.
19. Ware, *Holding Their Own,* pp. 74-78.
20. Ross, *Ladies of the Press,* pp. 317, 347-49.
21. Iona Robertson Logie, *Careers for Women in Journalism: A Composite Picture of 881 Salaried Women Writers at Work In Journalism, Advertising, Publicity and Promotion* (Scranton, Pa.: International Textbook Co., 1938), p. 5, 149.
22. Ibid., pp. 5, 146.
23. Ibid., pp. 21-22.
24. Ibid., pp. 134, 139-40.
25. Ibid., 154.
26. Ibid., pp. 155-157.
27. Ibid., p. 158.
28. Ibid., pp. 69, 161-62.
29. Ibid., pp. 172-74.
30. Ibid., pp. 176-77.
31. Ibid., p. v.
32. Marjorie Shuler, Ruth A. Knight and Muriel Fuller, *Lady Editor* (New York: Dutton, 1941), pp. 17-18.
33. Abbie A. Amrine, "This Is Our Day," *The Matrix* 27 (Oct. 1941), p. 15.
34. Ibid.
35. "Matrix Final" column, *The Matrix* 28 (Dec. 1942), p. 3.
36. Bernell Winn, "It's Ladies Day," *The Matrix* 28 (April 1943), p. 6.

37. Ibid.
38. Ibid., p. 7.
39. Marzolf, *Up From the Footnote,* p. 69.
40. Roberta Applegate, "Fran Harris: Pioneer Newscaster," *The Matrix* 28 (Aug. 1943), pp. 6-7.
41. Susan M. Hartmann, *The Home Front and Beyond: American Women in the 1940s* (Boston: Twayne, 1982), p. 20.
42. Ibid., p. 21.
43. Rosamond Risser Jones, "The Campus Beat," *The Matrix* 29 (April 1944), p. 16.
44. Stanley Frank and Paul Sann, "Paper Dolls," *Saturday Evening Post,* May 20, 1944, p. 95.
45. Joy Turner Stilley, "Unathletic Sports Editor," *The Matrix* 30 (Oct. 1944), p. 13.
46. Marzolf, *Up From the Footnote,* p. 75.
47. Rosamond Risser Jones, "The Campus Beat," *The Matrix* 31 (Feb. 1946), p. 30.
48. Joy South, "Field of Promise for Women," *The Matrix* 31 (Feb. 1946), p. 8.
49. As quoted in Marzolf, *Up From the Footnote,* pp. 75-76.
50. Carl W. Ackerman, "The Inside of a Newspaper Should Be Like the Inside of the Home," text of speech given in honor of members of the seminar on Women's Pages of the American Press Institute at Columbia University, June 6, 1949, Box 164, Ackerman Papers, Library of Congress.
51. *Gist, Journalism at Columbia University,* annual report of Dean Carl W. Ackerman to President Dwight D. Eisenhower, Sept. 1950, Box 191, Ackerman Papers, Library of Congress.
52. Adelaide H. Jones, "Women Journalism Graduates in the 1941-51 Decade," *Journalism Quarterly* 30 (Winter 1953), pp. 49-50. Unfortunately Jones did not give the total number of women surveyed.
53. Ibid., p. 50.
54. Ibid.
55. Ibid., p. 51.
56. Ibid., p. 52.
57. Midge Winters Sherwood, "No Such Thing as Part-time Mother," *The Matrix* 37 (Oct. 1951), p. 9.
58. Betty Angelo, "Career: Metropolitan Vs. Community Newspaper," *The Matrix* 39 (Oct.-Nov., 1953), p. 14.
59. Millie Willett, "Career Vs. The Home and Family," *The Matrix* 44 (June-July, 1956), p. 3.
60. "Recruiting Young Journalists," *The Matrix* 44 (Sept.-Oct. 1959), p. 10. See also "Recruiting Young People for Communications Careers," *The Matrix* 46 (Sept.-Oct. 1961), p. 26, and Charles T. Duncan, "Again Too Few Graduates To Go Around; Salaries Up," in *Journalism Quarterly* 34 (Fall 1957), p. 493-95.
61. Marzolf, *Up From the Footnote,* p. 74; Mary D. Keyserling, "Women Journalists and Today's World," *The Matrix* 50 (April 1965), p. 11.

62. William H. Chafe, *The American Woman: Her Changing Social, Economic, and Political Roles, 1920–1970* (New York: Oxford, 1972), p. 218.
63. Betty Conrad Allen, "Queen Smith, Dean of Society Editors," *The Matrix* 41 (Oct.–Nov. 1955), pp. 4–5; personal recollections of Maurine Beasley, a 1958 graduate of the University of Missouri School of Journalism.

# Chapter 3

# A New Majority, With Little Change in the Schools: 1961–1985

As the 1960s opened, the position of women in higher education was weaker than it had been three decades before. In 1960, women received 35 percent of all bachelors' degrees awarded; in 1930 they had received 40 percent. American women were pictured in the media as affluent housewives, fulfilled by their husbands, homes and children, although 36 percent of all women worked for pay. But the myth of the "happy homemaker" soon was challenged by a movement for women's liberation that had widespread impact on colleges and universities.[1]

As an outgrowth of the civil rights struggle for black Americans, women became increasingly politicized. Linked to the New Left, which opposed the Vietnam war, women's groups waged their own fight for equality. An odd coalition of feminists, who sought passage, and southerners, who wanted to ridicule the bill to death, were behind 1964 civil rights legislation that outlawed sex discrimination under Title VII, the equal employment section of the measure. When the bill took effect in 1965, it became illegal to discriminate against women in hiring and promotions.[2]

Journalism education, long considered a male bastion, was forced to look at the composition of its faculties in light of the new federal law. What emerged was widespread evidence of prejudice against women. In 1965 Roberta Applegate, who had left an outstanding newspaper career as a political reporter to teach journalism at Kansas State University, found that 76 women faculty members, representing 56 schools or departments of journalism, belonged to the Association for Education in Journalism (AEJ), the umbrella organization for all journalism educators. Of the 76, only seven had attained the full professor rank. Most were so isolated from participation in AEJ that only nine had attended the association's convention that year.[3]

In fact, Applegate discovered, male dominance of the educator ranks had not changed much since the 1930s. She noted that "thirty-five years ago, two Helens—Hostetter (Kansas State) and Patterson (Wisconsin)—stuck together for moral support whenever they attended conventions of journalism educators. At the start, they didn't have much trouble finding each other because frequently they were the only women college faculty members present."[4]

Applegate also reported two observations from male department heads about the lack of women faculty members. Charles E. Rogers, former head at Kansas State, cited "the fact that prejudice against women is still present to some degree." Hyde at the University of Wisconsin called for token hiring at least, since one-third of the students were women.[5]

Although the percentage of women students increased during the 1960s along with total enrollments, journalism education did not change dramatically. In 1968 the percentage of women stood at 41 percent of the student total. By 1970 there were 33,000 journalism majors in colleges and universities and the majority were male. The largest single group was in news-editorial. But old barriers for women were breaking down.[6]

In view of equal employment legislation, the Columbia University Graduate School of Journalism did away with its long-standing quota on women students, previously limited to 10 percent of the class. "Since there were few jobs on large newspapers for women, we had (we felt) no business making women qualified to be unemployed," recalled Professor Melvin Mencher. "My recollection is that *The Wall Street Journal* broke its sex barrier in 1970 when it hired Ellen Graham, but we stopped the quota system two years before," he continued. "The surprising thing is that though the women were 10 percent, they usually walked off with more than half the prizes. But perhaps it wasn't surprising: They were carefully selected."[7]

In 1972 three women journalism faculty members at Kansas State, Ramona Rush, Carol Oukrop and Sandra Ernst, presented results of the first formal study of women journalism educators at the annual convention of the Association for Education in Journalism. Key findings were:

- For the year 1970–71, there were 131 women members of the association, representing 11 percent of the membership of 1,200. These women were almost invisible within the organization. The official schedule for the annual meeting in 1971 did not show any woman on the convention program.

- No women were listed in the 1970–71 AEJ Directory as officials or even members of the association's executive committee, advisory board or standing committees. Thus, women were not represented at all in the organization's official structure. No woman had ever been president of the association.

- The percentage of women involved in *Journalism Quarterly,* the main professional journal for journalism educators, was low. From 1960 to 1971, only seven percent of the contributors of major articles were women, with 59 women compared to 886 men having articles published in the journal. The percentage of women contributing to the "Research in Brief" section was

slightly higher, with 10 percent of the articles (30 out of 290) written by women.
- The number of women faculty members nationally in journalism education was less than the number of women members of AEJ (which included professional journalists and students as well as teachers). In 1971-72, women constituted about eight percent of the total employed on journalism faculties. Only 10 were identified as having Ph.D. degrees.[8]

The lack of women faculty meant few role models for women graduate students in journalism and communication, Rush, Oukrop and Ernst found. Questionnaires sent by them to 101 women working on doctorate degrees at 16 universities elicited comments on the role conflicts faced by those preparing to be journalism educators. Fifty-seven percent out of 72 responding stated they had to "do more" than men to earn the respect of their professors and male graduate student counterparts. Some commented:

- "I feel that I am assumed to be dumb (because I'm female and look young) and must prove myself to be competent. Men, on the other hand, are automatically assumed to be competent unless proven stupid."
- "Both professionally and personally, women are suspect. It seems we must be better students than men and more womanly than non-student females."
- "I find that as a single woman one must be particularly careful to cultivate the wives and make it apparent I'm no threat to them—that I am interested in their husbands only professionally."[9]

As a result of the report, AEJ appointed a Committee on the Status of Women, which is still in existence. One of its first tasks was to follow up a study made by Theta Sigma Phi, which changed its name to Women in Communications and decided to admit men in 1972. (It acted one year after Sigma Delta Chi, which became the Society of Professional Journalists/Sigma Delta Chi, had voted to accept women.) The Women in Communications study showed that 81 percent of 170 journalism schools had one or no woman on the faculty. Women in Communications called for an affirmative action program to increase the number of women faculty.[10]

In 1973, for the first time in the history of AEJ, the organization held a plenary session to spotlight the status of its women members. A survey of 60 schools led to the following conclusions: "If you teach journalism in a college or university which has a sequence accredited by the American Council on Education in Journalism and you are a woman, you tend to be ranked lower, promoted more slowly and paid less than your colleagues who are male." Of the eight percent of journalism faculty members who were female, two-thirds were in the lowest ranks: instructor, lecturer or assistant professor. By contrast only one-third of the males were at the lower levels.[11]

The creation of the Committee on the Status of Women led to more research about the position of women within journalism education. A 1974 study showed that the numbers of women in journalism education took a funnel shape. At the undergraduate level it was large, with women making up about half of the enrollment, but the number of women decreased at the master's level and represented only 10 percent of the doctoral candidates.[12]

A shortage of qualified women to teach journalism was stressed in responses by 29 department heads to the effort by Women in Communications to urge employment of more women faculty members. They cited both lack of women with advanced degrees in communications and lack of readiness by academic institutions to recognize extensive practical experience as a valuable substitute for advanced degrees. Since Ph.D. degrees were required for most positions leading to the prestige and pay of a full professorship, women with distinguished professional careers were limited to lower-level jobs as instructors or assistant professors, which paid significantly less than non-academic positions.[13]

Interest in the position of women on journalism faculties marked only one aspect of attempts by women to elevate their role in the media during the late 1960s and 1970s. Women's groups attacked the content of women's publications. They followed the lead of Betty Friedan, whose best-selling book, *The Feminine Mystique,* published in 1963, accused traditional magazines of depicting women only as sex objects or subservient housewives.[14]

Women's portrayal and participation in the media became a well-publicized issue in March of 1970 in New York when feminists staged a sit-in at the *Ladies Home Journal.* The same week as the sit-in, women at *Newsweek* filed a complaint with the Equal Employment Opportunity Commission, the enforcement arm for civil rights legislation. They charged discrimination in employment because they were restricted to jobs as researchers while men held reporter-editor positions. An agreement between *Newsweek* and the women subsequently settled the complaint and allowed the women to advance.[15]

As the women's liberation movement spread, women became more assertive in demanding different treatment both as consumers of media and as working journalists. Feminist publications, ranging from *Ms.,* a national monthly, to mimeographed newsletters, sprang up. After the National Organization for Women challenged a license renewal for WABC-TV in New York in 1972 on grounds the station discriminated against women, feminist groups obtained agreements with stations in Pennsylvania, Colorado, New York, Tennessee and California. These contained promises to improve employment opportunities for women, and to take women's groups into account in programming. Newspapers did away with their traditional women's pages, replacing them with lifestyle sections aimed at readers of both sexes.[16]

More and more women poured into journalism schools. Lady Bird Johnson, the wife of President Lyndon B. Johnson, who held office from 1963 to 1968, helped publicize the major. Although she had never worked as a journalist, she held a degree in journalism from the University of Texas. "Not a day passes that I am not confronted with a situation, a group, a question that causes me to be grateful that I picked journalism for my major," she wrote in 1965. In 1967-68, journalism enrollment rose for the eighth consecutive year, with a total of 24,445 students enrolled in courses at 118 schools. This represented an enrollment increase of 9.4 percent, which exceeded the over-all college enrollment gain of 8.3 percent.[17]

Upon graduation women journalists still faced the prospect of lower pay and fewer chances for promotions than men. A 1970 survey of 616 members of Theta Sigma Phi showed that the women, many of whom had lengthy experience, made an average of $838 per month compared to $578 monthly for beginning journalism graduates. By far, the majority said they felt, or knew, they were not paid as well as their male counterparts for equal work.[18]

*The Matrix* reported, "In spite of laws against discrimination, some employers frankly tell their women employees that they cannot expect to make as much as men. Many women feel that they would be in serious trouble with their bosses if they openly insisted on equal pay for equal work."[19]

To help women cope with discrimination, women's studies courses were added to the curriculum in some journalism schools. The first began as a seminar for seniors and graduate students taught by Marion Marzolf, an assistant professor, at the University of Michigan in 1971. "Do women in journalism have a history?" Marzolf wrote on a sign posted on her office door, inviting students to explore the subject with her. Out of Marzolf's course came the first bibliography on women in journalism. Six years later she published the first contemporary history of women journalists.[20]

Women who were graduated with journalism degrees in 1966 and 1971 from three state universities, Louisiana, Missouri and Nebraska, were surveyed in 1977 on their careers and personal lives. The study found the majority both married and employed and committed to the successful mixing of marriage and family with a lifetime career.[21]

Their continued enthusiasm for journalism supported results of an earlier study which concluded that "...female (students) considered journalism more interesting than did males." That study reported in 1974 that men with journalism degrees were more likely to pursue non-journalism careers than women (going on to law school, for example). It concluded "...women students are more likely to be committed to pursue journalism careers than men."[22]

Yet observers of journalism education overlooked the growing numbers of women students. In a 1977 attack on journalism schools that appeared in the *Atlantic,* Ben H. Bagdikian, a media critic, attributed the swell in enrollment, which reached 64,000 students that year, to youth eager to emulate Carl Bernstein and Bob Woodward. These two young *Washington Post* reporters were credited with exposing the Watergate scandal that toppled President Nixon in 1974. While stressing their fame may have drawn students to journalism, Bagdikian ignored the fact that percentage increases in journalism enrollment were larger in the 1960s than in the 1970s.[23]

In an 11-page article, Bagdikian contended many journalism schools taught trivial trade skills "imbedded in a curriculum that discourages intellectual growth, prevents depth of knowledge, and denies the future journalists a broad perspective on society." He also argued journalism education was flooding the market with far more graduates than could find newspaper jobs. Nowhere in his critique did he refer to the changing nature of the student body, made up of an increasing number for whom Woodward and Bernstein were unlikely role models; those, that is, who were in the public relations and advertising parts of journalism programs.[24]

In the same year that Bagdikian's article appeared, the percentage enrollment of women in journalism schools surpassed that of men for the first time. According to Paul V. Peterson, journalism professor at Ohio State University and compiler of the major annual journalism enrollment survey, the proportion of women represented slightly more than 50 percent in 1977. In 1978 it reached 53.1 percent, compared with only 41.1 percent a decade before. That year Mary Gardner, professor of journalism at Michigan State University, became the first woman president of the Association of Education in Journalism.[25]

Since then the percentage of women has continued to increase. In 1983 it stood at 58 percent compared with 57.5 percent in 1981. While the comparable figure for 1982 was 58.6 percent, Peterson did not see the 1983 figure as representing a downward turn.[26]

"At best these figures are only estimates since some schools don't keep figures broken down by sex," Peterson said. His survey of 1983 enrollments showed a total of 82,649 journalism students listed by sex with 47,961 women and 34,688 men. In the 1984 survey, Peterson found the female majority to be about 59.2 percent out of a total of about 86,000 students. The minority enrollment was about 8 percent.[27]

In terms of graduates, women represented 61.5 percent of the 14,274 persons receiving journalism degrees in 1981–82. By contrast the percentage of women obtaining degrees in other professional fields traditionally considered male-dominated was far smaller for 1981–1982. Women represented 33.4 percent of law school graduates, 25 percent of medical school graduates and 11.4 percent of engineering school graduates. As expected, women continued to dominate in traditionally female fields, receiving 75.9 percent of all degrees given in education and 82.3 percent of all degrees given in library science, for example.[28]

The new predominance of women in journalism schools reflected the growing numbers of women college students in general. While higher education long had been the domain of men, women constituted the majority of undergraduates by 1982. According to Betty Vetter of the Scientific Manpower Commission, which made an annual statistical study of the numbers of women going into professions, it was not surprising that journalism had drawn an increasing percentage of women students.[29]

"When women started to get the option to do what they pleased, they went to college and they went into those non-traditional fields where they had been before," she explained in 1984. She pointed out women as a group tended to select fields where other women had gone before them, although in fewer numbers. Vetter projected the percentage of women in law schools soon would increase to the 50 percent mark.[30]

Peterson's surveys linked the growing percentage of women journalism students to the increase of enrollments in public relations and advertising sequences. In 1980 Peterson first observed, "...when sequences are analyzed, there is a clear indication that a growing percentage of students are enrolling in the advertising and public relations sequences, while the number in news-editorial is declining. The first two sequences are more heavily female populated as well."[31]

Peterson concluded that this shows "more females looking at nontraditional forms of journalism for careers." He also saw a reflection of the past. "I still think they see the newsroom as an all-male bastion," he said.[32]

The influx of women students did not bring an equal influx of women faculty members. In 1983 researchers at Syracuse University determined there was a striking imbalance between the percentage of women students and women faculty members. Based on a national survey, they found women students constituted 59 percent of enrollment at the undergraduate, 52 percent at the masters, and 36 percent at the doctorate level. But women represented only 20 percent at the faculty level. Only two accredited journalism programs were headed by women.[33]

The study also found 43 percent of women faculty viewed sex discrimination as a problem. Those who perceived it gave the following areas of concern: salary, 44 percent; appointment to administrative positions, 53 percent; tenure and promotion, 34 percent. Subtle discriminatory attitudes were cited by 59 percent, who said they had to do more than their male colleagues to earn respect from male faculty and administration.[34]

Responding to inquiries from the National Federation of Press Women in 1983, male heads of eight journalism programs said they wanted more women on their staffs but that they received relatively few applications from qualified women when openings were advertised. Most said few applicants had the required doctorate or master's degree and strong professional experience.[35]

"In addition to teaching strengths, women faculty are needed as role models and as advisers and counselors," commented Herbert Strentz, dean at Drake University. "We're presently conducting a search for two assistant professors and received only four applications from women in this national search," Walter Bunge, director at Ohio State University, noted. "The response from such a small number of women is not unusual in our previous searches, but it's disappointing."[36]

In terms of employment, women graduates appeared to experience somewhat more difficulty than male graduates in finding media-related jobs. The Dow Jones Newspaper Fund/Gallup survey completed in 1984 showed differences in the employment patterns of men and women who received bachelor's degrees in the spring of 1983. Among them:

- While women represented 64.1 percent, or 11,326 of the total of 17,670 graduates surveyed, they were less likely than male graduates to find media-related jobs. While 14.6 percent of the graduates as a whole found jobs in the print media, only 11.8 percent of the women did so.
- Although 9.4 percent of the graduates found jobs on daily newspapers, women were less likely than men to be in this category, with only 6.9 percent of the women reporting jobs on daily papers. An almost equal percentage of men and women, 4.8 and 4.7 respectively, found jobs on weekly newspapers.
- A higher percentage of women were unemployed than the graduates as a whole, with 14.2 percent of the women continuing to seek media-related work compared to 11.8 percent for the total group.
- A higher percentage of women graduates than graduates as a whole were employed in two categories—advertising and magazines—with 7.7 percent of the women finding jobs in advertising compared with 6.8 percent of the total and 2.5 percent of the women finding jobs on magazines compared with 1.9 percent of the total. In public relations 6.8 percent of the women found jobs compared to 7.3 percent for the total.
- In broadcasting 6.1 percent of the total found work in radio and 5.8 percent in television, while the comparable percentages for women were 5.5 percent in radio and 5.6 percent in television.[37]

The figures suggested women were less successful than men in moving from journalism school into the field. Were too many women fighting for too few jobs confronted by employers who preferred men? Was journalism education becoming a "pink-collar ghetto" field? What effect was the predominance of women graduates having on salaries in the field?

General sex discrimination in pay has been a well-documented fact. According to the U.S. Census Bureau, on the average women who work full-time, year-round were paid approximately 61 cents for every dollar paid to men in 1982. Median earnings in professional occupations with large concentrations of women fell short of median earnings in nonprofessional occupations with large concentrations of men. Registered nurses, for example, had a median income of $18,980, librarians $17,992 and elementary school teachers $18,148, compared to $21,840 for mail carriers, $17,732 for meat cutters and $21,944 for plumbers and pipefitters.[38]

The salary picture for male and female journalism graduates in 1983 showed no clear pattern of discrimination. The Newspaper Fund/Gallup survey broke down the weekly salaries of 1983 graduates into 12 ranges varying from $130 or less to more than $400. The percentage of women being paid in the lowest range was exactly the same as the percentage for the group as a whole—.9 percent. In the highest range, however, the percentage for the group as a whole was 5.5 compared to 3.9 percent for the women. In the middle range of salaries of $231 to $250 a week, women fared somewhat better than the group as a whole, with 14.3 percent in this category compared to 13.5 percent of the total.[39]

Yet journalistic salaries in general were not high and fears that women depressed pay scales did not appear unrealistic. Peterson commented: "Is it important that women dominate the field? I don't think so. But as males began to look at the salaries, they may give journalism another thought. Traditionally females have been willing to accept lower salaries than males."[40]

A 1982 study of women in educational communications, a branch of public relations, for example, showed that salary discrepancies existed between men and women respondents with comparable years of experience. Even at the lowest level of experience, two or fewer years in the field, men had a mean salary of $23,090 compared to $19,397 for females, a difference of almost $4,000.[41]

This suggested that journalism schools might be turning out an increasing number of graduates who would encounter sexual bias in their careers. Were they being properly prepared to recognize sexism and to overcome it? How adequate was mentoring? Academic and career advisement? Were women students being prepared to see themselves as potential managers, editors and policy-makers, not simply as technicians or entry-level editorial assistants? Were they being discouraged from careers in news-editorial work and counseled to go into public relations and advertising on the grounds that these areas were more appropriate for women? Were appropriate role models being provided? And, perhaps most important, what sorts of attitudes and expectations did the women students bring with them into journalism schools? Did these differ from the attitudes and expectations of the male students to whom journalism schools so long were geared?

If journalism education was not able to successfully prepare women to gain jobs traditionally given to men, then the future of the field seemed uncertain. In January, 1984, a national conference on journalism education was held at the University of Oregon as part of a two-year program to explore new directions for journalism education at a time of radical change in the mass communication industry. Participants, including both educators and journalism professionals, grappled with issues including curriculum, relationships between academia and professionals, faculty qualifications and the status of journalism units within university structures. After debate the group reaffirmed the liberal arts tradition in journalism education, which requires students at accredited schools to take 75 percent of their coursework in liberal arts and sciences and only 25 percent in journalism.[42]

The conference drew attention to the explosive growth in journalism programs and mass communications in the past two decades, which outstripped efforts to develop coherent academic models. It pointed out the changing employment picture for journalism graduates: Whereas newspapers once were the prime employers of graduates, this certainly was no longer true. Figures showed that advertising and public relations each claimed about one-fourth of the students enrolled in journalism; another quarter of the graduates did not remain in the communications field.[43]

The remaining quarter, about the same proportion as 20 years ago, entered news organizations, with expansion in radio and television offsetting decreases in jobs on newspapers and magazines. Yet newspapers continued to depend on journalism graduates. In 1981 the Newspaper Fund found that 83 percent of news-editorial people hired by newspapers directly from college campuses the year before had been journalism graduates.[44]

The Oregon conference did not consider the impact of the gender shift in enrollment. But no more pressing question confronts journalism educators. Since formal licensing requirements do not exist for journalists (unlike lawyers, doctors and some other professionals), employers are under no obligation to hire journalism graduates rather than individuals with college preparation in other fields. Some evidence already exists that employers are concerned about the declining percentage of male journalism graduates. In a report on a 1983 conference on professional support of journalism education, the American Newspaper Publishers Association Foundation drew attention to the dwindling proportion of men in journalism schools. "In the broadcast area it is becoming difficult to find male—especially black male—journalists," the report stated.[45]

In public relations, a female-dominated field, the percentage of those employed who majored in journalism apparently dropped during the period that journalism enrollments changed from predominantly male to predominantly female. According to the International Association of Business Communicators, the percentage of women communicators in its membership is growing—moving from 50.8 percent in 1977 to 59.8 percent in 1983. Yet over this same period the percentage of journalism graduates among its membership has declined—from 53 percent in 1977 to 38 percent in 1983. Journalism, however, has remained the single most common major for individuals in business communications.[46]

## ENDNOTES

1. Barbara Sinclair Deckard, *The Women's Movement: Political, Socioeconomic, and Psychological Issues* (New York: Harper & Row, 1983), p. 317.
2. Ibid., pp. 322-23.
3. Roberta Applegate, "Women as Journalism Educators," *The Matrix* 50 (June 1965), pp. 4-5.
4. Ibid.
5. Ibid.
6. Telephone interview by Maurine Beasley with Paul Peterson, March 26, 1984; Margaret Genovese, "J-Schools Try to Keep Up With Change," *Presstime* (Sept. 1980), p. 4.
7. Letter from Melvin Mencher to Maurine Beasley, Feb. 25, 1985.
8. Ramona R. Rush, "Women in Academe: Journalism Education Viewed from the Literature and Other Memorabilia," unpublished paper presented to the Association for Education in Journalism annual convention, Ft. Collins, Colo., Aug., 1973, pp. 13-17.
9. Ibid., pp. 18-20.
10. Ibid., pp. 22-24. See also "Journalism Faculties—Where Do We Stand?" *The Matrix* 57 (Fall 1972), pp. 20-21; Marzolf, *Up From the Footnote,* p. 261.
11. Marzolf, *Up From the Footnote,* pp. 261-62.
12. Ibid., pp. 263-64.
13. Ann Daly, "Journalism Faculty Women," *The Matrix* 58 (Winter 1972-73), pp. 20-21.
14. Nora Magid, "Women's Magazines in the Sixties," as excerpted in Maurine Beasley and Sheila Gibbons, *Women in Media: A Documentary Sourcebook* (Washington, D.C.: Women's Institute for Freedom of the Press, 1977), pp. 91-97.
15. "Action for Change: The Sit-in," in Beasley and Gibbons, *Women in Media,* pp. 98-108.
16. "Ms. Magazine," "Challenging Broadcast Licenses: WABC-TV," and "Negotiation Agreements: KNBC-TV," in Beasley and Gibbons, *Women in Media,* pp. 119-137, 142-146.
17. Mrs. Lyndon B. Johnson, "Woman's Tomorrow Is Here," *The Matrix* 50 (April 1965), p. 3; "J-Schools Continue to Grow," *The Matrix* 53 (Feb. 1968) p. 8.
18. Doris Quinn, "Are We Going for a Discount Price?" *The Matrix* 56 (Summer 1971), pp. 14-15.

19. Ibid.
20. Paper on "Seminar Journalism 500, 501," in Rush, "Women In Academe," p. 70; see also Marion Marzolf, Ramona R. Rush and Darlene Stern, "The Literature of Women in Journalism," *Journalism History I* (Winter 1974-75), pp. 117-128.
21. Wilma Crumley, Joye Patterson and Patricia Sailor, "Journalism Career Patterns of Women Are Changing," *Journalism Educator* 31 (Oct. 1977), p. 50.
22. Thomas A. Bowers, "Student Attitudes Toward Journalism As a Career," *Journalism Quarterly* 51 (Summer 1974), pp. 265-70.
23. Ben H. Bagdikian, "Woodstein U.: Notes on the Mass Production and Questionable Education of Journalists," *Atlantic* 239 (March 1977), pp. 80-92; Margaret Genovese, "J-Schools Try to Keep Up With Change," *Presstime* (Sept. 1980), p. 5.
24. Bagdikian, "Woodstein U.," p. 87.
25. Paul V. Peterson, "Enrollment Surged Again, Increases 7 Percent to 70,601," *Journalism Educator* 33 (Jan. 1979), p. 3. See also Peterson, "1984 Survey: No Change in Mass Communication Enrollment," *Journalism Educator* 40 (Spring 1985), pp. 3-9.
26. Paul V. Peterson, "Survey Indicates No Change in '83 Journalism Enrollment," *Journalism Educator* 39 (Spring 1984), p. 3.
27. Telephone interviews by Maurine Beasley with Paul V. Peterson, March 26, 1984, and April 11, 1985.
28. Telephone interview by Maurine Beasley with Tom Snyder, National Center for Education Statistics, U.S. Department of Education, March 26, 1984.
29. "The Classroom Climate: A Chilly One for Women?" Project on the Status and Education of Women (Washington, D.C.: Association of American Colleges, 1982), p. 1; telephone interview by Maurine Beasley with Betty Vetter, Scientific Manpower Commission, March 26, 1984.
30. Vetter interview.
31. Paul V. Peterson, "J-School Enrollments Reach Record 71,594," *Journalism Educator* 34 (Jan. 1980), p. 3.
32. Peterson interview, March 26, 1984; as quoted in Genovese, p. 5.
33. Survey results given in report by Judy Turk, Nancy Sharp, Sharon Hollenbeck, Linda Schamber, and Edna Einsiedel, S.I. Newhouse School of Public Communications, April, 1984.
34. Ibid.
35. "Enough Women on the Faculty?" *PW* (Press Woman) 46 (Feb. 1983), p. 1.
36. Ibid., p. 3.
37. Final tabulation, January 1984, Dow Jones Newspaper Fund/Gallup survey of 1983 journalism graduates, obtained from the Dow Jones Newspaper Fund, Princeton, N.J.
38. National Committee on Pay Equity, "The Wage Gap: Myths and Facts," (Washington, D.C.: 1983).
39. 1983 Dow Jones Newspaper Fund/Gallup survey.
40. Peterson interview, March 26, 1984.

41. Judy Kulstad VanSlyke, "Women in Educational Communications: Profile of Case Members, 1982," paper presented to the Committee on the Status of Women, Association for Education in Journalism annual convention, Athens, Ohio, July, 1982.
42. Tim Talevich, "Liberal Arts Tradition Backed at J-Education 'Summit'," *Presstime* (Feb. 1984), pp. 38–39.
43. Jonathan Friendly, "Journalism Educators Debate Strategies, Technology and Ties to the Media," *New York Times,* Jan. 23, 1984, p. A15.
44. 1981 Survey by Dow Jones Newspaper Fund.
45. Report on 1983 Conference for Professional Support of Journalism Education, (Reston, Va.: American Newspaper Publishers Association Foundation, 1983), p. 2.
46. International Association of Business Communicators, *Profile '79: A Survey of Business Communication and Business Communicators* (Syracuse, N.Y.: Syracuse University, 1979), p. 7; *Profile '83,* p. 4.

# PART II:

# One School Looks at Itself: The University of Maryland Study

## Chapter 4

## Alumni, Employers and Students Respond

Fairly recently at the University of Maryland College of Journalism there were relatively few students and they were mainly male. In 1968, for example, there were 120 majors, 80 percent of whom were men. In 1984–85, by contrast, there were more than 1,000 undergraduate majors and 69 percent were women. This was significantly greater than the national average of 59 percent. The majors specialized by sequence: news-editorial, public relations, advertising, magazine, photojournalism, broadcast news and science communication. In the advertising and public relations sequences, women represented about 80 percent of the enrollment.

Using the Maryland program as a case study, investigators sought to find out how well journalism education was serving the new majority. Information was sought from students, alumni and employers.

Was the college preparing women as well for the job market as it was preparing men? To what degree were women students and graduates having educational and employment experiences different from those of male students and graduates?

Did employers perceive the skill level of women graduates as different from that of male graduates? Did students, graduates and employers perceive sexism in operation, and if so, to what extent?

Beyond these questions, investigators were concerned with vital issues in journalism education. Will the predominance of women graduates mean that journalism education will be perceived as a second-rate educational program (since occupational programs for women traditionally have lacked the status of programs for men)? Will the communications industry hire journalism graduates or will it turn away from journalism education, hiring, for example, from schools of business administration or from liberal arts programs and providing on-the-job training for male employes? Will the influx of women journalism graduates further depress wages in areas where starting pay already is low? Have the women journalism graduates themselves been socialized in such a way they are handicapped in successfully moving beyond entry-level positions?

The initial step was to survey current students, alumni and employers of Maryland journalism graduates to see whether the experiences and attitudes reported differed based on sex.

The student survey included all potential graduates of the class of 1984. Of more than 280 questionnaires mailed out, 60 percent were returned.

In the alumni survey investigators mailed out a total of 642 questionnaires to a sample of male and female graduates beginning with the class of 1981 and including all other classes at three-year intervals back to 1951. Of these, 356 were returned, yielding a 55 percent response rate. About 53 percent of those replying were male, reflecting the large number of males in classes prior to 1975, when the balance tilted to women. A sizeable number of those who returned questionnaires agreed to complete an additional telephone interview of 30 minutes. Of these, 31 women and men were selected, proportioned among the 11 classes, to help interpret trends defined in the larger survey.

The employer sample was drawn from lists of newspapers, agencies or corporations where Maryland graduates were employed. There was a 57 percent response rate to the 251 questionnaires mailed out.

The survey explored the educational history and career aspirations of students and alumni, and the work history of alumni, including personal attitudes toward their careers. For all three groups attitudes about sexual bias in the classroom and workplace were investigated. Employers were asked to rate graduates by sex on specific areas of journalistic skills.

Findings from these three surveys of University of Maryland College of Journalism alumni (1951–81), students (class of 1984) and employers, supported expectations that attitudes within the three groups differ on journalism education and gender bias in the workplace. (Survey instruments are in Appendix C.)

Generally, graduates between the years 1951–81 perceived greater gender bias in the workplace than did employers, and students graduating in 1984 perceived greater bias than either group.

While educational preparation often differed significantly between males and females majoring in journalism at the University of Maryland between 1951–81, few differences remained by 1984.

Employers, generally, evaluated male and female journalism graduates equivalently and suggested the strengthening of several skills, particularly writing.

Female students in 1984 appeared to be as well prepared as males but had stronger career aspirations. In the alumni survey, factors influencing the choice of journalism as a major differed in degree by sex.

The overall findings suggest female journalism students and recent female journalism graduates are planning strategically for successful careers; and that female employers tend to recognize excellence in female employees to a greater degree than do male employers.

But they also show that journalism educators need to address the special problems of women in the labor market. This is borne out by comments made in the telephone interviews.

One graduate summed up the concerns of many in these words: "Equal pay for equal work is never addressed in the classroom. Helping women compete in the real world is needed."

Another remarked on the difficulties of career interruption: "The responsibility of family and childbearing is devastating for the careers of women in the journalism field. When you drop out of the job market for five years, it is hard to get back."

Others commented on the reaction of men to the influx of women. One said: "Men in the profession will protect their jobs more fiercely...men are feeling threatened and defensive..." Another said, "Pay has always been abominable in journalism and will get worse, as women always end up in low-paying fields. Where the money is, men will go."

## Highlights of Alumni Survey

- Alumni graduating from the University of Maryland between the years 1951–81 differed significantly by sex and age in a number of areas investigated.
- While only 36 percent of alumni transferred to the University of Maryland, female alumni tended to transfer later than males when they did transfer. In the selection of the university, alumni considered location, cost and reputation of the journalism program as important factors influencing the decision. Women tended to place greater importance on reputation, financial aid and parental and alumni recommendations than did males.
- Proportionate numbers of men and women went on to graduate school after college; however, men were twice as likely to earn a post-graduate degree. High income seemed to be correlated with advanced degrees.
- Sequence choices over time differed by sex. This can be accounted for by the increasing enrollment of women since the mid-1970s and the addition of new sequences. Consequently, greater proportions of women graduated in advertising, broadcast and magazine sequences while men dominated public relations and news sequences that have been offered traditionally. Those who graduated in public relations made higher incomes than those whose sequence specialization was news-editorial.
- When asked what influenced their decision to study journalism, alumni agreed that liking to write and creative opportunity, followed by value of job to society and liking to meet people, were of greatest importance. Women placed greater importance on liking to write, value of job to society, liking to meet people and the reputation of the college than men, while men placed greater importance on journalism as an "easy major." Recent graduates were more likely than earlier ones to cite prestige, money and creative opportunity as factors influencing their decisions to study journalism.

- Asked to comment on forms of discrimination they may have experienced in the classroom, about 20 percent noted the presence of sexual discrimination. Women were more likely to identify sexual discrimination than men.
- About 80 percent of alumni had a career/life goal while in college. Less than half said one person was the primary influencer in the choice of that career/life goal. Older alumni (40-49 years) mentioned a female as primary influencer 10 percent of the time, while younger alumni (20-29 years) mentioned a female 40 percent of the time. But on average, a male was the influencer 71 percent of the time.
- Upon graduation, about 90 percent worked full-time at some point. Those who got jobs first after graduation tended to make more money. Alumni agreed that the personal interview was of greatest overall importance in getting a job. Women placed greater emphasis on the personal interview, the quality of the resume, academic record, clip books, extra-curricular activities and pre-employment tests than males who tended to emphasize personal and professional contacts.
- Males were more satisfied with their jobs, incomes and chances for advancement than females. While alumni, in general, agreed that salary, freedom and autonomy, creative opportunity and career advancement were most important for career satisfaction, women placed greater value on creative opportunity than males.
- Women were 13 times more likely than men to have had career interruptions due to family responsibilities and seemed to suffer substantial income loss as a consequence. Women were out of jobs slightly longer and were twice as likely to change jobs as men.
- Alumni agreed that salaries of women doing journalism-related work are lower than those of men doing comparable work, and that men are promoted more quickly. They agreed that men are more likely to be hired over equally capable women for communications staff and other positions. Alumni also agreed that men are less likely than women to back down or seek compromises in office conflict situations. Less than half thought women are often hired as a result of affirmative action policies.
- About 70 percent disagreed with the statement that more men than women are hired as communications directors because they are better prepared for management, and a few more than half disagreed with the statement that men are more assertive in defining proposals and winning consent for decisions affecting the firm or agency. More than half disagreed with the statement that the way to get into management is to earn a post-graduate degree, and 80 percent agreed that prior job experience counts more than education in getting journalism-related work.

- Only 41 to 43 percent would encourage their sons or daughters to study journalism.
- Women agreed far more frequently than men with statements that salaries of women are lower than those of men and that men are promoted more quickly. They disagreed more often than men with statements that a woman would be hired over an equally capable male, and that men are better suited for management. They agreed more often than men that job experience counts more than a graduate degree.
- In general, men were more likely to have married and to have larger families than women.

## Highlights of Student Survey

- Students graduating in 1984 varied little by sex in their attitudes toward their educations, their careers or toward sexual bias in the classroom and workplace.
- Students did not differ by sex in their choice of sequences nor in the factors influencing their choice of journalism as a major. Most influential factors for both men and women were liking to write and liking to meet people, although females rated these factors significantly higher than males. Business and government were the minors of choice for both sexes, followed by sociology and English.
- Half of 1984 graduates participated in journalism student organizations, one-fourth participated in broadcast or print media organizations and three-fourths participated in internships.
- Almost one-third reported they had witnessed discrimination in the classroom based on sex. Few had observed other discrimination.
- Almost all students had career/life goals in college, although these generally were derived from a variety of sources rather than through the influence of only one person. One-third cited one person, and that person was most often a parent. More than half indicated that person was male.
- In assessing their overall journalism experience, about 83 percent considered it very or extremely good, and 90 percent said they would major in journalism again.
- Some 34 percent planned to go on to graduate school at some time and 94 percent planned to work full-time upon graduation. Only a few more than half were certain of the areas where they would find employment.
- Students ranked the following as important attributes for job satisfaction: career advancement, creative opportunity, freedom and autonomy and potential for promotion, followed by adequate salary and opportunity to apply specialized skills.
- Females placed greater importance on promotion, making a good salary and application of specialized skills than males did.

- While half of students indicated belonging to professional organizations was important to career advancement, females rated membership more important than males rated membership. Two-thirds of the students hoped to be staff directors rather than staff members. Half said they did not know what career interruptions they might experience, while 10 percent expected none. Of the 40 percent who expected career interruptions, only 23 percent expected interruptions for childbearing and family responsibilities and 17 percent for further education. About 50 percent expected a career change, but of those only about 5 percent expected to work in a field unrelated to journalism.
- Women students perceived greater potential for discrimination in the workplace than men on several items included in the attitude scale, although all recognized the presence of discrimination on the basis of sex. Women agreed more strongly than men with the statement that women doing journalism-related work were lower-paid than men doing comparable work and that a man would be hired over an equally capable woman.
- Most students indicated they believe that firms would prefer to hire a woman over a man for a staff position (rather than as a communications manager), that men are promoted more quickly than women, and that women are often hired through affirmative action.
- Students expressed the view that men are less likely than women to seek compromises in office conflict situations. However, most agreed that men were no more assertive than women in defining proposals and winning consent for decisions affecting the firm or agency. More than half did not agree with the statement that men are appointed directors because they are better suited for management.
- Half of students stated they thought that obtaining a postgraduate degree is a way to get into management, although 90 percent indicated that prior job experience counts more than education in getting journalism-related work.
- Less than half of the students reported they would encourage their children to study journalism. However, more would encourage their daughters than their sons.

## Highlights of Employer Survey

- Slightly more than one-third of employers said journalism was the most important undergraduate major for communication-related jobs. Almost 15 percent mentioned business, followed by history and math. The most frequently mentioned minors were government and English.
- Employers indicated the job interview was the most influential factor in getting a job. It was twice as important as other factors

such as clip-books or resumes, the next two most important factors. Far less important were tests, extracurricular activities, academic records and letters of recommendation. Other factors mentioned as important were experience, personal recommendations, writing ability and personality.

- Males and females were evaluated rather evenly on job skills, although males were usually evaluated a percentage point or two better than females. However, female employers evaluated female employees significantly higher than did male employers in reporting, photography, media relations, event planning, speech writing and sales. Male employers rated males significantly higher than did female employers in speech writing.
- Employers did not agree that women doing journalism-related work are generally paid lower salaries than men doing comparable work. However, female employers generally agreed with the statement.
- Employers also disagreed with the statement that firms are more likely to hire a man than a woman for a communications staff position. Almost half agreed that men are promoted more quickly than women, although proportionately more females agreed with the statement than males. Likewise, employers did not agree that men are more apt to back down or seek compromises than women in office conflict situations. Women employers disagreed in far greater proportions than men.
- Employers also did not agree that a woman would be hired over an equally capable man and were split on whether women are hired as a result of affirmative action policies.
- However, men were not considered to be more assertive than women in defining proposals and winning consent for decisions affecting the firm, and employers did not agree that more men are hired as directors because they are better prepared for management. Female employers disagreed on this point more frequently than males.
- Employers specified that a graduate degree is not the way to get into management positions and that job experience counts more than academic study in getting journalism-related work.
- In general, slightly fewer than half of the employers reported they would encourage their sons to study journalism while half would encourage their daughters to do so.

# Chapter 5

# Statistical Summary of Three Surveys

## Details of Alumni Survey:
## Classes of 1951-81

A purposive sample of University of Maryland College of Journalism graduates was drawn from records of alumni for whom addresses were current. The sample included all members of the class of 1981 and members of all other classes at three-year intervals back to 1951. Because class sizes and male-to-female proportions varied in the 11 selected classes, care was taken to see that when grouped by age and averaged, responses by age groups matched actual proportions by sex within each group. Returns varied no more than two percentage points from actual proportions by sex of graduates in those groups, with only one exception. Women in the 40–49 age group (1966, 1963, 1960 classes) were over-represented by 7 percent. Rather than weigh the sample, caution was exercised in interpreting data by sex for that age group. Caution was also exercised in interpreting data for the over-50 group, because the actual number of graduates was quite small for each class prior to 1960.

Of 642 questionnaires mailed, 354 were returned—a 55 percent response rate. A large number of those who returned questionnaires agreed to complete a 30-minute telephone interview. Thirty-one males and females from the 11 target classes were called. Conversations added depth and detail to help interpret the trends found in the larger survey. Four areas were investigated in the survey:

- Educational history and attitudes toward education.
- Work history and attitudes toward individual careers.
- Attitudes toward sexual bias in the classroom and workplace.
- Recommendations for journalism education.

If experiences of journalism graduates generally are similar to those in the study, there are a number of trends that journalism educators should consider in designing future curricula. Educators should note the needs of a large female population, which differ on a number of points from males. A large common ground, nevertheless, remains.

This survey indicates that male and female University of Maryland journalism graduates significantly differ on career choice, satisfaction and advancement. Differences may be related to differences in educational preparation and in attitudes toward the role of males and females in the workplace.

**Educational History**

Slightly more males than females transferred to the University of Maryland after earning nine credits. Only 64 percent who graduated enrolled as freshmen. However, the proportion of transfer students has steadily increased since 1955, ranging from a low of 30 percent in the 1950s to a high of 43 percent in the 1970s (Sig. = .01). Males tended to transfer earlier than females. Of those who transferred as freshmen, 77 percent were male.

Journalism graduates were asked to rate the importance of several factors that may have contributed to their selection of the University of Maryland as a place to study. In order of greatest importance those factors were: location (85.2 percent), tuition (79.1 percent), reputation of the journalism program (59.9 percent), entrance requirements (34.5 percent), friend's recommendations (34.5 percent), parents' recommendations (29.8 percent), financial aid (21.8 percent), recommendations of teachers/counselors (18 percent) and recommendations of alumni (17.8 percent).

Women were three times as likely as men to rate reputation as important in their selection process (Sig. = .0004). Graduates since 1976 were twice as likely to mention reputation as those prior to 1976 (Sig. = .0000). Women were slightly more inclined to mention financial aid as important (Sig. = .03). Recent graduates rated financial aid twice as important as those who graduated prior to 1976 (Sig. = .01). Likewise, women graduates since 1976 mentioned the importance of parental recommendations more frequently than did men. Women were more inclined to listen to alumni recommendations. The covariation between the importance of reputation, financial aid and parental recommendations among women and recent graduates reflects the presence of a female majority among graduates since 1976.

While men and women went on to graduate school in roughly the same proportions, men more frequently earned an advance degree (25 percent male to 9.3 percent female, Sig. = .0006). There was a positive correlation between graduate degrees and high income (Sig. = .0037).

Advanced degrees tended to be in marketing, business or public administration (42.6 percent), law (22.4 percent), humanities (15.5 percent) and communication (15.2 percent). Roughly equal numbers of men and women chose law, while slightly more men chose business-related studies. More men chose degrees in humanities and communication. Age trends showed recent graduates chose to study law or business more frequently than did other groups.

A breakdown of the seven sequences offered by the College of Journalism showed 39 percent of all respondents specialized in public relations, 32.7 percent in news-editorial, 8.6 percent in photojournalism, 7.7 percent in advertising, 3.4 percent in broadcast news, 1.1 percent in magazine and 1.1 percent in science communication. A small percentage of alumni completed more than one sequence. Women dominated the advertising, broadcast and magazine sequences while male graduates were twice as numerous in public relations. The only big shift in trends showed in news-editorial enrollments: Prior to 1976 about 50 percent of graduates finished in that sequence, compared with 25.7 percent since 1976. The balance has gone to new sequences (advertising and broadcast) and to public relations.

Those who trained in public relations did better financially than other groups. About 27 percent of public relations graduates made more than $45,000 per year, while only 12.1 percent in news-editorial (the next highest group) made more than $45,000.

About two-thirds of journalism graduates enrolled as journalism majors when they matriculated. Around 37 to 44 percent switched into journalism from other fields prior to 1976; whereas, only 26 percent of more recent graduates switched (Sig. = .0072). Students transferred to journalism from liberal arts (47.9 percent), science (19.3 percent) and business (22.7 percent). Men tended to transfer from business and science while women came from liberal arts.

Alumni were asked to rank factors influencing their decision to study journalism as a career. Factors that ranked extremely or moderately important were: liking to write (87.4 percent), creative opportunity (84.6 percent), value of job to society (56.6 percent), liking to meet people (55.1 percent), reputation of the journalism school (42.8 percent), prestige of the job (34.3 percent), recommendation of teachers or counselors (24.8 percent), recommendation of peers (21.5 percent), money (17.8 percent), recommendation of parents (16.7 percent), recommendation of media professionals (16.6 percent), and easy major (10.5 percent).

Females placed significantly higher emphasis than males on two categories: liking to write (73.4 percent extremely important to 53 percent; Sig. = .0025); and liking to meet people (36.8 percent extremely important to 16.2 percent; Sig. = .0000). Those who placed greater importance on liking to write and reputation of the college tended to make less income (Sig. = .0013 and .0089, respectively). Females were more inclined to be influenced by the recommendation of teachers/counselors than were males (Sig. = .0008). Males were more likely to choose journalism because it was an easy major (38.2 percent to 12.3 percent, Sig. = .0000). Those males who regarded journalism as an easy major made more money than others: $25,000 or more (Sig. = .0000).

When data were analyzed by age groups, significant differences appeared. Recent graduates placed greater importance on promise of prestige (Sig. = .0004), money (Sig. = .0265) and creative opportunity (Sig. = .0002). Some 30–50 percent of those thirty years of age or older indicated they chose journalism as an easy major, while 84.2 percent of those 20–29 said that factor was unimportant (Sig. = .0000).

A majority of alumni (83.3 percent) developed minors (12 or more upper-level credits) in only eight areas: business (23.5 percent), English (19.4 percent), government (16.5 percent), history (10.3 percent), sociology (10 percent), psychology (6.8 percent), sciences (4.5 percent), and foreign languages (2.3 percent). Cross-tabulation by sex and age revealed that men were more likely to select government or history, and women were more likely to minor in English and psychology (Sig. = .0135). When data were analyzed by income groups, those with minors in business, science, history and sociology earned higher salaries (Sig. = .0029).

Some 64 percent of respondents had internships while in college. About 16 percent more women than men had internships (Sig. = .0008). There was an expected difference in internship patterns by age. About 79 percent of graduates since 1976 had internships compared to 53 percent in other groups (Sig. = .0000). Since women graduates have been more numerous than men since 1976, internship differences by sex should be suspect.

Men and women graduates also participated in similar journalism-related extra-curricular activities, although women tended to make up a greater proportion of participants in the Society of Professional Journalists/Sigma Delta Chi (SDX) and the Public Relations Student Society of America (PRSSA). Only about 17 percent of graduates had no journalism-related extra-curricular activity. A majority (76.5 percent) had some contact with the student daily newspaper, *The Diamondback*.

Alumni were asked if, in their journalism classroom experiences, they detected instances of discrimination on the basis of sex, age, or race. A total of 19.3 percent mentioned sexual discrimination in the classroom, while 12.4 percent recalled discrimination on the basis of age, and 8.4 percent recalled discrimination on the basis of race. Women were more likely to report sexual discrimination than were men—25.2 percent to 15.0 percent.

About 80 percent of men and women reported having had a career/life goal while in college. Graduates since 1976 were more likely to have been goal-directed than those who graduated earlier, ranging from a high of 83.6 percent among 20- to 29-year-olds to a low of 52.6 percent among 40- to 49-year-olds (Sig. = .0130).

About 41.7 percent of respondents said one person influenced their choice of a life goal. No differences appeared by sex; however, significant differences by age showed younger respondents less likely to have had one person as a career/life goal influencer (58.3 percent for the 1950s to 34.8 percent for graduates since 1976; Sig. = .0067).

Alumni reported the person influential in career/life goal formation was male 70.9 percent of the time and female only 29.1 percent of the time. Trends over all classes showed that female influence has increased steadily for both sexes, ranging from a low of 10.5 percent among those 40-49 to a high of 40.5 percent among those 20-29. Women tended to name a male influencer 60 percent of the time and a female 40 percent of the time. Males tended to name a male influencer 80.7 percent of the time and a female 19.3 percent of the time (Sig. = .0095).

Those who had career/life goals identified the following persons as important: high school teachers (24.6 percent), parents (20.3 percent), college professors (18.8 percent), media professionals (14.5 percent), business professionals (11.6 percent) and peers (7.2 percent). Women were far more likely to choose a high school teacher (40 percent) than were men (8.2 percent). Men were more likely to consult business professionals (14.3 percent to 2.5 percent) and to choose peers (10.2 percent to 2.5 percent). High school teachers were mentioned about 20 percent more frequently among graduates 20-29 than in other age groups.

Alumni rated their experience with the College of Journalism as extremely or very good 57.9 percent of the time, somewhat good 36.6 percent of the time and not good 5.2 percent of the time. There was no difference by sex, nor age in the evaluation of the college. However, the higher the income of alumni, the more positive the evaluation of the college (Sig. = .0414). About 73 percent would major in journalism again. Of those who would not, 11.6 percent would major in business, 7.2 percent in liberal arts courses, 6.3 percent in radio, television and film, and 2.9 percent in science. Of those expressing interest in change, men were more likely than women to mention business (19 percent to 9.3 percent). General comments suggested the importance of skill development, internships and professional experiences for journalism majors while in college.

**Employment History**

Of those surveyed, 91.5 percent had been employed full-time since graduation, although not continuously. Some 38.6 percent had jobs lined up before graduation; 39.1 percent had jobs in less than three months after graduation; 13.3 percent had jobs within four to six months after graduation; 4.3 percent had jobs from 6 to 12 months after graduation and 4.1 percent took longer to find a job. No significant differences by sex appeared in employment patterns following graduation, although significantly more alumni who graduated in the 1960s had jobs waiting for them than in later years (ranging from 54 to 32 percent). Some 53.9 percent of those earning $45,000 or more had a job before graduation (Sig. = .0269). The first job after graduation was full-time for 92.5 percent of those reporting employment.

Alumni were asked how helpful several factors were in obtaining the first job. These included: personal interviews, clip books, letters of recommendation, resumes, academic record, extra-curricular activities, pre-employment tests, professional contacts and personal/family contacts. Ranked in order of importance, alumni identified the personal interview as extremely or very important (81.6 percent) followed by resumes (65.4 percent), professional contacts (54.8 percent), letters of recommendation (47.4 percent), clip books or tapes (44.8 percent), personal contacts (44.6 percent), pre-employment tests (44 percent) and extra-curricular activities (40.5 percent). Differences by sex appeared in six areas related to personal achievement. Women tended to believe interviews, resumes, academic records, clip books, extra-curricular activities and pre-employment tests to be somewhat more important than men in obtaining the first job.

Based on 78 percent of the respondents who identified where they were employed, 37.6 percent of alumni worked for corporate/financial institutions, 18.8 percent worked for daily or weekly newspapers or wire services, 12.4 percent for federal or state government, 8.9 percent for non-profit organizations, 6.9 percent for educational institutions, 5 percent for public relations firms, 5 percent for magazine/newsletters, 4.5 percent for broadcast firms, and 1.9 percent for advertising firms; 2 percent did not specify any of the above categories.

The categories above showed differences by sex in only a few areas. Education as a career field was slightly more female than male. Magazines/newsletters employed twice as many females as males, but newspapers had twice as many males as females. Differences by age showed greater proportions of 20- to 29-year-olds involved with radio and television, while greater proportions of 30- to 39-year-olds were involved with non-profit organizations than alumni in other age groups.

In the corporate sector 22.8 percent earned $25-34,000 and 29.7 percent earned more than $45,000; in education 52.9 percent earned $15-24,000 and 23.5 percent earned $35-44,000; in public relations 42.9 percent earned more than $45,000, and 28.6 percent earned $25-34,000; in government 32.4 percent earned $15-24,000, 17.6 percent earned $25-34,000, 26.5 percent earned $35-44,000 and 17.6 percent earned more than $45,000; in non-profit organizations 38.9 earned $15-24,000; 22.2 percent earned $35-44,000 and 22.2 percent earned more than $45,000; in news 36.6 percent earned $15-24,000; 17 percent earned $25-34,000 and 14.6 percent earned $10-14,000 and $35-44,000, respectively. Magazine and advertising cases were too few to report.

Of those who reported current employment, 36 percent worked for firms of 500 or more employees, 18.3 percent for firms of 1-10, 16.7 percent for firms of 10-50, 14.9 percent for firms of 51-150, 9.5 percent for firms of 151-300, and 5 percent for firms of 301-500.

Of the 70 percent who were extremely or very satisified with their jobs, males were more likely than females to be satisfied (74.9 to 63.3

percent; Sig. = .0008). Generally, the more income, the more satisfied were respondents (Sig. = .0000). Analysis by age showed that alumni age 40–49 were far more satisfied with their jobs (44 percent extremely satisfied) than were those 20–29 (23 percent extremely satisfied; Sig. = .0008).

As expected, satisfaction with income was related to satisfaction with the job. Some 72.6 percent were very or extremely satisfied with their incomes, and males were more satisfied than females—76 to 63 percent (Sig. = .0006). By age, the 40–49 age group tended to have higher satisfaction with income (Sig. = .0000).

Most alumni (77.5 percent) were very or extremely satisfied with chances for advancement, although males more often responded extremely satisfied (57.1 to 40.3 percent; Sig. = .0006). Younger males felt better about their chances for advancement than other males and females. Likewise, the higher the salary, the more likely respondents were to be satisfied with their chances for advancement. The highest percent of those saying "extremely satisfied" fell in the $25–34,000 group (Sig. = .0000).

A majority (57.9 percent) of graduates belonged to professional organizations: 25.7 percent belonged to only one, 18.5 percent belonged to two, and 12.7 percent belonged to three or more. There appeared to be a curvilinear relationship between age and membership in organizations. More graduates belonged to two or more organizations in the middle years of productivity (40–49) than before or after (Sig. = .0088). There was also a strong correlation between higher salary and the greater number of professional memberships (Sig. = .0000).

Graduates also attended career-related seminars, luncheons or meetings: 5.9 percent attended at least bi-monthly, 23.5 percent attended twice a year, and 35 percent attended once a year. About 77 percent of alumni had attended continuing education workshops or classes: 43 percent did so every three to five years; 34.1 percent did so every one to two years and 22.8 percent did so twice a year or more. Greater frequency of attendance at meetings and classes was also related to higher income (Sig. = .0197).

Alumni were asked to rate the importance of several categories that contributed to job satisfaction. Arranged in order of importance, alumni ranked the following as extremely important: creative opportunity (69.4 percent), freedom/autonomy (67.1 percent), career advancement (58.4 percent), adequate salary (57.8 percent), potential for promotion (48.7 percent), job security (45 percent), opportunity to apply specialized skills (42.5 percent), managerial responsibility (40.3 percent), recognition of colleagues (32.9 percent), recognition of superiors in the organization (31.8 percent), value of the job to society (28 percent), and prestige (22.8 percent). Women tended to place more importance on creative opportunity (76.3 percent extremely important) than males (63.8 percent; Sig. = .0116).

Trends showed that careerist concerns, as defined by Wilensky (1964), and Hage and Aiken (1968), are more prevalent among younger graduates. Freedom and autonomy were more highly valued than other factors among those making $15–24,000 (Sig. = .0312). Those 20–29-years-old were more concerned about job security and potential for promotion than older graduates (Sig. = .0079 to .0000). Younger graduates also placed slightly more emphasis on having management responsibility (Sig. = .0389).

Alumni were asked to identify whether or not their work was related to journalism in each of their last three jobs and whether their positions could be classified as staff member or staff director in each case. Some 30.6 percent of respondents held journalism-related staff positions; 21.6 percent held non-journalism staff positions; 25.8 percent held journalism-related director positions and 21.9 percent held non-journalism director positions. Of those holding journalism-related staff positions, 16 percent reported moving out of staff positions in one of their three most recent jobs (from 48.5 to 32.6 percent).

Presence of females in staff positions decreased from 59.2 percent to 38.9 percent over a three-job span. The presence of males in staff positions decreased from 39 percent to 22.8 percent over a period of three jobs (Sig. = .0178). Females outnumbered males in staff positions at all times, and those positions became proportionately more female. As would be expected, the older the graduate, the more likely he or she was to move from a staff-member to a staff-director position.

The proportion of women who were staff directors increased from 10 percent to 21.5 percent over three jobs, as compared with men whose proportion increased from 16.9 percent to 24.7 percent.

The picture differed in non-journalism related fields. In their most recent jobs, most graduates working in non-journalism jobs at director levels were men. The female to male ratio improved only slightly over a three-job span—moving from 3.3/16.9 to 11.8/31.5. Males dominated staff-director positions two to one.

There was no statistical difference in earnings between alumni working as staff members in journalism and non-journalism fields. Journalism staff salaries broke down according to the following categories: 41.1 percent made $15–24,000; 20 percent made $25–34,000 and 18.9 percent made more than $35,000. Of non-journalism staff members, 31.3 percent made $15–24,000; 18.8 percent made $25–34,000 and 18.7 percent made more.

However, journalism staff directors were paid less than non-journalism staff directors: 33.8 percent of journalism staff directors made $15–24,000; 28.2 percent made $25–34,000; 11 percent made $35–44,000 and 15.5 percent made $45,000 or more. Of directors in non-journalism related work, 17.7 percent made $15–24,000; 11.3 percent made $25–34,000; 19.4 percent made $35–44,000; and 41.9 percent made $45,000 or more.

About 67.2 percent of respondents reported they were not free to make decisions on their own in their most recent job, but rather, had to clear decisions, even though 46 percent claimed to be directors. Apparently, 15 percent of those in director positions held middle management positions and reported to a supervisor. It appears that greater numbers of those who were free to make decisions fell within the 20-29 age group while greater numbers of those who cleared decisions fell in the 40-49 age group. While this may seem counterintuitive, the younger group may have consisted of reporters who act on their own authority, while the older group may have been middle-level managers who feel more acutely the constraints of delegated or otherwise limited decision-making power (Sig. = .0471).

Approximately 43 percent of the respondents reported having had career interruptions. Reasons for interruptions included layoff, firing or quitting (33.8 percent); childbirth and family responsibility (24.5 percent); additional education (17.9 percent); military service (6.6 percent); illness (4 percent); other (9.3 percent) including travel, breaks, etc.

Differences by sex showed males, who exclusively experienced interruptions because of military service, were twice as likely to be ill and were also 1.5 times more likely to seek additional education. Men were slightly more likely than women to be laid off. Women on the other hand, were 13 times more likely to have interruptions for childbearing and family responsibilities. Some 41.5 percent of women who had interruptions fell in this category.

By age, the majority of those with interruptions for military service fell into the 40-49 age group; for illness, childbearing and layoff, the 30-39 age group; and for education, the 20-29 age group.

Those reporting interruptions due to childbirth, layoff, illness or education generally reported an income from $15,000 to $24,000. Some 70 percent of those with military interruptions made $45,000 or more.

The average length of unemployment did not differ significantly by sex. Women were unemployed for slightly longer periods: 64.7 percent of men were unemployed for less than six months to 59.6 percent of women; 25 percent of men were unemployed for less than seven to 12 months to 13.8 percent of women. In other words, 89.7 percent of men were back at their jobs in a year compared to only 73.4 percent of women. About 7.4 percent of men were out of work 1-2 years to 9.6 percent of women; 2.6 percent of men were out of work 3-5 years to 7.4 percent of women; and no men were out of work more than 5 years, while 9.6 percent of women were out of work more than five years. Of those who had a career interruption, 55.7 percent resumed the same career while 40.9 percent entered a new career and 3.4 remained unemployed. Women (63 percent) were more likely than men (47.8 percent) to resume the same career (Sig. = .0421). A total of 47.7 percent resumed work at a higher level while 34.9 percent resumed work at the same level and 17.4 percent at a lower level.

Some 69.9 percent of the respondents reported they would not change jobs in the next two years, while 30.1 percent reported they would. Women were twice as likely to change jobs as men (40 percent to 22.3 percent; Sig. = .0007). Those making $15-24,000 were most likely to change jobs (42.3 percent, Sig. = .0000).

Some 30.1 percent said they would remain in a journalism-related field and 18.8 percent said they would seek employment elsewhere. Men were more likely to say they would seek employment outside the field (21.1 to 15 percent), while more women would change within the field (41.6 to 19.5; Sig. = .0007). The older the respondent, the less the likelihood of change (Sig. = .0016).

**Attitude Scales**

Alumni were asked to agree or disagree with several statements about sexual bias in the employment situation. Based on their own experience or observation, 48.4 percent of graduates agreed, "Salaries of women doing journalism-related work are generally lower than salaries of men doing comparable work." About 28.8 percent disagreed and 22.8 percent claimed no experience. Women differed significantly from men (69.7 percent agreement to 31.4 percent). Men claimed no experience 30.9 percent of the time to 13.2 percent for women (Sig. = .0000). The lower the salary of the graduate, the greater the agreement (Sig. = .0060).

Alumni disagreed with the statement, "Firms or agencies are more likely to hire a woman than a man for a communication staff position (writer, etc.)," 41.0 percent to 33.9 percent; 24.2 percent claimed no experience. Likewise, 54.8 percent agreed, "Men are promoted more quickly than women in most firms or agencies;" 32.4 percent disagreed and 12.8 percent claimed no experience. Females agreed 70.6 percent of the time to 41.8 percent for males (Sig. = .0000).

Some 70.9 percent disagreed with the statement, "Men are more apt to back down or seek compromises in office conflict situations than women are," while 14.1 percent agreed and 15 percent claimed no experience. Older males were more likely to agree (Sig. = .0004).

Alumni disagreed 63.7 percent of the time with the statement, "If an equally capable woman and man applied for a job, the woman would probably be hired." Some 20.2 percent agreed and 16.1 percent claimed no experience. Significant differences by sex showed 74.5 percent of females disagreed to 54.9 percent of males; 9.4 percent of females agreed to 29.4 percent of males; and roughly equal numbers claimed no experience (Sig. = .0000).

However, 88.9 percent of all alumni agreed with the statement, "If an equally capable woman and man had applied for a job ten years ago, the man would probably have been hired." Only 5.4 percent disagreed and 5.7 percent claimed no experience.

Alumni disagreed 62.2 percent of the time with the statement, "The way to get into management-level positions is to earn a postgraduate degree," while 30.3 percent agreed and 7.1 percent claimed no experience.

Alumni agreed 45 percent to 37.6 percent, "Women are often hired as a result of affirmative action policies;" 17.4 percent claimed no experience. By age, the younger the alumni, the greater the tendency to disagree. Younger graduates admitted to no experience more frequently than older graduates.

Most alumni disagreed with the statement, "Men are more assertive than women in defining proposals and winning consent for decisions affecting the firm or agency;" 56.8 percent disagreed to 30.4 percent who agreed and 12.8 percent who claimed no experience.

To the statement, "More men than women are hired as communication staff directors because they are better prepared for management," 70.7 percent disagreed, 5.7 percent agreed and 23.6 percent claimed no experience. However, women tended to disagree at a higher rate, (83.7 percent to 59.6 percent) and claimed no experience at a lower rate (13.7 percent to 32.1 percent; Sig. = .0000).

Some 80.2 percent of alumni agreed with the statement, "Prior job experience counts more than education in getting journalism-related work;" 6.9 percent disagreed and 12.9 percent claimed no experience. Women tended to agree more frequently than men (86.8 percent to 74.9 percent, Sig. = .0043). The younger and lower-paid the graduate, the more likely there was agreement (Sig. = .0000).

With the statement, "I would encourage my son (if I had one) to study journalism in college," 45.1 percent disagreed, 41 percent agreed and 14 percent claimed no experience. The lower the income of the graduate, the greater the disagreement (Sig. = .0387). Likewise, 43.9 percent disagreed with the statement, "I would encourage my daughter (if I had one) to study journalism in college;" 43 percent agreed and 13.1 percent claimed no experience.

**Demographics**

- Sex: Males, 55.6 percent; females, 44.4 percent.
- Marital Status: 56.1 percent were married; 8 percent were formerly married; and 35.9 percent were single; 49 percent of women were married compared to 61.3 percent of men (Sig. = .0304).
- Children: None, 56.4 percent; one, 17.4 percent; two, 17.8 percent; three, 6.1 percent; and four or more, 2.3 percent. About 48 percent of men had no children and 69 percent of women; 14 percent of men and 14 percent of women had one child; 21.6 percent of men and 13.5 percent of women had two children; 10.3 percent of men to 1.9 percent of women had three children; 5.7 percent of men to .6 percent of women had four or more children (Sig. = .0000).
- Age: 39.8 percent were 20–29; 38.7 percent were 30–39; 15.2 per-

cent were 40–49; and 6.3 percent were 50 or older. The proportions by age and by sex very nearly approximated the actual proportion by age and sex of each alumni class. The 20–29 group was 60.4 percent female; the 30–39 group was 40.2 percent female; the 40–49 group was 28.3 percent female and the 50 or older group was 9.1 percent female.
- Income: 4.9 percent earned $4,999 or less; 3.1 percent earned $5,000–$9,999; 11.3 percent earned $10,000–$14,999; 30.3 percent earned $15,000–$24,999; 19.9 percent earned $25,000–$34,999; 13.5 percent earned $35,000–$44,999; and 17.1 percent earned $45,000 or more.

Males made significantly greater incomes than females (Sig. = .0000).

By age, 53.5 percent of those 20–29 earned $15–24,000, 20 percent earned $10–14,000 and $25–34,000; 29 percent of those 30–39 earned $25–34,000, 21 percent earned $35–44,000, and 15 percent each earned $15–24,000 and $45,000 or more; 40 percent of those 40–49 earned $45,000, and 15 percent made incomes in each category below to $45,000; 61 percent of those 50 or older made $45,000 or more. There was a positive correlation between increased age and increased income (Sig. = .0000).
- Minority Population: This group made up 5 percent of the sample, which is lower than current enrollment levels, but approximates the aggregate over the 20-year period.
- Place of Residence: Only 45.8 percent lived in Maryland; however, 85.3 percent said they did not have to leave the area to find employment.

# Details of Student Survey
# Class of 1984

Students eligible to graduate with a degree in journalism from the University of Maryland in 1984 were mailed questionnaires. Of the 280 polled, 168 responded for a 60 percent response rate. The rate of response for males and females who participated in the survey (74 percent female, 26 percent male) closely approximated the actual population of graduates (69 percent female, 31 percent male).

**Educational History**

Almost half (48.2 percent) of the students who responded to the questionnaire reported that they had transferred from another educational institution to the University of Maryland. Of those who had transferred, 39.1 percent had earned between 29 and 89 credits.

Students were asked to identify the importance of several factors affecting their decision to attend the University of Maryland. In order of importance, they were: location (75.1 percent), cost (69.1 percent), recommendation of relatives (61.7 percent), reputation of the College of Journalism (57.7 percent), entrance requirements

(38.1 percent), recommendation of friends or peers (29.7 percent), availability of financial aid (20.4 percent), recommendation of teachers or counselors (15 percent), and recommendation of alumni (15.5 percent).

Students were asked to indicate the sequence they followed while earning their journalism degree. Thirty-three percent studied public relations. Other sequences included advertising (16.1 percent), broadcast news (14.3 percent), news-editorial (13.7 percent), magazine (12.5 percent), photojournalism (7.1 percent) and science communication (.6 percent).

Students ranked the importance of variables that influenced their decision to study journalism. In order of importance, they were: liking to write (85.1 percent), creative opportunity (74.7 percent), liking to meet people (70.9 percent), value of the job to society (64.3 percent), prestige of the job (45.3 percent), reputation of the journalism program (42.4 percent), parent suggestion (33.8 percent), promise of money (33.4 percent), teacher/counselor suggestion (24.4 percent), friend or peer suggestion (19.7 percent), professional suggestion (17.1 percent) and easy major (8.4 percent).

Females were more likely than males to stress the importance of liking to meet people (78.2 to 51.1 percent; Sig. = .0000), and liking to write (66.9 to 46.5 percent; Sig. = .0149).

Students were asked to indicate the most important minor field in which they earned at least 12 credits. The top areas were business (26.8 percent), government (23.2 percent), sociology (10.7 percent) and English (10.1 percent). Others mentioned were history, psychology, foreign languages and science.

About 42 percent of students belonged to a student organization such as the Society of Professional Journalists/Sigma Delta Chi, the Advertising Club and the Public Relations Student Society of America, and 26 percent participated in internships at campus radio station WMUC and the *Diamondback,* the student daily. Twenty-seven percent reported that they had participated in several other communication-related campus organizations. A large majority of students (75.6 percent) reported that they had participated in an internship program of some sort.

Students were asked whether they had perceived discrimination in the classroom based upon sex, age or race. Some 29.2 percent reported that they had experienced discrimination based upon sex. Fewer said they had observed discrimination based upon age (11.9 percent) and race (8.9 percent).

When asked if they had a career/life goal in college, 86.7 percent of students responded "yes." Thirty-three percent indicated that they were influenced by one person. A parent was most frequently cited as the one person who influenced the student's career/life goal (33.3 percent). Others who were influential included: college professor (15 percent), peer (13 percent), communications professional (10 percent), high school teacher (8.3 percent) and business professional (3.2 percent). About 58 percent indicated that the person who had influenced their decision was male.

Students were asked to rate the journalism program at the University of Maryland: 14.4 percent indicated they felt the program was extremely good, 54.2 percent indicated the program was very good, 28.6 percent said the program was somewhat good, while .6 percent indicated that they thought the program to be not at all good. When asked if they would major in journalism again, 89.9 percent responded affirmatively.

Of the 8.9 percent of students who would not major in journalism again, most said that they would choose business or marketing as their undergraduate major. Others mentioned English, broadcasting, music and government.

About 34 percent of students indicated that they planned to attend graduate school after graduation.

Asked whether they planned to work upon graduation, 94.6 percent answered affirmatively: 21.2 percent indicated they hoped to work at public relations or advertising firms; 12.5 percent wanted to work in print news; 9.5 percent in broadcast news; 10.7 percent in a corporation; and 6.4 percent in government. The rest were uncertain.

Students indicated the following as most important to them in future jobs: career advancement (73.8 percent), creative opportunity (72.6 percent), freedom and autonomy (61.9 percent), potential for promotion (61.3 percent), adequate salary (56 percent), opportunity to apply specialized skills (54.8 percent), job security (50 percent), value of job to society (34.5 percent), recognition of colleagues (33.9 percent), managerial responsibilities and recognition of superiors in the organization (32.1 percent), and prestige (23.5 percent).

Females were more likely than males to place great importance on promotion and making a good salary (Sig. = .0011 and .0247, respectively). Women also placed greater emphasis on applying specialized skills (Sig. = .0284).

Students were asked to evaluate the importance of membership in professional organizations for their own career advancement. Fifty-five percent indicated that belonging to professional organizations was extremely important or very important. Females were more likely than males to rate membership as highly important (61 percent to 39 percent; Sig. = .0025). Students indicated that they preferred to be staff/directors (62.3 percent) rather than staff/members (37.1 percent) in the organizations where they expected to work.

Asked about their expected career interruptions, 10.1 percent did not expect to interrupt their careers for any reason in the future; 23.2 expected to interrupt their employment for childbearing and family responsibilities; 1.8 percent indicated that military service would interrupt their careers; 17.3 percent planned to pursue additional education in the future. Half said they did not know.

When asked if they anticipated a career change in the future, 50 percent indicated that they would change careers. Of those, 11.3 indicated that they would pursue a career in a related field; 4.4 percent indicated they would enter an unrelated field, while the remainder were unsure.

**Attitude Scales**

Students indicated that they agreed (55.7 percent) with the statement, "Women doing journalism-related work earn salaries that are generally lower than men doing comparable work;" 11.4 percent disagreed and 32.9 percent reported that they had no experience. A significant difference appeared between men and women on this scale: 67.9 percent of the women perceived salaries to be lower but 20.7 percent of the men did (Sig. = .0000).

Asked whether "Firms or agencies are more likely to hire a man for a communication staff position," 41.9 percent disagreed with the statement, 21 percent agreed and 27.1 percent claimed no experience.

Asked whether "Men are promoted more quickly than women in most firms or agencies," 53.9 percent agreed that they are, 16.2 percent disagreed, and 29.9 percent claimed no experience. Women agreed more frequently than men, 51.8 to 41.9 percent (Sig. = .0367).

With the statement, "Men are more apt to back down or seek compromises in office conflict situations," 61.8 percent disagreed, 4.8 percent agreed and 33.3 percent claimed no experience.

"If an equally capable woman and man" were vying for the same job, 57.7 percent of students said the woman most likely would not be hired; 14.9 percent disagreed; 28.1 percent reported no experience. Women disagreed more frequently than men (Sig. = .0156). Ten years ago, 89.2 percent of students agreed "The man would probably have been hired." To this women agreed more frequently than men (Sig. = .0307).

In response to the statement, "The way to get into management is to earn a post-graduate degree," 50.3 percent of students agreed; 29.7 percent disagreed and 20 percent reported no experience.

About 41.6 percent of the students agreed, "Women are often hired as a result of affirmative action policies," 28.3 percent disagreed and 30.1 percent reported no experience.

Some 55.8 percent disagreed with the statement, "Men are more assertive than women in defining proposals and winning consent for decisions affecting the firm or agency," while 21.8 percent agreed and 22.4 percent reported no experience.

And 62 percent of students disagreed with the statement, "Men are hired as communication staff directors because they are better prepared for management," 7.2 percent agreed and 30.7 percent reported no experience. Women disagreed with greater frequency (Sig. = .0138).

The overwhelming majority of students (86.1 percent) indicated they agreed, "Prior job experience counts more than education in getting journalism-related work," 7.3 percent disagreed and 6.7 percent reported no experience.

As to whether they would encourage their sons and daughters to study journalism in college, 49 percent indicated that they would encourage their daughters to study journalism while 36 percent would not, and 15 percent reported no experience. And 44.1 percent said they would encourage their sons to study journalism while 40.4 percent would not, and 15.5 percent reported no experience.

**Demographics**

- Sex: Female, 74.4 percent; male, 25.6 percent.
- Marital Status: 92.3 percent were single; 4.8 percent were married; and 3 percent were formerly married.
- Children: 96 percent reported no children; 1.2 percent had one child; 1.2 percent had two children; and 1.2 percent had three or more.
- Age: 95.2 percent were 20–29 years old; 4.2 percent were 30–39; and .6 percent were over 40.
- Ethnic Derivation: 86.7 percent were Caucasian; 5.4 percent were black; 3.0 percent were Hispanic; and 4.8 percent were Asian.
- Residence: 71.4 percent were Maryland residents. More than half (56.7 percent) hoped to work in Maryland; 40.9 percent hoped to work elsewhere; 2.4 percent were undecided.

## Details of Employer Survey

In another phase of the study, firms or agencies that had employed University of Maryland College of Journalism graduates were surveyed on their attitudes toward the quality of work of those graduates, the strengths and weaknesses of employees with journalism degrees as compared to those having other degrees, and gender-based differences in employee performance.

Of 251 questionnaires mailed, 132 were returned for a 53 percent response rate.

**Organizational History**

Of employers responding, 40.9 percent represented print or broadcast news media; 31.9 percent public information, public relations, government or non-profit firms; 19.1 percent corporate, financial or medical institutions; and 8.2 percent educational institutions.

Firms ranged in size from very small to very large. Those reporting less than ten employees equaled 15.7 percent; those employing 11 to 20, 13.7 percent; 21 to 30, 7.8 percent; 31 to 100, 27.5 percent; 101 to 150, 6.9 percent; 151 to 300, 21.6 percent; more than 300, 6.9 percent.

About 67 percent of those responding hired from 0 to 9 persons to do communications work; 11 percent hired 11 to 20; the rest hired from 21 to 300 communication professionals. About 72 percent said that 10 or fewer women were represented in the total workforce of their firms; 12.8 percent employed 11 to 20 females; 3.4 percent employed 21 to 30 females; and 2.6 percent employed more than 30.

About 65 percent of employers reported they currently employed University of Maryland College of Journalism graduates: 49.2 percent employed one; 23.1 percent employed two; 13.8 percent employed three; and 13.8 percent employed four or more.

About 53.8 percent did not report employing any female College of Journalism graduates. Of those who did, 73.2 percent employed one; 16.4 percent employed two; 7.3 percent employed three; 2.4 percent employed four and 2.5 percent employed five or more.

About 3.5 percent of employers reported either all male or all female employees; 23.4 percent reported equal proportions of male and female employees; 3.6 percent reported a 10 percent male staff as compared to .9 percent who reported a 10 percent female staff; 8.2 percent reported a 20 percent male staff as compared to 1.8 percent who reported a 20 percent female staff; 16.4 percent reported a 30 percent male staff as compared to 4.5 percent who reported a 30 percent female staff; and 26.4 percent reported a 40 percent male staff as compared to 10.9 percent who reported a 40 percent female staff. Males outnumbered females in general.

Employers mentioned journalism as the most important major for communications-related jobs 37.3 percent of the time; 14.7 percent mentioned business as most important; 13.4 percent mentioned sociology or psychology; 10.7 percent mentioned history; 9.3 percent mentioned math; 6.7 percent mentioned government; 4 percent mentioned English; 2.7 percent mentioned sciences and 1.3 percent mentioned languages.

Recommended minors included government (23.7 percent), English (18.4 percent), business (14.5 percent), science or engineering (11.9 percent), languages (10.5 percent), sociology or psychology (1.3 percent), math (1.3 percent), and other (15.8 percent). Male employers were far more apt to recommend business, government and history than female employers.

When asked what factors help in getting a job, 95.5 percent of employers rated the job interview as most important. Other factors ranked in order of importance included: clip books or tapes (48.6 percent), quality of resume (44.1 percent), pre-employment test (29 percent), extra-curricular activities (20 percent), academic record (19.8 percent), letters of recommendation (13.8 percent), and professional contacts (11.8 percent). Male and female employers responded differently on two criteria. Women employers considered clip books and letters of recommendation to be more important than did males (Sig. = .03 and .0007, respectively).

Other factors mentioned as important in open-ended questions included experience, personal recommendations, writing ability, personality and career goals.

Employers were asked to rate men and women on their skill levels in a variety of job-related activities. Men and women were given an "extremely good" rating with approximately the same frequency in reporting (extremely good, 32.5 percent of males and 29.5 percent of females), editing (33.8 to 30.8 percent), writing (30.8 to 29.6 percent), media relations (22.2 to 18.9 percent), event planning (20.5 to 16.3 percent), speech writing (16.7 to 11.4 percent), audio-visual production (13.5 to 11.4 percent) and sales (13.2 to 13.5 percent). Males were rated higher than females in publication design (18.8 to 9.1 percent) and photography (14.9 to 6.7 percent).

However, female employers evaluated women employees significantly higher than did male employers in reporting (69.6 to 30.4 percent extremely good, Sig. = .03); photography (66.7 to 33 percent, Sig. = .0066); media relations (70 to 30 percent, Sig. = .0057); event planning (85.7 to 14.3 percent, Sig. = .0007); speech writing (80 to 20 percent, Sig. = .0062); and sales (60 to 40 percent, Sig. = .0191). Male employers rated males significantly higher than did female employers in event planning (55.6 to 44.4 percent, Sig. = .0283) and female employers rated males higher than did male employers in speech writing (57.1 to 42.0 percent, Sig. = .0331).

Employers indicated that journalism graduates compare well with non-journalism graduates in the following categories: responsibility, work ethics, problem solving, initiative, creativity and flexibility. Female employers rated females higher than did males in problem solving, indicating that no women were deficient in that category (Sig. = .03).

Employers suggested improvements could be made in journalism education in the following areas: writing skills (58.5 percent), field experience (12.2 percent), production skills (9.8 percent), creativity (7.3 percent), public relations skills (4.9 percent), technical and computer skills (4.9 percent), internships (2.4 percent).

**Attitude Scales**

Employers responded to questions designed to measure differences in attitudes toward sexual bias in the workplace. Employers disagreed 51.7 percent to 48.3 percent with the statement, "Salaries of women doing journalism-related work are generally lower than salaries of men doing comparable work." However, 58.7 percent of male employers disagreed while 43.4 percent of female employers disagreed.

Employers disagreed 66.4 percent to 24.2 percent with the statement, "Firms or agencies are more likely to hire a man than a woman for a communication staff position (writer, editor, etc.);" 9.4 percent claimed no experience.

Some 45.3 percent agreed with the statement, "Men are promoted more quickly than women in most firms or agencies," while 39.1 percent disagreed and 15.6 percent claimed no experience. A significant difference appeared between responses of female and male employers: 37.5 percent of male respondents agreed while 55.4 percent of female respondents agreed (Sig. = .0471).

With the statement, "Men are more apt to back down, or seek compromises in office conflict situations than women are," 68 percent disagreed, 18 percent agreed and 14.1 percent claimed no experience. A significant difference in responses appeared between male and female employers: 56.9 percent of males disagreed while 82.1 percent of females disagreed (Sig. = .0018).

Employers disagreed 64.1 percent to 22.7 percent with the statement, "If an equally capable woman and man applied for a job, the woman would probably be hired." Employers claimed no experience 13.3 percent of the time. Employers agreed 83.6 percent to 9.4 percent that, if the same situation had occurred ten years ago, "the man would probably have been hired." Only 7 percent claimed no experience. Employers differed by sex: 77.1 percent of males agreed while 91.1 percent of females agreed (Sig. = .0194).

With the statement, "The way to get into management-level positions is to earn a post-graduate degree," employers disagreed 83.6 percent to 12.5 percent, and 3.9 percent claimed no experience. Employers were split almost evenly on whether, "Women are hired as a result of affirmative action policies:" 45.3 percent disagreed, 42.2 percent agreed and 12.5 percent claimed no experience.

Employers disagreed 70.3 percent to 22.7 percent with the statement, "Men are more assertive and logical than women in defining proposals and winning consent for decisions affecting the firm or agency;" 7 percent claimed no experience.

A significant difference appeared in the reactions of male and female employers to the statement, "More men than women are hired as communication staff directors because they are better prepared for management." Overall, employers disagreed with the statement 85.9 percent to 5.5 percent, while 8.6 percent claimed no experience. However, only 79.2 percent of male employers disagreed while 94.6 percent of female employers disagreed (Sig. = .0094).

Differences also appeared in regard to the statement, "Prior job experience counts more than education in getting journalism-related work." While 79.9 percent agreed and only 16.4 percent disagreed (and 3.9 percent claimed no experience), men agreed 84.7 percent to 73.2 percent for women (Sig. = .0473).

With the statement, "I would encourage my son (if I had one) to study journalism in college," employers were split: 44.5 percent agreed, 43 percent disagreed and 12.5 percent claimed no experience. To the same statement applied to a daughter, 50 percent agreed, 39.1 percent disagreed and 10.2 percent claimed no experience.

**Demographics**
- Sex: Males, 56.3 percent; females, 43.8 percent.
- Age: 11.9 percent were 20–29; 31.2 percent were 30–39; 34.1 percent were 40–49; and 21.4 percent were 50 or older.
- Job Title: Editor, managing editor or news director, 40.8 percent; personnel director, supervisor, manager or coordinator, 28.2 percent; director or general manager, 19.4 percent; president or CEO, 9.7 percent; educator, 1.9 percent.

- Level of Education: High school, 4.8 percent; college degree, 46 percent; post-graduate work, 21.4 percent; post-graduate degree, 25.4 percent; professional certification, 2.4 percent.
- Location of Firm: In-state, 39.6 percent; out-of-state, 59.4 percent.
- Size of Firm: Between 1 and 10 employees, 15.7 percent; 11 to 20, 13.7 percent; 21 to 30, 7.8 percent; 31 to 100, 27.5 percent; 101 to 150, 6.9 percent; 151 to 500, 21.6 percent; more than 500, 6.9 percent.
- Average Weekly Salary Offered (entry-level positions): Below $175 per week, 13.1 percent; $176 to $200, 9.6 percent; $201 to $250, 19.1 percent; $251 to $275, 8.7 percent; $276 to $300, 19.1 percent; and more than $300, 30.4 percent.

Differences between male and female employers appeared on one demographic characteristic. Significantly greater numbers of female employers worked for smaller firms employing from 1 to 29 employees (48.4 percent to 28.9 percent), while male employers worked for firms with employees numbering 101 or more (44.1 percent to 23.4 percent).

# Summary Tables
# Alumni, Student and Employer Surveys

## TABLE 1

**Frequency Distribution of Factors Influencing Selection of University of Md.**

*Moderately or Extremely Important in Percents*

|  | Alumni (1951–81) | | F | M | Students (1984) | |
| --- | --- | --- | --- | --- | --- | --- |
|  | N = | % |  |  | N = | % |
| 1. Location | (346) | 85.2 | | | (165) | 75.1 |
| 2. Tuition cost | (341) | 79.1 | | | (165) | 69.1 |
| 3. Reputation of journalism program | (341) | 59.9 | 61.8**** | 42.8**** | (166) | 57.7 |
| 4. Entrance requirements | (337) | 34.5 | | | (166) | 38.1 |
| 5. Friends recommend it | (339) | 34.5 | | | (166) | 29.7 |
| 6. Parents/relatives recommend it | (346) | 29.8 | | | (166) | 61.7 |
| 7. Financial aid | (340) | 21.8 | | | (162) | 20.4 |
| 8. Teachers/counselors recommended | (341) | 18.0 | | | (166) | 15.0 |
| 9. Alumni recommended it | (338) | 17.8 | | | (166) | 15.5 |

**** p < .0001

# TABLE 2

**Frequency Distribution of Factors Influencing Choice to Study Journalism**

*Extremely Important in Percents*

|  | Alumni (1951–81) |  |  |  | Students (1984) |  |  |  |
|---|---|---|---|---|---|---|---|---|
|  | N = | % | F | M | N = | % | F | M |
| 1. Liking to write | (345) | 87.4 | 92.2*** | 83.2*** | (167) | 61.7 | 66.9** | 46.5** |
| 2. Creative opportunity | (345) | 84.6 | 89.6** | 81.2** | (166) | 74.4 |  |  |
| 3. Value of job to society | (343) | 56.6 | 65.3** | 49.8** | (163) | 64.3 |  |  |
| 4. Liking to meet people | (344) | 55.1 | 65.1**** | 47.1*** | (167) | 71.2 | 78.2**** | 51.1**** |
| 5. Reputation of the College | (345) | 42.8 | 55.2*** | 32.8*** | (167) | 42.8 |  |  |
| 6. Prestige of the job | (347) | 34.3 |  |  | (167) | 45.3 |  |  |
| 7. Recommendation of teachers/counselors | (339) | 24.8 | 32.8*** | 18.4*** | (164) | 24.4 |  |  |
| 8. Recommendation of peers | (340) | 21.5 |  |  | (168) | 19.7 |  |  |
| 9. Money | (344) | 17.8 | 20.7* | 14.7* | (168) | 33.4 |  |  |
| 10. Recommendation of parents/relatives | (342) | 16.7 |  |  | (168) | 33.8 |  |  |
| 11. Recommendation of media professionals | (340) | 16.6 |  |  | (167) | 17.1 |  |  |
| 12. Easy major | (338) | 10.5 | 13.2**** | 38.2**** | (165) | 8.4 |  |  |

\* $p < .05$
\*\* $p < .01$
\*\*\* $p < .001$
\*\*\*\* $p < .0001$

# TABLE 3

**Frequency Distribution on Opinion of Journalism Program**

|  | Alumni (1951–81) | | Students (1984) | |
|---|---|---|---|---|
|  | N = | % | N = | % |
| 1. Rate your overall experience with the College of Journalism | (344) | | (164) | |
| Extremely or very good | | 57.9 | | 68.6 |
| Somewhat good | | 36.6 | | 28.6 |
| Not at all good | | 5.2 | | .6 |
| 2. Would you major in journalism again? | (262) | | (166) | |
| Yes | | 73.3 | | 89.9 |
| No | | 26.7 | | 10.1 |

# TABLE 4

**Frequency Distribution of Job Satisfaction Levels for Alumni (1951–81)**

*Extreme Satisfaction in Percents*

|  | F | M | N = |
|---|---|---|---|
| 1. Extreme satisfaction with job | 19.9** | 36.6** | (319) |
| 2. Extreme satisfaction with income | 21.3* | 28.6* | (321) |
| 3. Extreme satisfaction with chances for advancement | 40.3*** | 57.1*** | (316) |

\* $p < .05$
\*\* $p < .01$
\*\*\* $p < .001$

# TABLE 5

**Frequency Distribution of Factors Contributing to Job Satisfaction**

*Extreme Satisfaction in Percents*

|  | Alumni (1951–81) |  |  |  | Students (1984) |  |  |  |
|---|---|---|---|---|---|---|---|---|
|  | N = | % | F | M | N = | % | F | M |
| 1. Creative opportunity | (342) | 69.4 | 76.2* | 63.8* | (163) | 72.6 | | |
| 2. Freedom and autonomy | (340) | 67.1 | | | (161) | 61.9 | | |
| 3. Career advancement | (341) | 58.4 | | | (163) | 73.8 | | |
| 4. Adequate salary | (341) | 57.8 | | | (162) | 56.0 | 62.2* | 46.5* |
| 5. Potential for promotion | (337) | 48.7 | | | (163) | 61.3 | 70.0** | 44.2** |
| 6. Job security | (340) | 45.0 | | | (163) | 50.0 | | |
| 7. Opportunity to apply special skills | (341) | 42.5 | | | (162) | 54.8 | 60.8* | 45.2* |
| 8. Management responsibility | (338) | 40.3 | | | (163) | 32.1 | | |
| 9. Recognition of colleagues | (338) | 32.9 | | | (162) | 33.9 | | |
| 10. Recognition of supervisors | (333) | 31.8 | | | (161) | 32.1 | | |
| 11. Value of job to society | (339) | 28.0 | | | (163) | 34.5 | | |
| 12. Prestige | (337) | 22.8 | | | (162) | 23.5 | | |

\* p < .05
\*\* p < .01

# TABLE 6

**Frequency Distribution for Alumni, Employers and Students On Attitudes Toward Journalism and Sexual Bias in the Workplace**

**Note:** No opinion categories have been omitted. Columns do not equal 100%.

| | Alumni (1951-81) | | | Employers | | | Students (1984) | | |
|---|---|---|---|---|---|---|---|---|---|
| | N = | % | F | M | N = | % | F | M | N = | % | F | M |
| 1. Salaries of women doing journalism-related work are generally lower than salaries of men doing comparable work. | (348) | | | | (116) | | | | (167) | | | |
| Agree | | 48.4 | 67.7**** | 31.4**** | | 48.3 | 43.4* | 58.7* | | 55.0 | 67.7**** | 20.0**** |
| Disagree | | 28.8 | | | | 51.7 | | | | 11.4 | | |
| 2. Firms or agencies are more likely to hire a woman than a man for a communication staff position. | (346) | | | | (128) | | | | (167) | | | |
| Agree | | 33.9 | | | | 24.2 | | | | 21.0 | | |
| Disagree | | 41.9 | | | | 66.4 | | | | 41.9 | | |
| 3. Men are promoted more quickly than women in most firms or agencies. | (349) | | | | (128) | | | | (167) | | | |
| Agree | | 54.8 | 70.6**** | 41.8**** | | 45.3 | 55.4* | 37.5* | | 53.9 | 58.1* | 41.9** |
| Disagree | | 32.4 | | | | 39.1 | | | | 16.2 | | |
| 4. Men are more apt to back down or seek compromises in office conflict situations than women are. | (342) | | | | (128) | | | | (165) | | | |
| Agree | | 14.1 | | | | 18.0 | 82.1*** | 56.9*** | | 4.8 | | |
| Disagree | | 70.9 | | | | 68.0 | | | | 61.8 | | |

TABLE 6 — Cont'd.

|  | Alumni (1951-81) | | | | Employers | | | | Students (1984) | | | |
|---|---|---|---|---|---|---|---|---|---|---|---|---|
|  | N = | % | F | M | N = | % | F | M | N = | % | F | M |
| 5. If an equally capable woman and man applied for a job, the woman would probably be hired. | (342) | | | | (128) | | | | (163) | | | |
| Agree | | 20.2 | 74.5**** | 54.9**** | | 22.7 | | | | 14.9 | 61.7** | 46.5** |
| Disagree | | 63.7 | | | | 64.1 | | | | 57.7 | | |
| 6. If an equally capable woman and man applied for a job ten years ago, the man would have been hired. | (347) | | | | (128) | | | | (167) | | | |
| Agree | | 88.9 | | | | 83.6 | | | | 98.2 | 91.9* | 81.4* |
| Disagree | | 5.4 | | | | 9.4 | | | | 3.6 | | |
| 7. The way to get into management level positions is to earn a post-graduate degree. | (345) | | | | (128) | | | | (165) | | | |
| Agree | | 30.3 | | | | 12.5 | | | | 50.3 | | |
| Disagree | | 62.2 | | | | 83.6 | | | | 29.7 | | |
| 8. Women are often hired as a result of affirmative action policies. | (346) | | | | (128) | | | | (166) | | | |
| Agree | | 45.0 | | | | 42.2 | | | | 41.6 | | |
| Disagree | | 37.6 | | | | 45.3 | | | | 28.3 | | |
| 9. Men are more assertive than women in defining proposals and winning consent for decisions affecting the firm or agency. | (347) | | | | (128) | | | | (165) | | | |
| Agree | | 30.4 | | | | 22.7 | | | | 21.8 | | |
| Disagree | | 56.8 | | | | 70.3 | | | | 55.8 | | |

TABLE 6 — Cont'd.

|  | Alumni (1951-81) | | | Employers | | | | Students (1984) | | | |
|---|---|---|---|---|---|---|---|---|---|---|---|
|  | N = | % | F | M | N = | % | F | M | N = | % | F | M |
| 10. More men than women are hired as communication staff directors because they are better suited for management. | (346) | | | | (128) | | | | (166) | | | |
| Agree |  | 5.7 | | | | 5.5 | | | | 7.2 | | |
| Disagree |  | 70.7 | 83.7***** | 59.6**** | | 85.9 | 94.6*** | 79.2*** | | 62.0 | 67.5** | 46.5** |
| 11. Prior job experience counts more than education in getting journalism-related work. | (343) | | | | (128) | | | | (165) | | | |
| Agree |  | 80.2 | | | | 79.9 | | | | 86.1 | | |
| Disagree |  | 6.2 | | | | 16.4 | | | | 7.3 | | |
| 12. I would encourage my son (if I had one) to study journalism in college. | (339) | | | | (128) | | | | (165) | | | |
| Agree |  | 45.1 | | | | 44.5 | | | | 49.0 | | |
| Disagree |  | 41.0 | | | | 43.0 | | | | 36.1 | | |
| 13. I would encourage my daughter (if I had one) to study journalism in college. | (339) | | | | (128) | | | | (166) | | | |
| Agree |  | 43.0 | | | | 50.0 | | | | 44.0 | | |
| Disagree |  | 43.9 | | | | 39.1 | | | | 40.4 | | |

\*    $p < .05$
\*\*   $p < .01$
\*\*\*   $p < .001$
\*\*\*\* $p < .0001$

# Chapter 6

# Women in the Field Offer Their Views

After the Maryland survey team had identified some of the basic questions about "the new majority," the College of Journalism convened two roundtable groups for a full day of discussion on Sept. 28, 1984. For the background of participants, a preliminary position paper was prepared, based upon survey findings and questions that had emerged from other research.

The first panel consisted of women who had achieved substantial successes in their careers. The second panel consisted of current Maryland journalism students and four recent graduates. Excerpts from the two sessions follow.

## Participants in Roundtable One

DR. MAURINE BEASLEY, associate professor and project director, College of Journalism, presiding.

PROF. REESE CLEGHORN, dean, College of Journalism.

MS. MARY LOU FORBES, associate editor, *Washington Times,* Pulitzer Prize winner.

MS. MARCIA SLACUM GREENE, reporter, *Washington Post.*

MS. CAROL MUSGRAVE, public relations professional.

MS. ANNE M. RENSHAW, Renshaw and Associates (public relations).

MS. BEVERLY JACKSON, Jackson, Summers Associates (advertising and public relations).

MS. CHEREE CLEGHORN, vice president, public affairs, Washington Healthcare Corporation.

MS. JEAN GIANFAGNA, creative director, Bureau of National Affairs.

DR. LYNN M. HASKIN, national president, Women in Communications, and special assistant to the provost for academic planning, Temple University.

MS. SHARON DICKMAN, assistant metro editor, *Baltimore Evening Sun.*

MS. CLAUDIA TOWNSEND, city editor (on leave), *Washington Post.*

MS. NANCY MONAGHAN, national editor, *USA Today.*

MS. TONNIE KATZ, managing editor, *Baltimore News American.*

MS. RENEE POUSSAINT, news department, *WJBM-TV,* Washington, D.C.

MS. BONNIE JOE AYERS, editor, *Maryland Magazine.*

## Participants in Roundtable Two

MS. KATHRYN THEUS, director of undergraduate studies and associate project director, College of Journalism, presiding.

PROF. REESE CLEGHORN, dean, College of Journalism.

MS. KAREN WATERS, senior, advertising.

MS. SANDRA HAMORSKY, junior, broadcasting.

MS. CAROL HOXIE, senior, public relations.

MS. CLOVIS BARKDULL, senior, magazines.

MS. ROBIN CAUDELL, freelance writer.

MS. LAURIE JONES, senior, news-editorial, and writer for *Diamondback.*

MS. MELAINE CARROLL, freelance writer.

MS. CRISTAL WILLIAMS, general assignment reporter, *Easton* (MD) *Star-Democrat.*

MS. CONNIE HENEBERRY, account coordinator, Needham, Harper Worldwide Advertising

MS. CHRIS HARVEY, reporter, *Prince George's Journal.*

## Excerpts—Roundtable of Successful Career Women

DEAN CLEGHORN: You know, I think, essentially why we thought doing such a study as this was worthwhile. In the background paper for the roundtable you saw the statistics—nationally 59 percent of journalism school students are women, a reversal from only a dozen or so years ago. In our own school the figure is 69 percent female. We are a little ahead of the national trend and in both cases the percentage seems to still be rising, perhaps leveling off in our case, but I think still rising nationally.

Obviously we thought this had some real ramifications for us in journalism education and in particular for us at the University of Maryland. What does it mean for us in terms of how we teach or how we do other things in the school? Does it mean we should do anything differently? The fact is that we haven't really looked at any of what we do in that light. It's not that our curriculum hasn't changed; it's that we have never looked at it thinking in terms of a predominantly female profession that we will be serving. We want to know if there are specific things we should do about curriculum, if there are things we should do about student organizations, if there are other things we should do.

Why do this study at Maryland? We thought at first maybe this should be a national study at which we looked at all journalism schools and then decided that that might produce some rather thin results. What we wanted to do was to look at one journalism school that might be fairly typical of the larger ones and look at it in real depth.

If it were a totally untypical school that might not be useful to anyone but us, but in fact our size is approximately the same, a bit more or a bit less, as that of most of the major comprehensive journalism schools in the country. The distribution of students is not unlike those elsewhere. Some of you in the news world perhaps are surprised when you see a figure that says 20 percent of journalism schools graduates go into print news. It's not surprising nationally; it's just about what nationally journalism schools produce and just about what we do. So we think we can learn from looking at ourselves about some things that apply on the national level.

DR. BEASLEY: The pioneering stage of women in journalism is over. According to the Bureau of Labor Statistics, in 1977, of the working journalists in this country, 45 percent were women. Women are not only the wave of the future; they're the wave that is already there in journalism.

Does the group think that it's more difficult for women than men to move up from journalism school into the labor force? Could we talk about some of the problems that women have that are peculiar to them because of their social role and because of their sex?

MS. JACKSON: I'd like to comment on the role of combining the motherhood thing. I have two small children, ages five and nine, and don't forget my business is also nine and a half, almost ten years old. So clearly I've had the two babies while I've been creating this business. And I do think this reinforces what I have said before about developing the possibility of an entrepreneurial spirit because it isn't easy for women to come and go in and out of the work force.

There is that natural inclination to ask even though no one can verbalize it now because it's against the law: What are you going to do if you have a baby? What are your intentions if you're 26 years old, married and no children and so forth? No potential employers can ask you that; however, they're thinking it, and it's a real problem.

I do think still today that men come and go easier. A man who takes an hour or two to take his child to the doctor for an emergency or dental treatment or whatever is considered just the neatest, trendiest, most wonderful upscale yuppie father in the world, but a mother will tend to lie about it and say that she's on an assignment. She, in fact, would even come closer to saying, "I have a doctor's appointment," than to say, in a highly competitive field, "I'm taking my child to the doctor." I don't even tell my clients when I'm out doing something with the children and it's my business. It's just one of those things, play it down, put it in the background and it's just the way it is.

MS. FORBES: But aren't you putting your finger on something that lurks within yourself, that attitude? In other words shouldn't you just head on and meet the issue?

MS. KATZ: I was just going to say that we put much of the pressure on ourselves. I find at my office, which is very informal, that while I'm glad to have anyone go at any time to take a child here or there, to car-pool or go to dentist appointments, I find that I don't do that. I wait till 10 p.m. till I get home for dinner. My poor children are the ones that have to get themselves to the dentist. That's because I really do that to myself. But I think that women still put that pressure on themselves. And I'm not sure they have to.

MS. TOWNSEND: I think that's exactly true. At the *Post,* we've had a real wave of pregnancies in the last year. In the Metro section alone there were five women who were pregnant at the same time, a number of us who were editors. The poor metro editor was sort of in a state of shock about having half of his work force disappear. But the paper has been very good about offering maternity leave, offering people flexibility about how long they'd be gone and when they'd come back and about bringing people back into promotions when they come back. I had sort of anticipated being pushed off into the corner somewhere, you know, and viewed by the hierarchy as somebody who had a baby and, therefore, wasn't going to want to work hard. And they crossed me up by offering me a promotion, which caused me to have to sit down and think about what I wanted to do. Another woman who has come and gone since I have, left as an assistant Maryland editor and has come back as a Maryland editor with her new baby. So they are very willing to let people do whatever people will do and what they're finding as a result is that they're bumping into people who are not putting the pressure on themselves. I mean I sit and think about whether I'm going to let the baby stay home [with a sitter] till 10:00 at night and is that going to drive me crazy. One woman quit and became a professor at a journalism school because she felt that she could handle that pressure better than the pressure of the paper, and the paper would have been glad to have her back. So, for our case, it's not that people won't let us go or won't let us come back or don't treat us well; it is that the barriers have been broken down so far there's now room for people to take the responsibility for whatever choice they're going to make. And, to my surprise, I find that to be a little bit uncomfortable, and I think, other people have, too.

DR. BEASLEY: I think we should move on to the next question: What should the College of Journalism do to ease this transition? You're speaking in terms of pressure people put on themselves, of the feeling that women have guilt, perhaps; guilt over not giving enough to their job even though the company may be agreeable that they could give less than they do. Guilt over not being with the child, even though the child may or may not have a suitable substitute parent. How can a college of journalism address these questions in preparing women to enter the labor force? Should it be addressing the questions?

MS. MUSGRAVE: In moving from school into a career, I found that I got asked frequently "could I type" in interviewing for journalism-type jobs. And I think it's easier for women to go into entry-level positions after they graduate from school because there are so many of them that involve some clerical skills, and I found that it's easier for men to enter on a professional level than it is for women. I found that in my case. And as far as what the College of Journalism can do to facilitate women's entering into the professional world, I think the internship program is wonderful. I had something to show people as a graduate. I had clips. I had projects to show people.

I don't know how you can teach networking or how to find a professional position, but if you had courses that talked about management and networking and finding a professional position, I think that would be some help to students.

MS. KATZ: I think a real specific thing you could do that wouldn't take, I don't think, a lot of work, would be to look at the role models that you're providing. There are part-time people, full-time faculty members, women on panels and visiting lecturers. I think you have to provide role models in those positions.

MS. GREENE: Thinking back on internships, it's good if you would encourage the students while they are at Maryland to either work for the *Diamondback* [campus newspaper] or string for a local publication so that when they do go for an internship, they feel comfortable in that role and they're not sitting back waiting for someone to hand them an assignment. It's going to be more realistic if they come in knowing how to—feeling comfortable so that they push along with the other reporters or editors in terms of doing their daily job.

MS. RENSHAW: I would stress a work-study program. Perhaps that's being done at the university, whereby it's not just an internship where you come in in the afternoon but it's six months on the job, six months back at the university. I found myself having to go back to a graduate school mode because of the doors being shut, vis-a-vis, on the entry of women into the communications industry. And I foxed them out in Boston by getting turned down at one broadcasting station for a position and running back to school and earning a scholarship internship grant. I was back at the station within two weeks saying, "Here I am, and you're going to have to deal with it."

But I do feel that the men go after the options quicker than the women do. They will get out there and travel. They'll look far afield if they don't see anything on the local horizon. Women are root bound in some cases. Perhaps they need a college course called "reality one" or "reality two" that mentions such things as don't be encumbered by possessions, be able to pack and move if the opportunity presents itself; and that even means moving abroad because some of the best positions in management will come if you've had some experience outside in a foreign country and can speak another language and come back to this area.

MS. FORBES: I'd just like to address some of your realities there on getting a job. Many years ago you didn't even look for journalism experience when you were hiring people. Now I would say at the editorial assistant role or the entry-level job, you look for what applicants did on the college paper and that sort of thing. That certainly has changed in the last 20 years. So you do have an advantage to that extent with your journalism school experience now which people really didn't look for 20 years ago.

MS. POUSSAINT: I'm not sure what journalism schools can do to prepare women to combine a family life and a career. It is certainly a problem if you're serious about being a network correspondent. I think it's very difficult, particularly if you're at one of the bureaus where your work really involves a lot of traveling. In the Washington bureau most correspondents don't really travel that much except during campaigns. But if you're in the Midwest bureau or the Southern bureau based in Atlanta or even in Texas, you're on the road. I don't know of any woman correspondent working under those circumstances who has a family. I mean virtually all of them are single. A few of them who have been in the business for a long time and managed to get themselves into a position at a relatively stable bureau, like the Washington bureau, have put off childbearing, et cetera, et cetera, until they felt relatively secure with what they were doing. Leslie Stahl and Ann Compton are two people that immediately come to mind. But most of the women whom I know, who are in the business and are at the busier bureaus, are all single. And I don't really know how you could combine that kind of schedule with a family. I mean you just, you're never home.

MS. KATZ: I wanted to say, I think it's probably the best time for women in journalism that it has ever been.

I think that there are more women around. I think they are better qualified than we've ever had. I get about 150 resumes a month and I would say that, making a sweeping generalization, the women are more qualified than the men. The women I meet and interview are better—they're hungrier for the job and to me that's a real big qualification for the job, too.

DEAN CLEGHORN: I'd be interested in knowing whether you see any difference between men and women applicants in respect to the assertiveness that you've just described.

MS. KATZ: I do. I do believe that the women that we are interviewing are much more aggressive. They want the job more and that counts.

MS. MONAGHAN: I would agree with that. I think in my experience I have found that women are definitely more assertive in trying to get the job to get in the front door. Men have tended, the ones that I have interviewed over the years, to feel more like they deserve the job for nothing more than the fact that they may be a journalism graduate or have some nice clips to show and that because they're a man they deserve a reporter's job, whereas the women are hungrier. They're trying to prove that they can do the job that men think they can automatically do.

DR. BEASLEY: Does that mean the women will settle for less in order to get the job?

MS. MONAGHAN: That's also true.

MS. JACKSON: Absolutely, in PR, too.

MS. MUSGRAVE: I had an employer tell me that he hired mostly women because number one, they worked cheap and number two, they work long hours.

MS. MONAGHAN: I did that. With my first job I worked free for a year so I could get the job. I had a full-time job and I worked at night so I basically had two full-time jobs, one I worked for free. But I knew there was no other way to for me to get the job. I mean it was a new paper and, you know, I was a nobody. I had absolutely no experience whatsoever so I worked free.

MS. GREENE: I think there's a real danger if we settle for less because I know in your survey here, you're talking what's going to happen in the future in terms of pay and the job market with all these females that are going into journalism.

MS. JACKSON: That's right.

MS. GREENE: Just going back to '76 when I graduated from Maryland, a group of us would get together because there were so many people going into journalism because of Woodward and Bernstein, and we all discussed whether we would ever get jobs. I knew women at that time who sent out something like 100 resumes, and they were saying that, you know, it's going to be really difficult. Others said, "Well, I'll just—I'm going to stay in Baltimore, I'm going to stay in Washington and if I don't get a job, then I'll do something else." Instead, what I decided to do was to send out maybe ten letters to papers in the South saying that I'm interested in working in the South. I got in a car, borrowed $200 and went traveling in the South and decided I was going to get a job, and I just told the folks I'm coming your way at Christmas time and I'd like to sit down and interview with someone. And I did that. I think the journalism schools have to stress that some of the smaller papers are willing to hire you even if you don't have that basic experience because if I had not done that, I think maybe I would have settled for less. But instead I started on the *St. Petersburg Times,* which has a reputation for taking students right out of journalism school, and I started as a reporter and got some of my best experience there to move on to these larger papers. I think we can't settle for less and just what I hear makes me afraid that women will. Your case may be special but working free for a year—I don't know what that's going to do to the field eventually if more and more women have that attitude.

DR. HASKIN: As a professor, I always advise my students never work for free. If you work for free, what does that say about the quality of your work? If it's good enough to be published or broadcast, it's worth reimbursement. And I feel very strongly on that issue. But I don't think it's realistic to expect that we're going to see any major changes in the curriculum of journalism schools across the country, and the reasons are probably too long to explain in detail now, but if schools of journalism and communications want to stay accredited and want to maintain their reputations, they have to maintain a balance between the theoretical and practical courses that they can offer; and they also have to maintain a balance between the courses that they offer and the internships that they're allowed to give. So that's a problem of academe, that's something that academics will struggle with.

But what I think is, although we may not see major changes in curriculum, that journalism schools have a lot to teach.

So what I'm saying is I think more women need to be hired on faculties, and more minorities need to be hired on faculties, and they need to be promoted. They need to be in positions not only to be role models but to be the mentors that you talked about and to bring an infusion of some new ideas and some sensitivity. And I'm not suggesting that sensitivity only comes from women; there are sensitive men as well. And what the people who are in positions to hire need to do is to be sure that who they are hiring are sensitive people, and sensitivity isn't limited to women.

MS. CLEGHORN: Well, let me drop a bomb here. I agree generally with the trends that she described, but I was the beneficiary of a white male in a journalism faculty who took me and other females and assorted males. He didn't care. You could have been purple. If you were good, he would see to it that you did well. And he beat the hell out of you for two long years. The beauty of the relationship was you emerged clear on your basic skills. The way to prevail, the way to avoid being second class, is to be best, and if you are best, you don't have to take it from anybody.

Second, a white male professor, who has experience in the world with discrimination, will turn around and say as my professor said to me, do not—this is 1969—do not let them send you to talk to the women's editor. You tell them you do not know how to write those stories. You hold out for the city desk or you come home.

There are men who will do that for students. No student ought to emerge if she or he is really committed to the profession with less than full understanding of what his or her skills mean in terms of the market place, and they will defend themselves. They don't have to be run over, and they don't have to be second class. You know quality will out every time, regardless of sex.

MS. GIANFAGNA: I must say that my greatest concern and the thing that I would stress to the University of Maryland and all journalism schools to consider is that most of the people who apply at my company for advertising jobs cannot write.

MS. JACKSON: Same in our business.

MS. GIANFAGNA: It's absolutely shocking.

MS. JACKSON: It is.

MS. GIANFAGNA: I probably hire four or five advertising copywriters every year because we have a fairly high turnover for a number of reasons, but also, our program is growing, and I've hired advertising copywriters for agencies, and I'm shocked at the number of people who cannot put together a simple declarative sentence, who cannot spell, who will turn in samples where the client's name or the product's name is misspelled. It is shocking, but it's a reality. And I saw some of it in the classes when I taught here at Maryland. I'm not trying to criticize your program, but it's true, and it's not your fault. I think a lot of it is the American education system. By the time they get to college, they don't know how to write. You know, you're in trouble, you're in the remedial position. You're in the position to help them write.

The ability to write is crucial, no matter what you're going to do. If you're going to move into management, if you can't write, you're lost. You're absolutely lost. If you can't prepare presentations and written documents and proposals and marketing plans, you cannot function. You will not be moved up. They will not promote you. They will not make opportunities for you if you can't write. No matter what you're doing in advertising, whether it's graphics or account work or media work or whatever, if you're a poor communicator in writing, you aren't going to make it.

MS. FORBES: But there are [news] instincts that some people have. They just recognize what the story is and, of course, that instinct is developed and enhanced over the years, but you may have really a difficult time teaching that. It's exposure to a constant flow of human events that maybe will develop that more finely. But J schools can certainly focus on writing and accuracy; [teaching students to] get it right; be fair. They can judge [women] on other things, but they cannot deny [you] if you're good and, you constantly turn out a good product. You write the best obituaries in the office; you come up with a scoop out of police court every day. This is a great business for women for that reason because if you're good they can't deny it.

MS. POUSSAINT: I really feel sort of isolated here as a broadcaster because a number of the things that have been said about print don't really apply to broadcasting. And one of the things that you just said doesn't necessarily apply, that if you're real good, quality will out; broadcasting is not necessarily like that. And this is something that unfortunately journalism students are not told. I wanted to make a couple of points.

One is I absolutely agree with the writing, and part of that is my own background because I come out of that, and that's how I got into the business. But, in a very pragmatic sense, one of the few sorts of entry-level jobs that students can sometimes get at a broadcast station is as a news writer, and we at *WJLA* have had two news writing openings for the past five years—five years. We have been using freelancers because we can't find people who know how to write well for broadcast journalism. And it is one of those more amazing things about the business, that I find that most of the journalism grads who come to apply are very bad. I mean they—the verbs don't agree with the nouns, and they write these sentences that just go on forever, and you can't figure out what they're talking about. I mean they just have no realistic relationship with the craft. And for whatever you do in broadcasting, a good writing background is absolutely critical whether you're a news writer or a reporter or a news director or whatever; you have got to be able to write. Broadcast journalism is really headline writing. And it's headline writing very fast—half of it in your head—so that you compose a story as a story is going on, and by the time it's finished, you ought to be able to bang it out. And to be able to tell a story basically in a minute and a half is something that is very hard to do, and it's very hard to teach. But I think the journalism schools generally are failing in that area because if the caliber of applicant we get is any indication, they're just not teaching that skill, and I think it's crippling a lot of young people who come in the business.

The other thing, other point that I'd like to make is about expectations of people who come to apply in the field of broadcast journalism. The expectations are totally unrealistic. And that is largely the fault, I think, of broadcast journalism in that most of the young women that I have contact with who want to get into my business say—they don't come to me and say, "Tell me how to get in the business and be a good reporter;" they ask me, "Tell me how to get in the business and be a star." I mean literally they use the word "star." And I have counseled students at a couple of journalism schools locally and hired some people temporarily as writers and whatever. I found that in talking to them most of the young women have very little interest in pounding the pavement and chasing fire engines and getting scoops from the police department. Most of them are interested in being Jane Pauley. And I don't know how you get around that because unfortunately the business encourages a lot of young women to think that they can do that. That they can, if they're blond and cute, be a network anchor and make a whole bunch of money. And I can't tell them that they can't do it. And I can't say that because they can.

MS. CLEGHORN: Well, but one thing that journalism schools could say to—in terms of people's expectations—is to point out how few of those jobs there are and it's the same thing in the newspaper business. You know if you're an ambitious and successful person and if you would like to some day run the *Washington Post* or be Jane Pauley, either one, and you're sitting there in college and you're looking at what you're going to do, nobody ever sits down and says there's going to come a time in your life when you're going to be successful at some newspaper, and you'll be somewhere, and you'll be 35 years old and you'll be really good and there's one job, and there're 100 people who want it, and everybody's going to have to wait for Ben Bradlee to die, you know, and it doesn't have anything to do with anything else. And you need to realize that if that's where you're headed, that's the kind of competition you're going to be after; and somewhere you're going to have to make a decision to do something else or wait and hope that you're the lucky one. And if you're going to do anything else, if you're not going to get to be one of the three people who's a network anchor, what are you going to do for the rest of your life?

MS. DICKMAN: Just in terms of actually getting the job, I talked with Bill Hawkins, who's the metropolitan editor of the *Evening Sun* in Baltimore, and he said that he does have more women applicants than men for jobs, but recently we had some openings, and we made three hires, one white woman, one white man and one black woman. And that's generally how our hires go. And so even though the white, primarily white, women are among the largest group in this pool, they're not knocking each other off, but there's a lot of competition. In companies like ours where there's a small number of women, it is the pioneering days. In the beginning, when you said pioneering is over, you know, in one sense it is, but in another sense in the newspaper business, it's not....I was thinking about the power of communications and of journalism, and I don't think men are ever going to abandon journalism to women. I think, you know, there's going to be a big struggle there and I think men are going to be running it for a while.

DR. BEASLEY: If journalism is likely to become a sex-stereotyped occupation, and people are saying they're getting increasing number of women applicants to the profession, should efforts be made to recruit more males?

MS. DICKMAN: I think you've made the link that a lot of women means it becomes a second-class profession, and I don't agree with that.

DR. BEASLEY: Second class only in the sense of—

MS. JACKSON: Salary. That's what it's going to mean, like nursing and teaching, where you have to fight to the death to get adequate salaries that would match a man in the same career path. The other thing in corporations is that public affairs jobs do not necessarily mean a route to the top. And sometimes they do if they're [held by] men, but it's trickier if you're a woman. You're not in line to be president of the company. There're lots of women in public affairs jobs, but they are never going to be at the top, ever, not ever. So that's, I think, a problem.

MS. GIANFAGNA: That question kind of threw me, too. I don't think that we should necessarily try to recruit more men into communications, but I think the answer is just—I think we should not try to stem the tide of the flow of more women into the field. But what I think we need to be certain of is that as women and men enter the fields that they are paid equally to the extent possible, comparable pay for comparable work. I think the concern and probably the reason the research even dealt with this question is because if you look at the statistics, the fields which are predominantly women's jobs tend to be lower-paid than jobs where men are predominant.

MS. AYERS: Where the new territory is being hurt is on the management level. I think what you have to teach women there is how to negotiate for what the men are already getting. Once you reach a certain level you negotiate and also—

MS. TOWNSEND: You don't know what to ask for, that's the question.

MS. RENSHAW: Well, within the agency business there's a little bit more flexibility and it tends—an employer will take a look at the background of the person, the experience, which plays a large part in the salary that the person is going to command, and also past pay levels. But I also want to make a point here, take this opportunity to get the point across, about holding out for a larger salary and the risks involved. When you are interviewed for a job, and it's in the city you like to be in, it's with a business that you'd like to get experience in and you think the salary might be a little bit low, and you step back and say they ought to pay me more, and the firm says no, we can't, no, that's not possible and so you say no, thank you very much, but no, you're taking risks when you do that. Because you may not be able to find a good job fast enough to make up for the months that you may be without a salary.

MS. GIANFAGNA: I'd like to suggest, though, that if a company says no, we cannot pay you more than that, that very well may be the case. Beyond that, I think what we all need to be aware of is that there are a myriad of things that you can use in lieu of salary—educational benefits, secretary, car, health benefits, educational benefits for spouse or children—or more weeks vacation, professional development, paid conference dues, paid professional membership dues. When you start to add those things up, they can be significant. They can be several, many, thousands of dollars worth of benefits. And initially the company may be staying within its guidelines offering you only what they said they could offer you, but they can enhance the benefits to you without making other employees feel uncomfortable.

DR. BEASLEY: Do we risk flooding the market with an influx of women fighting for the same job and further depressing salaries? Those of you who have looked into the so-called pink-collar occupations such as beautician, store clerk, clerical worker, will find that economists say part of the reason the salaries in these fields are so low is because there are so many people willing to take the jobs. And I guess we are asking ourselves here: Are we turning out an increasing number of women students who are going to be fighting for the same jobs and thus the pay will be depressed?

MS. JACKSON: There are a number of fields like that also that have a slightly glamorous tinge to them. [Take] the people who work behind the counters in Garfinckel's, Bloomingdale's and all those places. If you only knew their salaries—I don't know how they even dress. Fortunately, they get discounts in the stores, which is one of the benefits. But there are some fields where they can just keep generation after generation attracting new kids and people who will stay on, work for pennies. It's not going to change because the economics of that industry is based on those low salaries.

MS. FORBES: But in the news business you have to have talent to survive. So I think we are living in an era when information is going to become increasingly important, and people will not get it in the traditional ways that we see now.

I think the people who are flooding into the information market will be involved in the processing and the packaging and the delivery of the quick information fix, which will become increasingly specialized.

DEAN CLEGHORN: There's a key point, I think. I think that we're going to have a sort of split-level profession which in part won't be a profession any more. And the journalism school has to decide what to do about that. But it seems to me that there's going to be so much information processing—and very clerical kind of work related to information—that we need to make clear that that's not what we're in the business of doing. And that's one way that women, if they're in the majority in journalism schools, may come out ahead. There may be a tendency for many women to be hired, assuming clerical levels in information. And what a journalism school presumably does is produce professionals who have not simply learned how to put words together and put them out on the machine, but who have also gotten a legal, ethical, historical context and value structure related to the profession. I think there is a potential trap, though, because journalism schools may decide to justify their size by doing a lot of information processing concentration and then feeding people out to clerical kinds of jobs. [If so] they're going to lose ground.

MS. POUSSAINT: Going on the basis that in the broadcasting industry image and reality often get fudged, I wanted to say that I think it is highly unlikely that with control of information really being as powerful as it is, particularly in my business, that men are going to give up control of the industry. They certainly aren't now. And the pattern is that women are still being clustered in the lower paying jobs. There is the bulk of the large influx of women that come into the broadcasting industry in the past few years. The bulk of them are not clustered in the producer ranks and assistant producer ranks. And many of those positions are not unionized. And they are getting smaller salaries than men doing comparable work in many instances, but they don't tell each other that. They ought to be networking. And that's something of a problem.

In some broadcast stations they do tell each other, and they get upset, and then they go and talk to management. Management tells them: Do you know how many other women want your job?

DR. BEASLEY: That's pretty powerful stuff.

MS. POUSSAINT: Yes. But it was interesting, there was an update recently. The National Organization for Working Women did an update on the status of women in the broadcast industry, an updated *Window Dressing on the Set,* and they found that for the most part there's virtually no increase of women reporters on the network levels and in larger markets. It's all sort of moving the same bodies around. Women reporters are getting on the air now, [but] the trend is less than in the past. There is a decline actually in the visibility and participation of women reporters on the air.

DR. BEASLEY: Why do you think that is? Or why does the group think that is?

MS. POUSSAINT: Men deciding that women were getting too much control, too much visibility, too much influence in the industry, and beginning to block certain channels of upward mobility.

Well, I have run into a number of younger women who really quite sincerely feel that the need for networking and "women's lib type activity" is not necessary any more.

MS. JACKSON: I've heard that, too.

MS. POUSSAINT: I mean they look around, and they see a whole bunch of women in the field and they say, you know, well, we ought to be able to make it on talent and qualifications. I don't see why we have to have women's caucuses and women's groups and talk to each other about our salaries. My salary is my own business. And that's fine for them. But the end result is there is a lot of interchange and a lot of networking and a lot of power in number activity that doesn't happen. And in the absence of that the trend seems to be just to increasingly stop up certain areas of increased power within the business and women are, at least in my business in many instances, being pushed backwards.

MS. GIANFAGNA: Can I ask an obnoxious question? You said before that a lot of the young women you ran into were more interested in being Jane Pauley than in being a reporter. Does that have anything to do with the fact that there aren't so many women reporters?

MS. POUSSAINT: Partly. One of the ways, I think that men are maintaining control of the industry in terms of not feeling that their positions will ever be threatened in terms of the real control is by hiring "Barbie dolls." I was at the Republican Convention and it was one of the more frightening phenomena I've ever been through, not because they're Republicans, but there was something that started hitting a number of reporters who'd been around for a long time. After about the third day, we realized that there was a certain reporter clone that had been hired by hundreds of stations across this country and they're all blond, and they're all under 26.

MS. MUSGRAVE: Under 26?

MS. POUSSAINT: All 25 and they all weigh—

MS. JACKSON: And you couldn't tell them apart, they all looked—

MS. POUSSAINT: —under 117 pounds. They're sort of thin and their hair is all the same length. And I mean it's funny, but after a certain point, it gets scary because you'd meet one in the hall and say, "I met you yesterday, didn't I?" It wasn't the same one. And at one point there were five of them standing together talking to each other, and you really had a hard time telling them apart.

MS. JACKSON: Somebody ought to write this up.

MS. POUSSAINT: It's funny, but it's scary because they are reporters. And they were all hired, the bulk of them were hired by men who want a certain kind of look and a certain kind of woman, and those women are not going to threaten those men in terms of—

MS. JACKSON: True.

MS. POUSSAINT: —control of the industry, in terms of management positions, in terms of changing anything. And they will be discarded as easily as they were hired, [replaced] by some other "Barbie doll" type. And what really became frightening was I discovered in talking to a number of my former colleagues from the networks, women reporters who've been in the business for 10-15 years, that they are now getting calls from vice-presidents of network organizations telling them that they don't want them on the air because they don't like their looks.

MS. JACKSON: Oh, God.

MS. POUSSAINT: And one network reporter who has covered Beirut, who has covered a number of places, told me that she has been put through three different wardrobe consultants, sent to four different hairdressers in the past six months because they want her to begin to look like the "Barbie dolls." And it is a very disturbing phenomenon, and that is one way that the males in the industry who are doing the hiring are controlling their own positions and the power in the industry because as long as you can divert women by making them compete on a physical basis, they're never going to get into any sort of position of power to start really managing the industry.

MS. MONAGHAN: I think, if there's anything that journalism schools can do, it's to give women and men options, but we're talking about women here, so we need to have people who tell them the realities of newsrooms: That if you get there men, some men, are likely to want you to go to work on the women's page. Women need to be told don't do that. Women need to know the reality of how you get in the front door, what the real world is going to be like when you get out there and how many job options you're actually going to have. I've had people just out of journalism school come to *USA Today*, and expect that they're going to be Carl Bernstein, you know, when they come through the door. It seems to me that that's the responsibility of the journalism school—to make realities known to the students.

The electronic information issue I was really interested to hear about. Certainly Gannett and *USA Today* have a major project underway. And it does appear to be the wave to the future, yet I fear that journalism schools wouldn't take part in that because they believe it is a clerical function, and I think that we're going to be in serious trouble if the information delivery of the future, which is going to be electronic, suddenly is seen not as a professional function but a clerical function. I would really hate to see journalism schools feel that they wouldn't want to prepare people for that field or entry ultimately into that field because I don't think it's going to be done in clerical functions.

DEAN CLEGHORN: I didn't mean to suggest that journalism schools shouldn't pay attention to that and acquaint students with it, but I meant that there is an awful lot of tabular work, as you know. *USA Today* has more of it than anybody almost. It's got to be done by somebody and it just doesn't seem to be fitting work for a journalism graduate. And it seems to me if a journalism graduate is involved with that system, then that should be in a managerial capacity, a judgmental one. What we hope students get is not skill only but also values of judgment, legal capacities and so on. That was the distinction I meant. I didn't mean we'd ignore that and stick to the old typewriter.

DR. BEASLEY: What I hear here is that journalism schools are not sufficiently informing students about the realities in the field, not telling them about the careers of the future, and it seems to me, that maybe what you're saying is that people who teach in journalism schools don't really know what's going on in the field today.

MS. GREENE: Just sort of piggybacking on what Renee was saying in terms of business, there seems to be an assumption in your question just because all of these females are now majoring in journalism that they're going to sort of take over the profession. And I just wondered if that's going to really happen because for one thing, as our research points out, a number of those majors are not in the news-editorial sequence, where evidence shows a lot of the jobs are going to be in the future. To throw out a couple of statistics, the 1983 survey from the ASNE [American Society of Newspaper Editors] shows that of the major newspapers in the country in terms of editors there are 93 women and 1,027 men; in terms of executive editors, 16 women and 230 men; managing editors, 120 women and 893 men. And the bottom line is there're 89.4 percent men compared to 10.6 percent of women in top management. I don't think that's going to change overnight.

MS. AYERS: But getting back to how to prepare someone, I think one of the things that we can look at is you go in there with a set of good clips and that's fine, but part of what you have to learn to do is to sell yourself through the interview; and how much experience are the women getting in interviewing—techniques of being interviewed and being an interviewer? So I think this is one of the things that the schools have to look at as far as preparing someone for the job market goes.

DR. HASKIN: I think if what we don't like is stereotypes, that we have to be careful to try to avoid stereotypes ourselves. And I think the message that students need, young women and young men need to hear, is that out there in the work world, there are supportive women and there are supportive men. And you have to learn to distinguish between them because a young man can learn from a successful woman; a young woman can learn from a successful man. They can have same-sex mentors or opposite-sex mentors, but I think the important thing is to seek the individual, to look at the strengths and qualities that you admire and aspire to. To that end, one of the things that Women in Communications is doing is unveiling very shortly a new five-year strategic plan to offer role models for the women and men who are members of Women in Communications, and I personally have recruited lots of high-level men and women to be role models for the organization and for the young professionals coming up.

MS. POUSSAINT: You know, I think that women have a tendency to behave differently in career situations, depending on whether or not they perceive an unspoken quota system at the organization for which they work. I think that if a woman is applying for a job or trying to move up in an organization where she knows that there are a certain number of slots that women are "allowed to get into" that her perception is that she has to get rid of one of the women in order to take her place. I think women behave very differently when they feel that they are working for an organization that doesn't have that kind of unspoken quota. I think that in the broadcast industry there is often an unspoken quota and as a result, women are often placed in positions of having to sort of do each other in in order to get a job or move up in the organization. And I think what we have to impress upon young women coming up is that that is inherently a no-win situation and that the alternative strategy, which to my mind works a hell of a lot better, is for women to organize to expand the jobs and get rid of the quotas so that there will not be that necessity for destroying each other in order to survive.

MS. RENSHAW: In the public relations field here in Washington, I am running across a great deal of this business of women not wanting to network. That it's almost like being labeled, if you are part of a women's organization in your own field. And there are many women, and this goes to some of the women at the PRSA [Public Relations Society of America], who say we are beyond that. We are all working together in this wonderful field of public relations and there is no, should never be any such thing as special women's programs, that kind of business. But many of the well-known men in the field easily transfer their skills from one agency to another. When these jobs open, it's the men who fill them because the men are the friends. And that word about the job opening at a top level never gets to the women who might be within the professional organization on a par with these people and perhaps have skills that far excel the men's.

MS. CLEGHORN: In terms of what journalism schools can do for students, I think it's very important to focus on what jobs really have significant sex differences. I'm a little concerned about a global view that seems to suggest if women predominate in a profession it automatically descends to second-class status. I think the thing that Renee described is so insidious that it is very important to be clear about where there are sex differences and where women are being exploited so that kids don't come out with some sort of global paranoid view of the whole world being out after women because, in fact, that's probably not always the case. It's important to zero in on where it's real. And I think in newsrooms it's far less real. And in public relations generally, it's a much more benign environment for women than what Renee has described, and what I've heard other TV people say.

DR. BEASLEY: Do women need specific assistance which could be provided in a college of journalism to allow them to move up the career ladder? We know that most of the women in journalism tend to be clustered in the lower-paying areas because of lack of experience or because sexism has continued on or whatever, perhaps because of career interruptions. Our research shows that women who interrupt their careers do not fare too well when they return. What could we be doing in college or should we be doing to give women a specific aid in moving up the career ladder?

MS. JACKSON: Somebody mentioned negotiation a while ago. Maybe there could be some curriculum developed for being in the business of journalism and negotiating a contract. If you're a free-lance writer, for instance, you have to be able to negotiate with editors and deal with kill fees and know how to be reimbursed for your expenses and all these things. But you don't learn that in journalism. You might learn it on your internship if you had an unusual situation. But probably not. But something could be taught about the business of going out into the world and being prepared for managing a budget possibly.

DR. HASKIN: Because the curriculum is so crowded, there's not a lot we can do except perhaps to encourage students to take the bulk of their electives in a particular area such as business courses or economics or marketing or something like that to get a specialized skill beyond the high quality writing and other journalism skills that they come out with. I think the extra kinds of things are helpful: the workshops, the seminars, the associations with professional organizations, hearing outside speakers and so forth. But I return to the point that I made earlier: That is, I think you can teach a lot of the things that we're talking about today without a course, without a specific workshop. They can come up in a casual discussion—if you're interviewing somebody or you walk into a situation, how do you handle this or whatever. Is it different for a woman than a man? A question like that from a student can initiate a discussion that a professor can lead if that professor is comfortable leading that discussion. And that can come from a sensitive man or a sensitive woman, as I said before. But it won't come up if there's not a wide variety of ideas. It won't come up, I think, if there's not a diversity of people doing the teaching. So I think it's important that we have the diversity represented on faculties so that these ideas and discussions can occur.

MS. POUSSAINT: I have a comment that goes against actually some of the things that we've been saying earlier about how aggressive a lot of women are in the fields that we're talking about. One of the things that I discovered, particularly in local broadcast stations, is that there are any number of women who will get into jobs, the lower-paying jobs, and they don't understand how to get out of them. They don't understand how to market their skills, they don't understand how to be assertive as opposed to—what is the—

MS. MUSGRAVE: Aggressive.

MS. POUSSAINT: Aggressive or what, you know, how do they in a sophisticated way market themselves within the organization. And they remain stuck at certain levels when they could move, but they don't understand how to make the process happen. Recently I was involved in setting up an informal kind of evening-at-home workshop thing for about five black women employees at my station who were in that kind of position. And all of them were graduates of journalism schools, and they're all sort of in the assistant producer assignment desk area. And they kept seeing other people getting promoted and given opportunities to move up that they weren't getting. And some of them had attributed it automatically to racism. They said, "I'm not getting the opportunity 'cause I'm black." And a couple of us who have been in the industry for a while said, "Wait a minute." It's not all racism, part of it has to do with you and how you market yourself and how you take advantage of opportunities and how you slip in the door and write this story ahead of somebody else who's coming in an hour later and giving it to so-and- so, or how you go to a manager three months before the March on Washington and say, "I want to be a field producer out in the field three months from now," when somebody else might show up two months in advance and say, "I want"—you've already gotten it. There are a number of things that they don't understand about how to move up within the organization and really push themselves forward; and I think, a lot of women who are not naturally assertive will find themselves boxed into positions, and they will assume it's because "I'm being discriminated against because I'm black," and it is not necessarily the case. Some of it still exists certainly and I'm the first person, you know, to get on a soap box about it, but some of it is the woman's inability because she has not been taught how to function within the network once she gets there.

MS. DICKMAN: And I think that's true more for women, so when you talk about sensitive men and sensitive females, I still think you still have to do more for the women and—

MS. POUSSAINT: For the women, yes.

MS. DICKMAN: I think when you look at one of these findings about women you see they are more likely than men to say liking to meet people and liking to write influenced their decision to enter journalism. And I think it's hard to take that mentality and say, could you be an editor, could you be a manager, what other skills do you have, you know, besides your ability to write. And you can learn at seminars and other things to broaden your outlook but it's hard to focus; men I think can do that better.

MS. KATZ: I think there's something else, too, and I'm sort of embarrassed that I have to say this. We have people come to us looking for jobs and interns who come to us who don't realize that journalism is a profession. When somebody comes—a student intern—into the office ready to go on assignment in a pair of shorts and a pair of sandals and a cut-off top, you know, they represent us and we can't have that. We have to—I'm not saying you have to wear a suit with a little bow, but I'm saying you have to be professional in the way you conduct yourself. And I think this certainly applies to men, as well as women. And I think students should be told that.

DR. BEASLEY: There's a considerable body of literature on areas you all have been touching on, on the difference in male communications style versus female communications style. And there is, out of that material, considerable literature to suggest that many women don't know how to articulate their desires for promotion and not only not how to articulate but then how to carry out their articulation once it's made.

MS. AYERS: I think tying in with what Renee was just saying is you have to look at the women themselves because some of them maybe still have not determined, yes, that they do want a career. There was a study done not long ago, of some high school women about to go into college in the Midwest that showed that many of them did not perceive themselves as having to work beyond, let's say, five years. So they were looking to an immediate job situation that would get them through until their prince came along and they were saved and put into the home. And this is not a reality today because you look at the women in the work force, the percentages, and why the women are working. They're working because they have to. And somehow this is not being imparted. It's sort of a negative thing, but this has to be imparted to the young women even before they get into college and in their early college years that, hey, you may be working because you have to, not because you want to. And then long-range goal setting is a necessity. So then they're going to have to accept it. I think we have to bring that off the written page and verbalize it because people don't want to sit down and read a book.

MS. GIANFAGNA: I have found that many of the women that I've hired and worked with have been afraid of confrontation. The ability to confront and to successfully confront someone or a situation or a problem is crucial to moving up in management. And most of the women that have the problem with confrontation have the biggest problem confronting men. And if men are in a position of power where they have the opportunities that you're trying to move up into; and if they say no when you want a promotion and you can't confront them on it and come back with persuasive argument about why you should be the person who should get the job, you're not probably going to get there very fast. So, one of the things that I try to work with with the women who work for me, I try to counsel them on how to confront people and successfully do it and not be terrified, not get the butterflies in your stomach and just be panic city when you have to deal with a man in a confrontation situation. You have to master it. And it's very difficult for women, especially women who want to be liked. And many women come into business wanting to be liked. And it's lovely, but it isn't going to happen.

MS. RENSHAW: One of the points that I wanted to make in a piggyback of what Renee said also is that we have to look at careers much like businesses look at a five-year plan and the ten-year plan that they have to put out in order to chart what they hope will be great profits. And we really have to get into the minds of young people how crucial are their early years. How fast they have to move out into the work experience, hopefully, even with going to college and grad school. And how they really have to have a direction.

So we have to be fairly realistic that we've only got so many years in this life, and if we are aggressive, we want more money, we want a lot of experience, we should have some goals set for ourselves. And we really don't do that. And maybe we haven't been getting the point across early enough as maybe even in grade school. Another thing that struck me with college graduates, and I am just amazed, the number of young people who go out for a job and have really little thought these days of the work ethic. And that is an attitude about business and it even extends itself to caring about the employer because it so often is the case that they come in, you know, and they say I want you to hire me and I am the very best there is in news writing or in producing and such is the case, but do they take an interest in the employer? Do they care about that business' profit and loss situation?

MS. FORBES: I cheer the career-path concept, but I do think that journalism offers something for everyone and not everyone's going to get to be a network anchor or something like that; and in fact, an overly ambitious career path can even serve to undercut the mission of a good newspaper reporter. The greatest reward of all in the business is that every day you can put something under your shoulder and say I did something important in this town today. If you do that to the best of your ability and you're head and shoulders above the rest, the path of your career will ever go upward. I sincerely believe that. Whereas you allow ambition in the news business to become your primary goal, I think it may even destroy what you do.

MS. POUSSAINT: Oh, I'm not suggesting that ambition should be your primary goal at all. I do not necessarily share your beliefs that good will win out in the end. I do not necessarily believe that people who are the most talented necessarily rise to the top.

In the best of all possible worlds, it ought to happen that way but lots of times it doesn't. One final thing that I wanted to say was I had a very disturbing experience doing a series a couple years ago. One component of the series looked at women in new roles. I conducted a sort of roundtable discussion with college students who were all seniors at George Washington University. And the topic was really sort of how they plan to combine career and home situation. Most of their mothers had been sort of pioneers in their fields. And women who had tried to have it all and do it all. To have the family, raise the family, be high-powered or something and every single one of those girls had a very strong reaction to living that kind of lifestyle. And they did not see their mothers as a positive role model. And their solution to the problem of "having it all" was that each and every one—it didn't matter whether they were going to be a lawyer or doctor or they were going to be president of General Motors—the game plan was that they were going to work for five years, get married, have two children, stay at home for four years until the kids were in pre-school and then go back to their high-powered jobs without losing a beat. The job was going to be there and they were going to be back in that position and everything was going to be just fine and they were going to be married to men who would share things 50–50. I hope that is not representative, but it was scary. And I think that not just journalism schools but schools in general, if they are allowing young women to go out into the work world thinking that this is a reality, they're doing them a terrible disservice.

## Excerpts—Roundtable of Students and Recent Graduates

MS. THEUS: What I would like to hear you give us by way of introduction is what you're currently doing, if you're a student or not, and what you expect to be doing in five years.

MS. WATERS: My names is Karen Waters. I'm a senior in advertising. Currently I'm in the Advertising Club and doing an internship. Five years from now I hope to be heading way up the ladder in the field of advertising, specifically marketing research.

MS. HAMORSKY: My name is Sandra Hamorsky, and I'm a junior in broadcasting. So I have a little bit more time here. What I'm going to do in five years, that's a good one. If all goes well, I'd like to either be working on a major metropolitan daily newspaper or preferably, so that it goes in line with my sequence, I'd like to be working in a local TV station either as—preferably as a beat reporter.

MS. HOXIE: My name's Carol Hoxie. I'm a senior in the public relations sequence and I'll be graduating in December. And as for five years from now, it will be something along the lines that I will have finished my graduate education: It will either be a master's in communication or an MBA. And I may be somebody's mommy by then, and I hope to, at least, have had my first job. So that's what I hope to accomplish in the next five years.

MS. BARKDULL: My name is Clovis Barkdull, and I am also a senior journalism major. I'll be graduating also in December. Five years from now—ultimately I would like to do something along the lines of conservation news in line with my magazine sequence.

MS. CAUDELL: My names is Robin Caudell. I'm a 1980 graduate of this university. Presently I'm doing freelance work, not in print journalism per se, but more creative like poetry, prose, things like that. And in five years I'd like to have completed my first book.

MS. JONES: My name is Laurie Jones. Right now I'm writing for the *Diamondback*. Five years from now I'd like to be a reporter on a paper somewhere in New England, probably Providence or Boston.

MS. CARROLL: My name is Melaine Carroll. I graduated in 1982. Right now I'm freelancing, writing and researching chapters on journalism textbooks and researching and writing about the drug culture in D.C. In five years I'd like to be pursuing graduate work, and in a role where writing would be demanding and fulfilling.

MS. WILLIAMS: I'm Cristal Williams. I'm also a recent graduate, graduated May 1984. I'm now working for the *Star-Democrat* in Easton, Maryland, general assignment reporter. And in five years I think I'd like to stay in newspapers for a while and probably be a reporter for one of the larger metropolitan dailies.

MS. HENEBERRY: My name is Connie Heneberry. I'm with Needham, Harper Worldwide. We just changed our name: Needham, Harper Worldwide Advertising and I'm, right now, I'm an account coordinator. In five years I hope to be an account supervisor in an ad agency, heading up the account management on a group of accounts.

MS. HARVEY: My name is Chris Harvey, and I'm a 1980 graduate of the journalism college. Right now I'm a reporter covering county government for the *Journal*. It's a five-day-a-week paper. Five years from now I think I'd like to be working on some type of a small national magazine where I'd be able to do more in-depth writing than I'm currently doing.

MS. THEUS: The first question that was dealt with is: Is it more difficult for men than women to move from journalism school into the labor force? Now what you heard, I think if we recap a bit, is that some felt it was harder for women than men; that women who made it seemed to be hungrier, a little bit more assertive perhaps than men; that women bosses may enable women to move into the labor force; on the other hand women bosses might, in some cases, be obstructionists, more so than males. How would you respond to that question?

MS. HARVEY: I think one of the biggest things for the people first getting out of school, it's not so much whether you are a man or a woman, it's how much experience you have while you've been in school—what you've done.

MS. HENEBERRY: In my advertising agency it's the same. It's the entry-level positions—it doesn't matter what sex you are, it's what's on your resume.

MS. WILLIAMS: Well, I haven't been at the *Democrat* that long but from what I can tell it seems like the same general thing—that they are looking for someone who's really qualified, not for whether you are a man or whether you are a woman.

MS. THEUS: Am I hearing you say that women may not have a more difficult time getting a job if their resumes and their recent experiences are competitive? If there is a transition problem for females, how might the College of Journalism address that problem in preparing students to move from student to employee?

MS. WATERS: The one suggestion I heard this morning that I think is fantastic, maybe not feasible, is a work-study program. The internship program's great, but it's hard because I'm also working. I have classes and I'm doing an internship, so I can only devote two or three afternoons a week to it. And to be able to have it mandatory, to take a half a semester off and do a job full-time in the field you want and then to come back to school and maybe even make it into the senior thesis paper, that kind of thing, I think that would be really a big help.

MS. CARROLL: I don't know if this is directly related, but it was a point I wanted to bring up. It doesn't really deal with the male, female type of issue. But some friends of mine that graduated when I did, and that was 1982, we were discussing this, and we felt we had the technical skills, but we lacked marketing skills, and that was marketing ourselves. And that was brought up over and over again, the interviewing, the assertiveness, negotiating techniques. Also little things like a portfolio.

MS. HOXIE: I was wondering if there might be some possibility of having more recent and up-to-date statistics on what's happening in the job market in the journalism field, in all the different sequences. Who's hiring, you know, what percentages and the salary ranges because a lot of times if you don't have that information right and you're out there interviewing, you don't have much to go on in terms of knowing whether you're being offered a really good salary or whether it's really a pittance or whatever.

MS. THEUS: There is an indication on the part of the professionals you heard this morning that moving from the entry-level ranks into management may be difficult for women, and they attributed some of the problem to sexism that remains. On the other hand they also attributed part of the problem to women not being able to negotiate a contract, or articulate their career paths and goals, often because women seem to be ambivalent about where they want to go. They also indicated that perhaps women aren't given sufficient role models, aren't given mentors, or the college does not help provide mentors, and that networking is not taught. I'd like for you to respond to the mentor, networking, role-model aspect of the college and how it might help you. How do you perceive your professors and guest speakers who come into your classes as role models?

MS. JONES: I definitely think that's a great idea to bring more professionals in to speak to classes and things because I know at home in our local paper there's a columnist I've always liked a lot. When I was home for a couple of weeks, I just decided to call him and take a chance and see if he'd give me some advice. And he did, he was really nice, and he told me so many things that no one else had ever told me. I think it's a great idea because a lot of the teachers you have have been out of the field for a while and—they're good teachers and all, some of them, but if they're not right in the field then, it's not the same thing as hearing it from someone who is working now.

MS. HARVEY: One thing, this is really off the wall, but I mean there were so many men teachers when I was in the news-editorial sequence. And it seemed like everybody was divorced. They were giving the impression what a horrible profession, horrible, you know, no home life. And I don't know if it was just because they were men and what their particular situation was but every male teacher I had in a writing course, it seemed like they were all divorced and they all had these horrible social lives. And it leaves you with this kind of sick impression of the profession that you're getting ready to enter into. [You wonder], what's it going to do to you?

But it was just one thing of having so many men in there. Maybe if there had been more women teachers, they would have all been divorced, too.

One thing I wanted to add also when you were talking about the mentor thing, I found a problem getting someone—teachers are always so busy when you're in school and working. The biggest help that I had was when I joined Sigma Delta Chi. It seems that you can really get a lot of contacts when you join a professional association. I got in one for advertising. I know other sequences have organizations, too. And those contacts really helped me. There are a lot of women and they have professional organizations that hook up to students. You get to see more women who are actually out there working.

MS. CARROLL: As far as the females on the staff went, they, to me, were the real role models. I felt, I mean, a lot of the mentors were men, but the women role models were irreplaceable to me. For instance, there's one of them that even after I graduated, I've gone and stopped in her office and asked a particular question, and that's just something that I feel is very important. But mentoring is there if the students want to take advantage of it because the teachers I've asked have been very accommodating.

DEAN CLEGHORN: Let me ask a question of just the students here that goes back to something that we discussed this morning; and that is, what sort of ways do you think your family situations are going to affect your work lives? What sort of plans do you think you will have? Do you expect to be out of the workplace and then back into it five years later or 10 years later?

MS. HAMORSKY: Remember the scenario Renee Poussaint described? That's me. I thoroughly figured that I would work, I would get married, I would leave the work force to raise my children and then re-enter the work force; however, I didn't expect to do it without missing a beat.

DEAN CLEGHORN: How far into the work career will you be, do you think, when you get out?

MS. HAMORSKY: We'll put it this way. When I decide to start a family, I will leave the work force. It will come to that. Not necessarily when I get married, but when I start to have a family, I will leave the work force because that's important to me. And I think that—although the point was made that they cannot ask—your employers or potential employers cannot ask you that question, they are certainly thinking it, yes, I'm sure they are.

DEAN CLEGHORN: But do you think that your choice of a sequence is related to what you perceive as family difficulties and a career? Have you chosen a sequence partly on the basis of how you think it would affect that?

MS. HAMORSKY: No, certainly not me. I'm in the broadcast sequence, and Renee was talking about being gone 26 days out of 30 a month and I'm aware of that, fully aware of that. It never really affected my decision to pursue a broadcast career.

MS. HENEBERRY: I know and a lot of my friends and people that I work with know that we're going to be leaving the work place. I sat here and said I want to be an account supervisor, but I know if I get married, I'm going to want to—it's like you're blind to it. It's almost like you're pretending to know that that's not going to have anything to do with it. You want everything. You can't have everything, you really can't. It's so hard for women.

MS. HOXIE: I think you can have everything, but you have to make some adjustments about what it is that you're actually going to have and what you may not have is an account supervisor job five years out, you may not have it for seven or eight until you get over— I don't know how many children you want....

MS. HARVEY: I just couldn't picture myself in the job that I'm doing now and having children because you just work 50 or 60 hours a week, you work at night, you work on weekends. I just don't think it would be fair, you know, single—married with no kids that would be fine but to have little kids around, I would just have to take an easier job.

MS. BARKDULL: I'm, you know, in school and I'm doing an internship and I'm married, so I know what it's like to be pulled in 90 different directions, and, I think, it's important when you start running across all the different pressures of being pulled in the different directions, what you feel you can handle.

MS. CARROLL: Something I notice, being a recent graduate, and I'm dealing with smaller papers, daily, I mean weeklies, monthlies, newsletters, I've noticed that's where the women are [who previously left to have families]. And I would quit and change and they would stay. And one of the women I met—she's a very talented reporter, she's had five years experience on a daily paper—she stopped, she raised kids, and now she's scared to get back. So she stays at the same paper. She's over-qualified for it. And as I'm going from place to place, I see it over and over again. They're staying at the weeklies and smaller papers.

They're wanting to go on [but] they were uncomfortable in going to larger papers and seeking employment. That's fine if they are happy, but I've spoken to women who were dissatisfied.

MS. WILLIAMS: Well, one of the things that I have thought about more since I have been working is, I guess, to postpone getting married.

MS. CARROLL: I was just going to say maybe one of the things the college could do. You're discussing bringing in outsiders. Perhaps included in that group could be women who have children who are journalists. Like, for example, Anne Compton of ABC.

DEAN CLEGHORN: We were thinking also of the possibility, I don't know how feasible this would be, of workshops for those recently returned or returning or maybe even about to leave the work force.

MS. HARVEY: And just having employers say what they look for and want out of you, you know, if you are going to try and come back.

MS. THEUS: It sounds to me like the college, if it did anything in this area, could identify ways that persons wishing to leave the work force might negotiate re-entry prior to leaving perhaps.

MS. HAMORSKY: That's self-marketing again.

MS. THEUS: Does this frighten you in any way, the possibility of entering into a field in which you will be competing for places?

MS. HOXIE: The only reason it would scare me is if I really thought that the whole field of communication was narrowing or for some reason didn't have more openings expanding as time went by. But it seems from the trends in society that if anything we have more need for communication than we ever did before.

MS. THEUS: And you wouldn't necessarily recommend the recruitment of males, therefore, for journalism education?

MS. JONES: I don't think you're ever going to need that. They were saying there's power involved.

MS. HARVEY: The thing that bothers me is the salary. I think maybe it's more noticeable on the littler papers especially because, well, on the weekly-type papers there seem to be a lot more women but you mentioned that. Young women and people who are married and have come back to the field. And the salaries are so much lower than at the larger papers.

MS. HENEBERRY: I just don't want anyone to think that women get—that men don't make more than women. Men make more than women in jobs.

MS. BARKDULL: I was just going to say in terms of wearing your womanhood on your sleeve, I think what they meant more than that, is you should be very aware of what's going on, and you should be ready to handle it, but don't let them know that you're aware of it. That you're handling it.

MS. THEUS: What was the single most important conclusion or challenge regarding the tilt in female enrollment that you heard today in all of the roundtable?

MS. JONES: I think one thing I keep getting out of this is holding workshops for the negotiating and the interviewing and for both trying to get a job and later for re-entering the work force. And also almost as important as that, I think the journalism college should try emphasizing more English classes because I think it's so important when you're learning how to write to read good writers and you can't help but learn from that.

MS. CAUDELL: I agree with the marketing because you have to make someone believe that you're good, so I think you have to believe that you're good, that you're a professional and let things come from that.

MS. BARKDULL: I was just going to say I think the idea of bringing professionals in and having them orient the students as to what is out there is good. I mean this is going to sound really dumb, but do you know I didn't realize that you negotiated raises or things like that?

MS. HOXIE: All I wanted to say was an emphasis on work-life realities from the seminars and workshops, and also through more effective use of speakers in the classrooms. And you need to understand why businesses do what they do and what kind of the bottom line the situation is.

MS. HAMORSKY: At the risk of sounding redundant, I think the self-marketing workshops are going to be crucial, I really do. And one of the things that's really interesting and I realize—I mean I have always thought I was pretty savvy and pretty bright, but I had never heard of networking before today. I'd never heard the term. I've always thought, they told us, it's important to make contacts and use them. What they need maybe as well to provide through the journalism colleges as well as the students' societies is opportunities to make these contacts.

MS. WATERS: Because of the level I'm in at my education, I'm more concerned with career counseling and the opportunities of meeting more people in the profession. But I also definitely think that more writing, more English is very important.

MS. CARROLL: Same. Everyone knows my answer, that's for sure. It's focusing on the reality of the occupation we're pursuing.

MS. CAUDELL: Also maybe the realities of life because I think of the way things fall for me that when you're in college, it's like you're sheltered, you're being cushioned, you know, and then you're out there and all these things hit you and you doubt yourself, your work and everything. And that's a rude awakening for some who have just been kind of in a haze, you know, all the time that they've been here.

MS. HOXIE: I think the other thing students should be aware of is that when you take an entry-level job, whatever salary you negotiate and accept you're going to be stuck with for quite a while unless you're willing to take another job because the chance of being able to negotiate a significant increase in your same job is fairly low. So it's good to really negotiate for as much as you possibly think you're worth in the first job and, you know, for any other jobs after that and realize that if you want to make big bucks beyond that, you're going to have to be willing to take a different kind of job or move sideways or something.

DEAN CLEGHORN: Let me thank you, too. I have to confess my nightmare, which is that journalism will become even more female and all of our students will go off and marry male engineering students and have to have a break in their career and never get back to it. That's my nightmare. So help us not to let that happen, okay?

# Chapter 7

# Four Challenges That Were Identified, and What May Be Done About Them

Four issues were identified from the roundtable discussions of the surveys for further exploration. They pointed to the need for women journalism students (1) to acquire better basic writing skills, (2) to find suitable role models, (3) to learn how to persuade employers so women will not settle for less than men, and (4) to make plans for successfully combining family life with careers.

Discussion of these needs follows, with recommendations.

## Acquiring Better Basic Writing Skills

In recent years there has been increasing concern about the skills of journalism school graduates. A 1979 survey found magazine editors unhappy with journalism graduates, and a 1980 survey found editors of daily and weekly newspapers equally displeased. Homer T. Ford, managing editor of the *Dowagiac* (Mich.) *Daily News,* summed it up, "If carpenters were as poorly trained, the students wouldn't know how to use hammer and nails."[1]

Four-fifths of those hired by newspapers directly from college are journalism graduates. But, reflecting some dissatisfaction, a publication of the American Society of Newspaper Editors advised members in 1985 to look beyond journalism schools. "Don't restrict yourself to journalism-school graduates," the handbook on newsroom management stated. "You may find an expert in history, economics, English or government who can write more lucidly than almost anyone on your staff."[2]

Journalism educators have viewed with dismay the level of skill displayed by many students. Tests to evaluate students' spelling, grammar and other language skills frequently are given but have provided no easy answer. Numerous questions have arisen: Should students be required to pass the tests before or after enrollment in basic writing, reporting and editing classes? Are the tests accurate predictors of success? What types of remedial programs should be set up? Are these tests fair to minority students? Experience at the University of Central Florida, for example, showed that only 73 percent of 434 journalism students (or fewer than three out of four) who took a standardized English usage test were able to pass it on their first attempt.[3]

Journalism education was never intended to operate as a mass remediation program for large numbers of students. Writing in the Winter 1985 issue of *Journalism Educator,* Dave Berkman, chair of the department of mass communication at the University of Wisconsin, Milwaukee, posed the problem. "Journalism education in this country is in deep trouble," he stated. "It is in deep trouble for much the same reason that higher education, in general, is in such dire straits." He meant, of course, that journalism schools have been victimized by the shortcomings of the educational system in general.[4]

Remedial education in the basic language skills, though, is to some extent a necessity if journalism schools are to fulfill their mission. Some have begun to bear down harder. The need for this is obvious from the feedback constantly heard from professionals in the field, and heard in especially strong voices at the roundtable discussion of successful women professionals who were assembled for this report.

Journalism students need to be told, emphatically, that professionals in the field place writing skills above almost all other aspects of their journalism education. That is true whether the advice comes from a newspaper professional or from someone successful in public relations, broadcast news or advertising. The professionals usually are clear that they mean the kind of writing that is embodied in good reporting.

Even those who have mastery of basic English skills may find the language of news writing foreign, and this may apply especially to women. Journalism is written in terms of winning and losing, conflict and controversy, as Catherine S. Covert, a journalism professor at Syracuse University, pointed out. She cited examples from a journalism history textbook: "The press wins a beach-head," "the rise of the fourth estate," "the press and the expanding nation," "the race for news," "a revolution in communication." This is the language of male "winners," not that of women as a group, Covert maintained.[5]

The old newsroom sobriquet "sob sister" conveyed women's position in relation to male journalists, Covert noted. Women were supposed to write stories with heavy emotional content, but these stories and women reporters were "only marginally relevant to the rational [male] business of the newsroom day." According to this line of thought, the preference of women journalism students for sequences other than news-editorial reflects the social conditioning of women.[6]

American journalism itself has celebrated "independence and individual autonomy," Covert stated. These are male values—symbolized in the image of men as strong, self-reliant and assertive. By contrast women have developed relationships over the centuries based on "concord, harmony, affiliation, community," Covert continued. These values, which emphasize consensus more than controversy, may be better suited to the fields of public relations and advertising than to news. Perhaps the nature of news itself will change, at least some, when women are the majority in newsrooms.[7]

It may seem odd, in a report on women in journalism education, to begin a series of recommendations with this: Improve basic writing skills. Certainly this is an admonition that applies to male as well as to female graduates. Yet to omit it from these recommendations would be to ignore what probably was the most ringing message from our discussions with professionals in the field: participants in the roundtable, as well as employers of journalism graduates in general.

Is there anything gender-specific about this? Given Catherine Covert's analysis, there is, in the sense that male and female students may view journalistic writing in different ways. If the female students are less conflict-oriented and less drawn to writing news as a series of conflicts, they may choose writing fields that are outside the mainstreams of journalism; or if they do enter journalism, they may change what is considered news.

In teaching writing to these young women, it may be well for instructors and the textbooks they use to emphasize that news reporting has evolved in recent years and often takes on the character of feature writing. If this helps young women to see that they may be creative and may emerge as the excellent writers sought by many editors, this motivation may move them forward in their careers—whether they move into journalism or into one of its related fields involving writing.

**Specific recommendations:**

- All students should be required to meet a minimum standard of basic language proficiency, including punctuation and grammar testing, before graduation. This probably should be apart from regular course requirements. Journalism instruction should end with an "exit" examination, but only if individual schools have systematically alerted their students of deficiencies revealed by language skills tests before their senior year.
- Schools of journalism and mass communication should make new efforts to attract highly motivated students. This might be done by requiring all accredited schools to establish minimum admissions standards for their students apart from those required by their universities.
- Instructors and textbooks should be directed more consciously toward developing high aspirations on the part of students. Because female students tend to lower their aspirations as they go through college, this is especially important for them.
- Graduation requirements should assure not only an adequate number of journalism courses specifically devoted to writing but also should include writing courses offered by English departments, probably beyond general university requirements.

## Finding Suitable Role Models

At first glance finding suitable role models may not appear to be a major problem. Two solutions quickly present themselves: Employment of more women instructors and closer contacts between professional women journalists and students. On examination, however, neither solution is as simple as it initially might seem.

Obviously successful instruction is based on more than the sex of the instructor. "If I say that only women can teach women students, then I also am saying that I can't teach men students," commented Pam Brown of Rider College. That is not a statement that she, or other women faculty members, are willing to make. Sensitive faculty members of both sexes are needed to help dispel what the Association of American Colleges has called an "institutional atmosphere, environment or climate" that can impede women students' full personal, academic and professional development. According to the association's Project on the Status and Education of Women, the classroom climate for women can be quite "chilly."[8]

While much of the overt sexism that once marked higher education, including admissions quotas, lack of women's athletic scholarships, segregated faculty clubs and discrimination in financial aid, has vanished, women students still may be exposed to subtle bias that undercuts their career aspirations. "Some studies indicate that men faculty tend to affirm students of their own sex more than students of the other sex, and often perceive women students primarily as sexual beings who are less capable and less serious than men students," the project report stated. In addition, patterns of male-female interaction from the society at large, which condition women to seek support and reassurance from men, may carry over into classroom settings. Women as well as men may display prejudice toward women. Female instructors, for instance, may unconsciously limit eye contact to men, as if only the males are expected to respond to questions, while men instructors may use a tone that communicates interest when talking to male students but speak in a condescending manner to women.[9]

In journalism the vocabulary of the news field itself carries blatant sexual overtones. Front-page news stories that detail action are referred to as "hard news," while feature stories that appeal to the emotions are called "soft news." Traditionally men reported the "hard news" and women the "soft news." By assigning women students feature stories, for example, and men straight-news stories, instructors perpetuate a sexist climate in campus newsrooms. The same holds true in teaching assignments. If men faculty members are assigned to general reporting courses, and women faculty members to feature writing and introductory news writing, students receive the same message—that women are consigned to subordinate places in news operations.

The problem of creating an equitable classroom learning climate is especially acute in academic areas considered "masculine fields," according to the project report. Although journalism education has a preponderance of women students, only one out of five instructors is female. While women students may be taught just as competently by males as females, nevertheless the lack of women faculty reduces opportunities for women to develop formal and informal contact with same-sex role models of achievement. One study shows that contact of this type is highly significant in the development of professional identity. It indicated that women Ph.D.'s who themselves had women dissertation advisors produced more scholarly publications than those advised by men.[10]

The imbalance of women faculty also means that women journalism students have relatively few opportunities to take coursework dealing specifically with women and the media. Although a few men have developed courses in this area, most of the classes offered have been designed by women. Course goals include raising the level of aspirations of women students by making them aware of (1) the history of women in journalism, (2) the sex-role stereotyping common to media portrayal of women and (3) the problems of discrimination in media careers.

"We believe there should be at least one course on media and women offered on a regular basis at every institution that teaches communications," Dr. Donna Allen, director of the Women's Institute for Freedom of the Press, wrote in an introduction to a collection of syllabi for 68 such courses. These were added in journalism departments during the 1970s after Marzolf pioneered with her course on the history of women journalists at the University of Michigan.[11]

Allen identified 39 schools offering these courses: Antioch College, Baltimore Center; Arizona State University; California State University at Hayward; College of the Holy Cross, Worcester, Mass.; Eckerd College, St. Petersburg, Fl.; Florida A & M University; Goddard-Cambridge Graduate School, Cambridge, Mass.; Governors State University, Park Forest, Ill.; Humboldt State University, Arcata, Calif.; Ithaca College; Michigan State University; Niagara County Community College, New York; Northeastern Illinois University; Ohio State University; Oregon State University; Pennsylvania State University, University Park; Pennsylvania State University, Delaware Campus; Point Park College, Pittsburgh; Ohio University; Sonoma State University, Calif.; Stanford University; Glassboro State College, N.J.; St. Peter's College, Englewood Cliffs, N.J.; Towson State University, Towson, Md.; University of California at San Diego; University of Denver; University of Maryland; University of Michigan; University of North Carolina; University of Nebraska, Lincoln; University of Northern Iowa; University of Oklahoma; University of South Florida; University of Texas at El

Paso; University of Washington; University of Wisconsin at both Eau Claire and Madison.[12]

While this list represented a cross-section of schools teaching communications, it did not cover more than a sprinkling of the 200 schools that teach journalism/communications in the United States. These offerings still meet with the skepticism that greeted their arrival in the curriculum prefaced with comments such as: "But what would you teach in such a course?" or "We only teach serious subjects here," or "Our courses already cover women," or "No one would enroll in such a course."[13]

Enrollments, however, have not turned out to be an issue, but scheduling has. For example, a course, "Women, Minorities and the Media," taught by Zena Beth McGlashan at Pennsylvania State University drew 40 when first offered in 1978, 70 the following year and 98 in 1979-1980. But sometimes women and the media courses are taught at infrequent intervals because they are viewed as "frosting" on a curriculum made up of more essential ingredients. Yet such courses can be extremely valuable in aiding women students to develop the positive self-image necessary for professional success.[14]

"This course made me proud to be a woman," a student in public relations told an instructor at the University of Maryland after completing a course in women and the media. The instructor, who had written her dissertation in graduate school under a black woman professor, was shocked. It had never occurred to her that any woman would not be proud of her sex.[15]

Women's studies courses within journalism schools also help make women aware of how they use the media in their own life. According to Doris A. Graber, there are differences in the way men and women select news items for attention and in their rankings of what is and what is not important. In a study based on newspaper and television usage during the 1976 Presidential campaign, she discovered, "Women recall less information than men and are less specific in their comments and descriptions about the information that they recall."[16]

She concluded, "Women must realize that politics concerns them as much as men. Not only must they continue to watch the same issues as men, but they must watch them with equal attention to detail." In addition, she emphasized, "Women must also become more aware of the role they must play in pressing for politics that advance women's interests. This requires greater attention to news concerning women's issues."[17]

Women and the media classes offer an opportunity for journalism schools to educate students in coverage of women's issues. Speaking at a plenary session of the 1984 AEJMC convention, Dr. Allen emphasized, "At present mass media do not know how to cover women's issues." She pointed to a study by Dorothy Jurney and Catherine East, "New Directions For News," which concluded, "If the way newspapers have covered recent issues and events of importance to women can be taken as a measure of general performance, then it would seem papers have often failed to carry out their primary purpose [of informing readers so they can make judgments on crucial questions]."[18]

The "New Directions For News" study was distributed by the American Society of Newspaper Editors. It reported on coverage by 10 leading newspapers of alimony and child support questions, enforcement of Title IX (the law expressly prohibiting discrimination in education), the Equal Rights Amendment campaign, the 1977 National Women's Conference at Houston, pay equity and the World Conference of the U.N. Decade for Women. Jurney and East discovered news articles on these subjects in some newspapers demonstrated "inadequate, unfair or total lack of recognition of the issues." They called for journalists to develop new ways of defining news that would include the effect of change on daily lives of readers.[19]

But women in media courses, as presently constituted, are no panacea for the problem of motivating large numbers of students. They reach only a small percentage and often are taught by women themselves on the lowest rungs of the academic ladder. Throughout journalism schools, as in higher education in general, women are disproportionately represented in the lower ranks. As a 1984 article in the *Chronicle of Higher Education* pointed out, "Despite an increase in the proportion of assistant professors who are women, there has been little change over the last decade in the proportion who are full professors." That percentage has stayed around 10 percent. The chances are exceedingly small that a journalism student will be instructed in a women and the media class by a woman who is a full professor and, therefore, a role model who has attained senior status in the academic world. It is far more likely that the teacher will be in the junior ranks—an assistant professor or graduate student instructor.[20]

To expose a larger number of students to women's issues a women's news component must be added to general and special topics reporting courses. This would allow for greater discussion of ethical concerns related directly to woman and the news. To date journalism educators (perhaps because 80 percent are male), have tended to ignore questions dealing with women. Among notable exceptions was a survey done by Carol E. Oukrop at Kansas State University on reporting of rape cases. Employment of more women faculty could be expected to lead to more extensive research pertaining to women and the news.[21]

Apart from having women faculty as role models, women students at most journalism schools are encouraged to develop contacts with successful professionals in the field. These contacts generally fall into three categories: (1) Speakers brought to campus; (2) women met during off-campus internships; (3) women met through involvement in professional organizations which have student chapters. Students, however, may not find adequate role models through these contacts, valuable though they may be.

First, the gulf between the professional and the student may be too wide to be bridged by visitors to a campus. Sometimes the professional may offer comments that students simply fail to understand or do not want to hear. A Washington television anchorwoman who spoke at the University of Maryland, for example, disturbed a small group of women students by criticizing male television managers who hire young women reporters for their looks and not their abilities. The anchorwoman was referring to what she perceived as a callous attempt to exploit women on the basis of their appearances instead of offering them genuine opportunities to develop into respected broadcast journalists. The students, however, misinterpreted the remarks.

"She's saying 'beauty and brains don't mix,'" one young woman, herself an attractive blond, commented later to a woman faculty member. "I don't think that's fair." The student also noted that the anchorwoman was married but saw her husband, busy with his career in another city, only twice a month. "That's not my idea of a marriage," the student said.[22]

Second, internships and professional organizations may offer opportunities for students to find role models, but they can prove disillusioning. During internships for the first time students may encounter the reality of the journalistic field—that relatively few women are in positions of control. The same student who was upset by the comments of the anchorwoman said she had run across few women in sportswriting, her chosen field. "Although we're being told it's not the men's occupation it once was, it still is a man's world," she said. "I've worked at the *Diamondback* [University of Maryland student daily], the *Prince George's Journal* [a suburban daily] and the *Washington Post*. What I've seen at all of them is men. The last time the *Diamondback* had a woman editor was 11 years ago."[23]

This young woman had attempted to make contact with professional journalists by being active in the University of Maryland student chapter of the Society of Professional Journalists/Sigma Delta Chi [SDX]. But she found it a financial strain. She complained that members of the Maryland professional chapter of the society wanted students to pay $35 to attend a regional meeting "and to work, too, [at the conference].... I just paid Mom and Dad back the $200 I borrowed from them to go to the national [society] convention." Her expenses there came to nearly $500 above the travel subsidy provided by the national organization, she said. "I came back all fired up about SDX, but there wasn't anybody to share it with.[24]

"When I was 16 or 17 years old, I was really gung-ho on a career," this young woman continued. But now she is thinking more and more about getting married and having children. She would like to stay home with them, but "realistically I know I may not have the option," she added. "A lot of us [women students] swore a career was what we wanted. It's funny to watch our attitude change as we get older. Now more people are concerned about a family but they believe they have to finish school before they move on to another commitment."[25]

This student typifies the young woman whose aspirations actually decline during college, partly because of lack of positive role models. Seeking to be recognized for her femininity, as well as her intellectual ability, she has searched somewhat vainly for examples of what she wants to be. Finding few, she is dreaming of a retreat to the world where women have traditionally reigned supreme—the home. Yet realistically she knows she can expect to enter the labor force.

College experience can have a bruising effect on the aspirations of even the brightest young women. A recent study, by two University of Illinois researchers, found a sharp drop in self-esteem and estimates of their own intelligence among top women students following one year of college. This study of 45 women and 36 men, who had achieved high grades in high school, determined that 23 percent of the men and 21 percent of the women considered themselves "far above average in intelligence" as high school seniors, but that after one year of college only 4 percent of the women still rated themselves in that category compared to 22 percent of the men.[26]

In contrast is a study by the Women's College Coalition of nearly 5,000 graduates of 48 women's colleges. It found that these alumnae were nearly unanimous in agreeing that women's colleges fostered self-confidence among their students. The graduates, who came from the classes of 1967 and 1977, as a group appeared to be successfully combining careers and marriage. They include women like Cathy Black, publisher of *USA Today,* who is a graduate of Trinity College in Washington. In a *Washington Post* column, Judy Luce Mann pointed out, "The majority of women's colleges are headed by women, and women hold a higher proportion of tenured faculty and top administrative positions there than they do at coeducational institutions. Women students are constantly exposed to role models of female achievement."[27]

In summary, provision of role models for women students is essential if journalism education is to produce successful journalists. Educators must move immediately to ensure that women students are given positive examples of attainment.

**Specific recommendations:**

- Journalism educators should address the question of the classroom climate for both sexes. This can be done by such means as sponsoring workshops, publicizing the issue in professional and campus media, and administering surveys to measure men's and women's perception of sex-based differences in classroom situations.

- Efforts should be made to achieve gender balance on faculties, to meet affirmative action goals and to insure that at least some role models are available for both sexes as a way of facilitating their movement from college into professional jobs. The status of all faculty members should be reviewed to determine whether both sexes are given the same opportunities for tenure and promotion.
- Courses in sex roles and the media should be recognized as important elements of the curriculum and units on sex-role issues and stereotyping added to existing courses.
- Systematic programs should be set up, perhaps in combination with professional organizations such as the Society of Professional Journalists/Sigma Delta Chi, Women in Communications and the Public Relations Society of America, to bring professionals of both sexes to journalism schools to act as mentors for students. While numerous guest speakers appear in journalism classrooms now, additional efforts are needed to provide mentors in all schools.
- Student chapters of professional organizations should be involved in efforts to insure role models for both sexes in journalism schools.

## Persuading Employers, and Not Settling for Less

Sex-segregated pay scales are at least as old as the Bible. Verses one to four in chapter 27 of Leviticus refer to a conversation between Jehovah and Moses in which adult men are valued at fifty shekels of silver and adult females at thirty shekels—a ratio strikingly similar to the differences in male and female pay scales today. Perhaps this discrepancy can be explained by the greater ability of males to perform the hard manual work needed in a primitive society. But today technology has made physical strength obsolete in most occupations and certainly in the field of journalism.[28]

Why do women still receive less pay than men in American society? Much of the answer lies in the fact they are vying with each other in a narrow range of jobs considered socially acceptable for women. In an analysis of labor market problems, Ralph E. Smith, an economist for the Urban Institute, stated: "In fact, occupational and industrial concentration of female workers in a few 'women's' jobs is the biggest problem facing women in the labor market today. One-third work in clerical occupations. Another quarter work in the fields of health care (not including physicians), education (not including higher education), domestic service and food service." The extreme form of occupational segregation which kept women at work at home ended long ago, but the majority are still confined to "women's work," Smith concluded.[29]

Women's occupations generally provide below-average pay and limited opportunities for advancement, tending not to require a long-term career commitment or geographic mobility. Lack of commitment is crucial to understanding the problem of women establishing a meaningful identity in a society that devalues them, according to sociologists. "The system of sexual stratification which prevails in American society not only burdens women with domestic responsibilities that draw them away from the economic marketplace, but accords higher value to masculine endeavor, making maleness itself a condition of intrinsic worth," two sociologists stated in a study of nurses conducted in California. They found as students the nurses did not exhibit serious commitment, having chosen nursing because of short-run opportunities and expecting their jobs to be secondary to marriage and child-rearing. These were the activities through which the women planned to establish socially-approved identities.[30]

As the study of the nurses pointed out, important factors in pay discrimination include the attitudes and preparation of women workers. If women continue to enter "women's occupations," then pay and working conditions can be expected to decline further, according to Nancy S. Barrett, former deputy assistant secretary for economic policy and research, U.S. Department of Labor. Her recommendations, growing out of an Urban Institute project:

- Young women should receive counseling on career planning and the opportunities in non-traditional occupations;
- Changes should be made in the organization of the workplace to help women maintain job continuity as well as to encourage men to enter predominantly women's jobs and vice versa.[31]

Employer discrimination, based on devaluating the work of women, must not be minimized. This can be seen in studies of the earnings of women versus men in the public relations field. This field is changing rapidly from being male-dominated to female-dominated. In 1968, women constituted 25 percent of the public relations labor force, as defined by the U.S. Department of Labor under the category of "public relations specialists and publicity writers." Since 1977, when the Department of Labor first began keeping more precise statistics on the occupation, the number of women has increased about 2.2 percent a year. At this rate two-thirds of all practitioners are projected to be women by 1990.[32]

With the influx of women has come increasing concern about pay discrepancies between males and females. In a 1981 study conducted in San Diego, women practitioners were found to earn lower salaries than men, even when the influences of education, professional experience and tenure with current employers were taken into account. The study showed male practitioners earned an average of $31,310 annually, while females earned $22,250. Although the men were better educated, had more extensive professional experience and had been with their current employers longer, when these indicators of preparation for advancement were equalized, the salaries for men and women remained significantly different. After the equalizing adjustments were made, male practitioners earned average yearly salaries of $29,590 while females earned $23,820, a difference of $5,770 annually.[33]

A 1982 national study of members of the Public Relations Society of America found striking salary differences between male and female practitioners. Men earned average salaries of $43,220 while women made only $27,820. Female salaries increased to $30,810 and male salaries dropped to $41,470 when the influences of education, professional experience and length of time with present employer were controlled. But a $10,660 difference in salary still remained.[34]

These two studies also showed that women were occupationally segregated into the role of communications technician. The San Diego study found 36.2 percent of the women practitioners were communications technicians, compared to 22.2 percent of the men. In the national study, 34.1 percent of the women were communications technicians, while only 21.3 percent of the males were in this category. Technicians, who carry out tasks such as preparing booklets and writing press releases, earn lower incomes than practitioners who play broader roles and enter into management decision-making.[35]

The study concluded that there may be "conscious sex discrimination among the predominantly male managers who make hiring and promotion decisions." It also raised another question: Do women "self-select the communication technician role with greater frequency than men?" If so, the study concluded, "corrective action involves not only the profession but society as a whole."[36]

As an occupation, public relations is a communications profession allied to news reporting, broadcasting and advertising. At the undergraduate level, students are taught to place technical communications skills within the context of public relations management, according to James E. Grunig, professor of journalism at the University of Maryland. "Eventually," he stated, "most professionals and educators believe, the master's degree will be required for management positions."[37]

But at the entry level in public relations and advertising there may be little difference between clerical jobs and those leading into professional work. For that reason women may have an initial edge. "Secretaries have the best mobility and advancement and no man wants to start off as a secretary," commented a 1981 male journalism graduate of the University of Maryland, now employed in an advertising agency.[38]

Women are driving men out of entry-level jobs in communications and depressing the market, a 1969 woman graduate said. "These are second-choice careers for men because women will do the job for lower wages, so why should men enter a 'pink ghetto?'"[39]

One way of trying to make sure a field does not lose status by becoming all-female is to deliberately recruit men to enter it. This was done in the case of the profession of social work, for example. During the 1930s, the School of Social Service Administration at the University of Chicago made a deliberate effort to attract "good men" by giving them a disproportionate share of the scholarship aid available. The dean, Edith Abbott, believed that the general reputation of social work would be elevated if it were not an all-woman field. Even if considered advisable, similar plans would not be acceptable today because of laws forbidding discrimination in education. (It also should be noted that social work became a "women's field" in spite of favoritism toward male students.)[40]

At the technician level, public relations exhibits characteristics typical of jobs generally held by women. According to Barrett, these include lack of authority, as well as vicarious, rather than direct, satisfaction, gained by helping "bosses" succeed instead of competing for oneself on an individual basis. In addition, technician jobs may include repetitive tasks, which women sometimes are said to be better able to perform than men.[41]

As both the San Diego and national studies determined, there is increasing discrimination against women in pay as they move up in public relations. A woman graduate of the University of Maryland expressed it this way: "The perception of women as managers by men is poor. There is no equality between men and women managers."[42]

It appears essential in journalism education to give women students greater preparation to move into management. A 1978 alumna of the University of Maryland put it this way: "Journalism school did a good job with skill-preparation mechanics but it taught no workplace-setting skills. It has the 'ivory tower' syndrome." She called for "assertiveness" training.[43]

Widespread mergers and consolidations now underway in the communications industry mean that there will be an increasing need for middle and top management in corporate organizations. Yet women as a group can be expected to have difficulty moving into management roles. In part, this may be due to differences in the communications style of men and women.

This point was made in the first study of the effects of sex-role socialization on women entering journalism careers. The study was undertaken at the University of North Carolina in 1980. It sought to examine the effects of increasing numbers of women moving into the journalistic field on the composition of management positions traditionally filled by men. Through surveys of 180 journalism students, 57 men and 123 women, the study examined how these individuals perceived themselves in terms of traits associated with masculine socialization versus feminine socialization. Masculine traits included being assertive, independent and leadership-oriented, while feminine traits included being dependent, nurturing and passive.[44]

The researcher, Katherine C. McAdams, theorized that two traits associated with femininity, low career aspiration and lack of willingness to confront others when communicating, would be likely to impede progress toward management positions. Her study found that journalism students of both sexes measured high in traits associated with both masculine and feminine socialization. The women, however, measured significantly higher in feminine socialization than did the men.[45]

McAdams concluded: "Significant positive correlations were found between masculine socialization and career aspiration and willingness to confront. A significant negative correlation was found between feminine socialization and willingness to confront." The implication, in her view: "...more women will be offered management jobs [in the years ahead]; but based on high measures of feminine socialization found in this study, it may also be predicted that some women will not accept management positions, while others will accept them and then move on because of difficulties on the job."[46]

In the daily newspaper business, women constitute an increasing percentage of reporters, but fewer than 12 percent were classified as editors in 1985, according to a study by Dorothy Jurney for the American Society of Newspaper Editors. Great discrepancies exist in pay between male and female managers. A 1983 study reported top women newspaper managers earned about 60.1 percent of men's salaries for comparable jobs, with the actual dollar gap given as $18,147 annually.[47]

Even women who already are part of newspaper management appear to have difficulty in articulating their goals in a realistic way. A study of 59 women who attended management training sessions held at the University of Colorado (1980), Texas Christian University (1981) and the University of North Carolina (1982) found that these women did not state their career goals in terms of their organizations. Ninety percent of the women stated goals in terms of themselves.[48]

Typical responses: "to move into top management on the editorial side," or "to move to a policy-making position." But the women did not mention the behavioral steps in terms of organizational goals that would allow the performance review necessary to achieve such ambitions. Ardyth B. Sohn, assistant professor of journalism at the University of Colorado, who conducted the study, concluded, "It is difficult to see how managers could expect to be promoted or hired for a particular job in the next five years without setting some organizational goals."[49]

The study also found that the women, whose average age was 33, were indeed a dedicated group. Eighty percent worked on daily newspapers. Over half were single with 25 percent never having married, and 71 percent childless. When asked whether they thought they had made "personal sacrifices" because of their career goals, 66 percent said they had, but only 7 percent resented making them. The largest number (50 percent) mentioned failed or never developed relationships as their "sacrifices."[50]

But even though they had built their lives around their careers, they were not expecting to be promoted quickly. Not one mentioned she hoped to make it to a top-level position in five years. Sohn commented, "If top management is looking for women who will give maximum hours to the job, this is a good group to consider. In addition, they are not too expensive, with all this dedication only costing employers [an average of] $20,000 in annual salary."[51]

In summary, there is no clear answer to the problem of women being forced "to settle for less," except perhaps to alert journalism students to the fact that this exists. Women need to be told the fact that woman's progress in the job market has not matched the pace of rising expectations. In 1977, for example, the median income of female college graduates, including those with advanced degrees, who worked full-time, year-round, was below the median income of male high school dropouts.[52]

But this does not mean that journalism education should accept the status quo. Raising the consciousness of women may be the first step in enabling them to insist on fair pay. A 1982 survey of 200 recent journalism graduates of the University of North Carolina with experience on newspapers determined that the men and women had remarkably similar experiences except in two important respects: salary and years worked since graduation. The average salary classification for women on a 1–to–6 scale was 1.98, while the average category for men was 2.34. In addition, when the careers of men and women who were graduated the same year were compared, the men had more job experience than the women. This was explained by James H. Shumaker, director of journalism placement at the University of North Carolina, "Women don't stay. They drop out, then come back. Or they move [because of their husbands' jobs]."[53]

Unequal starting pay may be due to several factors: Unequal job responsibilities; cultural bias by employers who give men more because they think they need to support a family; low expectations by women themselves. According to one study, "Men know that women underrate themselves.... women will be considered cheap help as long as they accept less than they are worth." One item on the North Carolina survey bore out this thesis that women undervalue themselves. Women rated themselves less able to meet deadlines then males.[54]

Perhaps women tend to bargain poorly with employers as a result of differences in the language used by men and women. According to experts, woman's speech is less certain, more euphemistic and lacking in power when compared to the language of men. Its emphasis on courtesy and correctness is characteristic of subordination. Woman's communication pattern relates to woman's traditional function of serving the family and maintaining harmony in home relationships.[55]

**Specific recommendations:**

- Journalism education should inform students of the fact they

are likely to encounter sex discrimination in pay and promotions. It should make sure students are aware of legal remedies, if they exist, and cultural constraints that limit advancement.
- Journalism students should be taught how to prepare for interviews and women, in particular, acquainted with techniques of negotiations with employers through more assertive styles of communication.
- Journalism students should be prepared to move into management ranks, receiving instruction in economics and business administration.
- Journalism educators should conduct research by gender into the rate of advancement of graduates into management.

## Reconciling Career and Family Life

The headlines appear ominous. Women journalism students see them with increasing frequency these days. They tell the story of highly educated women who have succeeded with their careers only to encounter upsetting conflicts. Sample headlines: "New Study Finds Children of Working Mothers Suffer in School;" "Hittin' It Big & Kissin' It Goodbye: No Kids, No Job—Women at Home Just for Themselves;" "Parenthood and Career Overtax Some Women Despite Best Intentions—Many Find Job Stress Rising, Productivity Declining; Loyalty Sometimes Shifts." These articles present the problems of shifting roles—difficulties of child care, career burnout, conflicts as women try to juggle demanding careers and family duties.[56]

In the *Boston Globe,* Caryl Rivers Lupo, co-author of a book on career planning for women (*Lifeprints: New Patterns of Love and Work for Today's Woman*), discussed the "message" emerging from this type of news article. "It's nothing but the old bigotry, only now it's candy-coated," she wrote. "The new scare stories are simply an updated version of the old myth that women will get sick if they do too much (important) work."[57]

Lupo said that in the 19th century conventional medical thinking held that women's brains and reproductive organs could not develop simultaneously "so women must be kept away from too much thinking." In addition to scaring women from achievement by raising the possibility of threats to their health, societal pressures intimidate women by construction of a superwoman image requiring them to do everything perfectly, Lupo concluded. "Does anyone call a man who has a good job and a family 'Superman?'"[58]

Issues of this type rarely are addressed in journalism classes or in college courses in general except for those in women's studies. Yet nothing is more germane to the question of career planning for women journalism students. Socially conditioned to think in terms of romance, marriage and children, many women in college do not face the reality of what they will be doing for most of their lives. The answer is an obvious one that women are acculturated to minimize and overlook. It is, pure and simple, that an overwhelming majority of women will be working most of their adult lives.

This point is stressed in a report on U.S. women workers prepared by the Women's Bureau, Department of Labor. The facts:

- Of all women 18 through 64 years of age in 1981, workers constituted 62 percent, compared with 91 percent of men.
- Women accounted for 43 percent of all workers.
- The more education a woman had, the greater the likelihood of paid employment, with three out of five women having four or more years of college represented in the labor force.
- The average woman 16 years of age (in 1977) could expect to spend 27.7 years of her life in the work force, compared with 38.5 years for men.
- Women workers with four or more years of college had about the same income as men who had only one to three years of high school—$12,085 and $11,936, respectively, in 1981.
- The majority of women work because of economic need. Two-thirds (66 percent) of all women in the labor force in March, 1982, were single (25 percent), widowed (5 percent), divorced (11 percent), or separated (4 percent), or had husbands whose earnings in 1981 were less than $15,000 (21 percent).
- About 55 percent of all children under age 18 (32 million) had working mothers in March, 1982; 46 percent of all children under age 6 (8.5 million) had mothers in the labor force.
- The influx of women into the work force during the 1970s has resulted in nearly equal labor force participation rates for women by race/ethnic origin: 53 percent for black women (5.4 million), 52 percent for white women (40.2 million), and 48 percent for Spanish-origin women (2.2 million).[59]

The implications for women journalism students, particularly those in metropolitan areas, is unmistakable. Most will be working most of their lives. The question for some is whether they will be journalists or will move into another occupation. For graduates the initial competition of the job market may come as a shock. One 1975 graduate of the University of Maryland recalled with rueful amusement "the handout [mimeographed material] on journalism professionalism when I graduated stressing journalism as a profession similar to law or medicine." She found that "not true in the real world. No one cared that I had a journalism degree."[60]

Even more deflating is the prospect of returning to journalism after taking time out for child-rearing. "I know I'm losing ground while I'm at home for five years," a 1972 graduate said. "I can't keep up in the field if I try to work part-time...I might bag journalism altogether...who'd take me after all this time out?" Yet this news-editorial graduate has an impressive record. She is a former press secretary for members of Congress and has obtained a master's degree in political communication.[61]

Those who stay out for long periods may give up all hope of getting back in. "The interruption (10 years) ruined my journalistic career," a 1966 graduate stated. "A new goal was set—nursing, more flexible for women with children."[62]

The impact of a career interruption on women journalists was noted by men graduates, who, like the women, were contacted for telephone interviews. One man, who was graduated in 1978, said he never understood feminist complaints of discrimination until he went to work for a "sexist" news organization in Washington. There, he said, he witnessed "a lot of tokenism, women not treated as well as men, or as seriously." He discovered, "Time off was pointed to as a lack of serious commitment, a weakness of women." He saw how maternity leave "served to differentiate the sexes, and men enjoyed [seeing] it, especially men 40 and over."[63]

One possible solution to the problem of enabling women journalism graduates to combine careers with family responsibilities would be to set up workshop and short courses to enhance the ability of alumnae to return to the job market. Such programs could correspond to those offered by nursing schools to allow graduates to retrain prior to returning to the labor force. They represent the response of a feminized occupation to the needs of an intermittent work force. Yet retraining is unlikely to provide a means of allowing women to compete more equally with men.[64]

A better solution lies in developing greater commitment in women journalism students and in devising means of restructuring jobs so it is not necessary for women to have relative long periods of career interruptions. "Journalism is not a good field to take a career interruption in," a 1978 woman graduate said. "It's not a traditional woman's field in which you can pick up and go back in. You need to be there, keep your hand in. In public relations, you're into management; gaps in your career are looked at closely."[65]

A 1966 woman graduate, who only interrupted her own career in public relations for three months and now has her own business, expressed the issue this way: "Interruptions are difficult for both sexes. They are harder for women because they miss out on valuable training, contacts, developments when they go out for long time periods. They gave me the choice of who to hire at my last job and I never hired anyone who had a spotty job record."[66]

Extensive literature exists on the subject of women's vocations. It suggests that aspiration itself is a powerful stimulant to career success. If woman truly are committed, they may be able to avoid the kinds of interruptions that force them out of career fields. A study of women and well-being, financed by the National Science Foundation and conducted by the Wellesley College Center for Research on Women, found that the women who scored highest in terms of mental and physical well-being were married, had children and worked at high-prestige jobs.[67]

Therefore it becomes the task of journalism educators to help women develop high aspirations. Historically this has been difficult, in part because the news business, like most institutions, has been male-dominated. Two studies of news values, one in 1979 and one in 1977, showed that standards of newsroom behavior on newspapers, whether exhibited by males or females, were male standards.[68]

One researcher found that among accepted news values was the discrediting of news stories in which the principal actor was a woman, even when the decisions on the stories were made by women editors. McAdams pointed out that women seemed particularly likely to conform to newsroom norms. She theorized: "Perhaps this is essential to their survival in the newsroom, since at entry they are farther from the established norm than their male counterparts simply because they are female. Like men who are promoted, women who advance have assimilated the values of their superiors, most of whom are male." Therefore, she said, women have had to adopt a way of thinking, communicating and acting contrary to their feminine socialization.[69]

Yet the latest findings on women and broadcast news operations hold some encouraging news for journalism education. The media elite—those who hold positions of power in major news organizations—are chiefly white males in their thirties and forties, a study five years ago by Stanley Rothman of Smith College and Robert Lichter of George Washington University showed. They discovered, however, that one in five is female.[70]

Also women are making some progress by moving up from reporter to news director, according to Vernon Stone, former director of the journalism school at Southern Illinois University. Stone's annual survey of women in broadcasting showed that in 1983 women were 11 percent of news directors compared with 8 percent in 1982 and 1 percent in 1972. The proportion in news in all television markets did not increase in 1983, however, in Stone's survey, remaining at about 31 percent. Similarly a study released in 1984 by the Women's Media Project of the NOW Legal Defense and Education Fund determined that the percentage of news reported by women on nightly national network news shows had increased less than one percent in the past decade.[71]

Nevertheless, the names of women television newscasters have become celebrated across the United States: Barbara Walters, Connie Chung, Lesley Stahl, Diane Sawyer, Jane Pauley. Their presence on national television makes them far more visible role models for other women than successful women in the print media, advertising or public relations. The presence of women in television newsrooms means that the news is being changed in subtle ways, according to Jean Gaddy Wilson, a lecturer at the University of Missouri School of Journalism, who has been conducting the first comprehensive study of women in the media.[72]

Women in broadcasting interviewed by Wilson repeatedly told her that women bring a different acculturation to the workplace, simply because they have grown up female. "I know that in the news profession, stories about rape, stories about children, stories about wives, stories about the family that were formerly the province of *McCall's* and *Redbook* are now routinely seen on television screens," Sylvia Chase, a *ABC* correspondent, told Wilson. Chase attributed this to the outgrowth of the women's movement of the 1970s.[73]

Another encouraging sign is some job restructuring within the communications industry to accommodate two-career couples. *The Kansas City Star,* for example, used to have a strict rule that one member of a couple had to leave the paper if the couple married after meeting on the job. But in April, 1984, that policy was changed when the newspaper's top feature editor became engaged to an editor of its Sunday magazine. The newspaper ended its ban on employing spouses, and it also removed the magazine from supervision by the feature editor so the husband would not be supervising his wife. Action came after the couple served notice neither would voluntarily leave the job.[74]

On occasion women in the communications industry have banded together for creative solutions to child care problems, although much more action is needed. In Washington, D.C., for example, parents working at local radio and television stations have established the Broadcasters Child Development Center to provide regular and after-hours care for children of broadcasters with variable work schedules. Such efforts, however, are rare. On a national level, most members of Women in Communications are married and have children, according to a 1983 marketing survey, but these women tend to work at small private firms where child care and/or on-site care do not exist.[75]

Journalism education could help in this regard by acquainting students with issues involved in corporate assistance to employes with children. Today about 80 major corporations, such as IBM, Polaroid and Proctor and Gamble, offer help including referral services, sick leave when children are ill, vouchers to pay for child-care, working parents' seminars and flexible benefit plans with child care as an option. Some businesses also are considering on-site child care centers to increase employes' productivity and decrease absenteeism and tardiness.[76]

In summary, journalism education should not tacitly allow women students, as in the past, to let their college years be dominated by dreams of a home and family likely to remove them from the labor force during a pivotal period for career development. Today we are entering a new information age when as Buck, Ogan and Rush put it, "Technological developments in satellites and computers will transform our work, our educational processes and systems, and the way we carry out our day-to-day lives. According to Robert Theobald, who coined the term, "the communications era," new technology will offer hope for women to break into decision-making roles in society. "Many women appear to find the patterns of process and cooperation required for the communications era easier than many men," he wrote. Another expert, Jessie Bernard, has contended the ethos of the feminine experience, which stresses collaborative and cooperative ventures, to be "more constant [than that of men] with the emerging high technology, post-industrial or communications era."[77]

Regardless of the validity of these predictions, obviously major shifts in the social roles of men and women are taking place. Journalism education must recognize these and strive to help women students develop new ways of looking at the issue of family versus career instead of becoming mired down in outworn, either/or arguments.

**Specific recommendations:**

- Journalism educators should undertake studies of the communications industry to assess the changes made in personnel practices as the result of more women entering the field. These studies also should cover inclusion of child-care provisions.
- Journalism educators should make sure that all students have accurate information about the position of men and women in the labor force today and encourage them to make realistic long-range plans addressing issues of professional and personal concerns.
- Journalism educators should research the introduction of new technology into communications industries with emphasis on their responsiveness to needs of both men and women workers.
- Journalism educators should survey communications employers to discover their perceptions of changes in the structure of family life and the corresponding impact on the communications industry.

## ENDNOTES

1. Ken Harvey and Ronald E. Smith, "News Execs Urge Major Overhaul of Journalism Training Program," *Editor & Publisher,* March 6, 1982, p. 10.
2. Bob Witty, "Hiring," in *Newsroom Management Handbook* (Wash., D.C.: American Society of Newspaper Editors Foundation, 1985), p. 3.
3. Fred Fedler and Philip Taylor, "Two-Year Analysis Discloses Effects and Problems of Required Grammar Tests," *Journalism Educator* 37 (Summer 1982), p. 20.
4. Dave Berkman, "Student Quality Fall Affects J-Schools," *Journalism Educator* 39 (Winter 1985), p. 33.

5. Interview by Maurine Beasley with Pam Brown, Rutgers University, March 30, 1985; Catherine L. Covert, "Journalism History and Women's Experience: A Problem in Conceptual Change," *Journalism History* 8 (Spring 1981), p. 4.
6. Covert, "Journalism History and Women's Experience," p. 3.
7. Ibid.
8. Interview by Beasley with Brown, March 31, 1985; "The Classroom Climate: A Chilly One for Women?" p. 2.
9. "The Classroom Climate: A Chilly One for Women?" pp. 2-3, 7.
10. Ibid. pp. 11-12.
11. Donna Allen, "Introduction," to Dana Densmore, ed., *Syllabus Sourcebook on Media and Women* (Washington, D.C.: Women's Institute for Freedom of the Press, 1980), p. v.
12. Ibid., vii.
13. Ibid., p. v.
14. Ibid.
15. Comment to Maurine Beasley by Colleen Moore, May 1975, College Park, Md.
16. Doris A. Graber, "Agenda-Setting: Are There Women's Perspectives?" in Laurily Keir Epstein, ed., *Women and the News* (New York: Hastings House, 1978), p. 32.
17. Ibid., pp. 34-35.
18. Text of Speech by Dr. Donna Allen as part of panel on "Shifting Priorities in Mass Communication Education," plenary session, national convention, Association for Education in Journalism and Mass Communication, Gainesville, Fla., Aug. 8, 1984; "New Directions for News," (Washington, D.C.; Women Studies Program and Policy Center, George Washington University, 1983), p. 3.
19. "New Directions for News," pp. 3-4.
20. Bernice R. Sandler, "The Quiet Revolution on Campus: How Sex Discrimination Has Changed," *Chronicle of Higher Education,* Feb. 29, 1984, p. 72.
21. "Dr. Carol Oukrop Survey Brings Women's Rape Reporting Concerns Together With Editors' Viewpoints," *Media Report to Women* 12 (Sept.-Oct. 1984), pp. 12-13.
22. Comments to Maurine Beasley by a graduating senior, March 18, 1985, College Park, Md.
23. Ibid.
24. Ibid.
25. Ibid.
26. Survey in *USA Today* as quoted by Judy Luce Mann, "Choosing the Best College," *Washington Post,* April 10, 1985, C3.
27. Ibid.
28. Nancy S. Barrett, "Women in the Job Market: Occupations, Earnings, and Career Opportunities," in Ralph E. Smith, ed., *The Subtle Revolution* (Washington, D.C.: The Urban Institute, 1979), p. 34.
29. Ralph E. Smith, "The Movement of Women into the Labor Force," in Smith, ed., *The Subtle Revolution,* p. 10.

30. Steven D. McLaughlin, "Sex Differences in the Determinants of Occupational Status," *Sociology of Work and Occupations* 5 (Feb. 1978), p. 21; Ellen Lewin and Joseph Damrell, "Female Identity and Career Pathways," *Sociology of Work and Occupations* 5 (Feb. 1978), p. 36.
31. Barrett, "Women in the Job Market," pp. 58–61.
32. David M. Dozier, Sharon Chapo and Brad Sullivan, "Sex and the Bottom Line: Income Differences Among Women and Men in Public Relations," paper presented to the Public Relations Division, Association for Education in Journalism and Mass Communication convention, Corvallis, Ore., Aug. 7, 1983, p. 1.
33. Ibid., p. 15.
34. Ibid., p. 17.
35. Ibid., pp. 17, 22.
36. Ibid., pp. 24–25.
37. James E. Grunig, "Hard Thinking on Education," *Public Relations Journal,* April 1985, p. 30.
38. Telephone interview with Edward Towdy, Jr. by Kathy Lemke, May 14, 1984.
39. Telephone interview with Marilyn Lyman-Jaumoville by Kathy Lemke, May 14, 1984.
40. Hasia R. Diner, "Service and Scholarship: Seventy-five Years of the School of Social Service Administration of the University of Chicago, 1908–1983," unpublished paper completed in Dec., 1984, p. 45.
41. Barrett, "Women in the Job Market," pp. 46–48.
42. Telephone interview with Candace Mayo by Kathy Lemke, May 9, 1984.
43. Telephone interview with Janice Colvin by Kathy Lemke, April 30, 1984.
44. Katherine C. McAdams, "Some Effects of Sex-Role Socialization on Women Entering Journalism Careers," unpublished master's thesis, University of North Carolina, 1981, pp. 29–41.
45. Ibid., pp. 44–46.
46. Ibid., p. 56.
47. Dorothy Jurney, "Percentage of Women Editors Creeps Upward to 11.7—But Other Fields Continue to Progress Faster," *ASNE Bulletin,* Jan. 1986, pp. 8–9. See also, Christine L. Ogan, Charlene J. Brown and David H. Weaver, "Characteristics of Managers of Selected U.S. Daily Newspapers," *Journalism Quarterly* 56 (Winter 1979), pp. 803–09; Christine Ogan, "Life at the Top for Men and Women Newspaper Managers: A Five-Year Update on Their Characteristics," a working paper, Indiana University, 1983.
48. Ardyth B. Sohn, "Goals and Achievement Orientations of Women Newspaper Managers," *Journalism Quarterly* 61 (Autumn 1984) pp. 604–05.
49. Ibid.
50. Ibid., p. 604.
51. Ibid., p. 605.
52. Barrett, "Women in the Job Market," p. 32.
53. Draft of unpublished paper by Katherine C. McAdams, June 1984, provided to Maurine Beasley, pp. 10–12.
54. Ibid., pp. 12–13.

55. McAdams, "Some Effects of Sex-Role Socialization on Women Entering Journalism Careers," pp. 21-23.
56. As quoted in Judy Luce Mann, "Working," *Washington Post,* June 29, 1983, C1; Stephanie Mansfield, "Hittin' It Big & Kissin' It Goodbye: No Kids, No Job: Women at Home Just for Themselves," *Washington Post,* Feb. 26, 1985, C1; Barbara Toman, "Parenthood and Career Overtax Rising, Productivity Declining; Loyalty Sometimes Shifts," *Wall Street Journal,* Sept. 7, 1983, Al.
57. Caryl Rivers Lupo, "If You Ask Me: Superwoman's a Myth...," as reprinted in *Washington Post,* June 20, 1984, B5.
58. Ibid.
59. "Twenty Facts on Women Workers," press release, Women's Bureau, U.S. Department of Labor, 1982, pp. 1-3.
60. Telephone interview with Penny Graf by Kathy Lemke, May 7, 1984.
61. Telephone interview with Loretta Robinson by Laurie Evans, June 24, 1984.
62. Telephone interview with Eileen Burke by Kathy Lemke, April 30, 1984.
63. Telephone interview with William Lucas Walker by Kathy Lemke, May 21, 1984.
64. Barrett, "Women in the Job Market," p. 60.
65. Telephone interview with Sarah Meehan by Laura Evans, June 12, 1984.
66. Telephone interview with Dawn S. Ford by Kathy Lemke, May 14, 1984.
67. McAdams, "Some Effects of Sex-Role Socialization on Women Entering Journalism Careers," pp. 19-21; Lupo, "If You Ask Me: Superwoman's a Myth..."
68. McAdams, "Some Effects of Sex-Role Socialization on Women Entering Journalism Careers," p. 24.
69. Ibid.
70. As cited in Jean Gaddy Wilson, "Are Newswomen Changing the News?" *Ms.,* Dec. 1984, p. 45.
71. Ibid., pp. 45-46.
72. Ibid., pp. 50, 124-26.
73. Ibid., p. 126.
74. Monica Langley, "Office Marriages Win More Firms' Blessings, But Problems Crop Up," *Wall Street Journal,* Oct. 16, 1984, p. 1.
75. Louise Ott, "Child Care Issue Gains Momentum," *Pro/Comm* 5 (Jan.-Feb. 1985), p. 1.
76. Ibid., pp. 1, 10.
77. Elizabeth Buck, Christine L. Ogan, and Ramona R. Rush, "Women and the Communications Revolution: Can We Get There From Here?" English translation of paper published in *Chasqui,* publication of the Centro Internacional de Estudios Superiores de la Communicacion para America Latina, Quito, Ecuador, (July-September, 1982), p. 2. Quotations from Robert Theobald, "The Communications Era from the Year 2000," *National Forum* 60 (1980), and Jessie Bernard, "The Female World and Technology in 2020," *National Forum* 61 (1981) cited on pp. 25-26.

# Epilogue

# Next Steps for Professionals and Educators

In addition to the points and recommendations made on preceding pages, we offer these conclusions and general recommendations:

Women in general are still at a disadvantage in the American workplace, for many reasons. As consciousness of overt discrimination has increased, some old barriers have been breached. But many elements still deter women in job placement, salaries and promotion. Among them are vestiges of blatant discrimination, more subtle assumptions about women and what is appropriate work for them, career interruptions for family reasons, a shortage of role models in the leadership of many employment fields, and self-limitations resulting from differences in female and male acculturation.

With the tilt in journalism school enrollments to almost two-thirds female, educators and professionals in the field have compelling reasons to act upon these disturbing prospects:

- Journalism and related communications fields may become "pink-collar ghettos" in which salaries and status are lowered in relation to other major professions. Female-dominated fields such as teaching, social work, nursing and librarianship traditionally have been lower-income professions. Although salaries in journalism-related fields (some of which already are noted for low pay) may not decline, there should be concern that they will not rise as they might if these fields remained predominantly male.

- Schools of journalism and mass communication have been experiencing strong surges in demand and enrollment, largely but not entirely because of the female tilt. A number of the accredited programs consequently have become more selective. But if salary and status in journalism-related fields decline relatively and those fields become less competitive, some of the most important work of a democratic society will become less attractive to students gifted in intellect, resourcefulness and general ability.

Throughout our history, journalism has been a male-dominated profession, even when millions of men were in war-time military service. It is clear that women will become a majority in journalism and its most closely related fields, though probably not soon a majority in the top management ranks. The import of this has not been properly examined or understood in the field.

Nor has there been a comprehensive study, until this report's limited exploration, of the implications of the "new majority" for schools of journalism and mass communication. Our findings point to the need for much more work to determine how educators should meet the new challenge.

In addition to the four specific challenges previously listed, here are our general recommendations for the next steps to be taken by professionals in the field and educators:

1. Major professional organizations in the field should give high priority to the implications of the "new majority." Programs at national meetings and professional journals should explore this subject in depth.

2. Managements of media organizations, in their training programs and personnel processes, should specifically examine ways in which the interests, professional growth and long-term satisfaction of the "new majority" may be encouraged in a field still dominated by males in management.

3. Professional development programs, such as workshops and seminars that deal with professional growth, should address the aspirations of women and the need for better management approaches to bringing them into a fuller partnership. In part, these should address the special problems women face in reconciling careers and family life.

4. Organizations of educators in journalism and mass communication should bring the subject of the "New Majority" to the fore in their programs and publications. The need for more female faculty members should be addressed systematically, with special efforts to identify women professionals in the field who might enter academic life and attention to ways in which more women may be attracted to graduate programs that produce faculty members.

5. It has been established that the career aspirations of women tend to decline while they are in college. This subject should be examined further with the help of journalism educators and professionals in the field. Programs should be put in place in the schools to provide realistic career advice for both female and male students, with special attention to the evident problem of declining self-esteem among many young women while they are in college.

6. Further studies should be undertaken dealing with (1) male-female differences in priorities for job satisfaction in journalism and related fields, (2) factors influencing both males and females to choose education in schools of journalism and mass communication, (3) trends in salary levels as they may be affected by an infusion of women during the next five years, (4) how the news may be affected by differences between male and female perceptions and acculturation and (5) how newspapers and other news organizations appeal to women as readers and viewers compared with how they appeal to men.

# Appendices

# Appendix A

# Chronology of "Firsts" by Women in Journalism Education

1886 — Martha Louise Rayne sets up the first school of journalism in the world in Detroit while male journalists scoff.

1909 — Seven students at the University of Washington in Seattle found Theta Sigma Phi (now Women in Communications), a journalism sorority. Elsewhere, male students had organized a journalism fraternity that excluded women: Sigma Delta Chi (now the Society of Professional Journalists/Sigma Delta Chi).

1910 — Mary Paxton (later Keeley) graduates with a bachelor's degree in journalism from the University of Missouri, making her the first woman in the world to receive a journalism degree.

1918 — Minna Lewinson, a student at the Columbia University School of Journalism, becomes the first woman to receive a Pulitzer Prize (sharing the award with another student, Henry Beetle Hough, in a special category of newspaper history).

1923 — Helen Patterson, one of the first women members of the American Teachers of Journalism, starts her 34-year teaching career at the University of Wisconsin, where she originates a course called "Writing For Homemakers."

1936 — Eleanor Carroll becomes the first woman faculty member to be hired at the Columbia University School of Journalism, where she advances to the position of associate dean.

1943 — Women enroll for the first time in a special typography program at Northwestern University's Medill School of Journalism. They train for newspaper production jobs, replacing men serving in the World War II armed forces.

1946 — Helen Hostetter, former editor of the *Journal of Home Economics,* receives a full professorship in journalism at Kansas State University, giving her a claim to being the first woman to attain this rank in academic journalism. She gets less pay than her male colleagues.

1950 — Marguerite Higgins becomes the first woman journalism school graduate to win a Pulitzer Prize for reporting. Her alma mater, the Columbia University Graduate School of Journalism, uses this headline in its annual report: "Marguerite Higgins, Girl Reporter, Covering War on the Korean Front Asks No Favors Because of Her Sex."

1972 — Three women educators, Ramona Rush, Carol Oukrop and Sandra Ernst, present the first formal study of women journalism educators at the annual convention of the Association for Education in Journalism. Their findings: Women constitute barely eight percent of the total employed on journalism faculties in the United States, and of these only 10 hold Ph.D. degrees.

1977 — Dr. Marion Marzolf, assistant professor of journalism at the University of Michigan, publishes the first modern history of women in journalism, *Up From the Footnote.*

1978 — Dr. Mary Gardner, professor of journalism at Michigan State University, becomes the first woman president of the Association for Education in Journalism.

# Appendix B

# Selected Previous Research on Women Journalism Students and Graduates

1938 — Iona Robertson Logie of the Hunter College High School in New York publishes a book based on a survey of 881 women journalists of whom 57 percent are journalism graduates. The findings: Widespread sex discrimination against newspaperwomen in salary and advancement.

1952 — Adelaide H. Jones, a journalism instructor at Drury College in Springfield, Missouri, gathers data on 1941 women graduates of 13 journalism schools to study their professional and personal lives during the decade after graduation. Her conclusions: "The proportion remaining in gainful employment decreased steadily to a low of 26 percent in 1949, which can be explained only by the high marriage rate of the group and subsequent interruption of employment for reasons due to marital status.... The journalism graduate...lived much more happily with her husband and family than with her profession."

1974 — Thomas A. Bowers, assistant professor of journalism at the University of North Carolina, surveys 185 journalism students, about half of whom are women, and discovers the females express more interest in journalism as a long-term career than do the males.

1977 — Wilma Crumley, professor of journalism at the University of Nebraska, Lincoln, Joye Patterson, associate professor of journalism at the University of Missouri, and Patricia Sailor, director of the School of Home Economics at Louisiana State University, report on a study of journalism alumnae at their universities five and ten years after graduation. They find the women express a strong commonality of interests along these lines: (1) continuing enthusiasm for journalism; (2) rising career aspirations; (3) commitment to the successful mixing of marriage and family with lifetime careers.

# Appendix C
# Survey Instruments

## JOURNALISM ALUMNI QUESTIONNAIRE

Questionnaire _____

Date _____

IN ORDER FOR THE COLLEGE OF JOURNALISM TO EVALUATE ITS CURRICULUM (AND TO LEARN MORE ABOUT HOW ITS GRADUATES FARE IN THE WORKPLACE), PLEASE COMPLETE THE QUESTIONNAIRE AT THIS TIME. IT WILL ONLY TAKE A FEW MINUTES. THEN MAIL IT TODAY IN THE PRE-PAID ENVELOPE ENCLOSED. *YOUR PARTICIPATION IS VERY IMPORTANT.* ALL ANSWERS ARE CONFIDENTIAL.

**PART I: EDUCATION**

THE FOLLOWING QUESTIONS CONCERN YOUR EDUCATIONAL HISTORY. MARK ONE ANSWER FOR EACH.

1. Did you attend any college and earn nine credits before entering the University of Maryland?

    ____Yes        ____No

2. If yes, how many credits had you earned when you transferred?

    ____I did not transfer        ____58–89 credits
    ____9–28 credits              ____90+ credits
    ____29–55 credits

3. How important was each of the following in choosing the University of Maryland rather than another college or university? Indicate whether each was extremely important, moderately important, somewhat important, or not at all important to you.

|  | Extremely Important | Moderately Important | Somewhat Important | Not at all Important |
|---|---|---|---|---|
| a. Location | ____ | ____ | ____ | ____ |
| b. Reputation of journalism program | ____ | ____ | ____ | ____ |
| c. Cost of tuition/board | ____ | ____ | ____ | ____ |
| d. Availability of financial aid | ____ | ____ | ____ | ____ |
| e. Entrance requirements | ____ | ____ | ____ | ____ |
| f. Recommendation of friends/peers | ____ | ____ | ____ | ____ |
| g. Recommendation of alumni | ____ | ____ | ____ | ____ |
| h. Recommendation of parents/relatives | ____ | ____ | ____ | ____ |
| i. Recommendation of teacher/counselor | ____ | ____ | ____ | ____ |

4. What year did you receive a Bachelor of Science degree in journalism (since 1970) or business or public administration (prior to 1970).

　　____1981　　　　　____1963
　　____1978　　　　　____1960
　　____1975　　　　　____1957
　　____1972　　　　　____1954
　　____1969　　　　　____1951　　　　　$\overline{22}\ \overline{23}$
　　____1966　　　　　____Other

5. What is the highest level of education you have completed since earning your B.S.?

　　____College graduate　　　____Post graduate degree
　　____Post-graduate work　　　(Specify degree and major)　　$\overline{24}$
　　　　　　　　　　　　　　_____
　　　　　　　　　　　　　　　　　　　　　　　　　　　　$\overline{25}\ \overline{26}$

6. As an undergraduate, what was your sequence within the journalism area?

　　____Advertising　　　　　____Photojournalism
　　____Broadcast News　　　____Public Relations
　　____Magazine　　　　　　____Science Communication
　　____News-Editorial　　　　____Other (Specify)_____　　$\overline{27}\ \overline{28}$

7. Did you ever have a major other than journalism? If so, what was it?

　　____No　　　　　　____Yes (Specify)_____　　$\overline{29}$

　　　　　　　　　　　　　　　　　　　　　　　　　　　　$\overline{30}$

8. How important was each of the following in influencing your decision to study journalism?

| | Extremely Important | Moderately Important | Somewhat Important | Not at all Important | |
|---|---|---|---|---|---|
| a. Promise of money | ____ | ____ | ____ | ____ | $\overline{31}$ |
| b. Promise of prestige | ____ | ____ | ____ | ____ | $\overline{32}$ |
| c. Creative opportunity | ____ | ____ | ____ | ____ | $\overline{33}$ |
| d. Value of job to society | ____ | ____ | ____ | ____ | $\overline{34}$ |
| e. Seemed like easiest major | ____ | ____ | ____ | ____ | $\overline{35}$ |
| f. Communication professional suggested it | ____ | ____ | ____ | ____ | $\overline{36}$ |
| g. Peers/friends suggested it | ____ | ____ | ____ | ____ | $\overline{37}$ |
| h. Parents/relatives suggested it | ____ | ____ | ____ | ____ | $\overline{38}$ |
| i. Teachers/counselors suggested it | ____ | ____ | ____ | ____ | $\overline{39}$ |
| j. Like to meet people | ____ | ____ | ____ | ____ | $\overline{40}$ |
| k. Like to write | ____ | ____ | ____ | ____ | $\overline{41}$ |
| l. Reputation of journalism program | ____ | ____ | ____ | ____ | $\overline{42}$ |

9. What was the most important *minor* field of study in which you earned 12 or more advanced credits? Mark one.

　　____Business, management,　　　____Engineering or computer science
　　　　accounting　　　　　　　　　____Mathematics
　　____Government　　　　　　　　____Psychology
　　____History　　　　　　　　　　____Sociology
　　____English　　　　　　　　　　____Foreign language
　　____Physical or biological　　　　____Other (Specify)_____　　$\overline{43}\ \overline{44}$
　　　　Science　　　　　　　　　　____None

10. Were you involved in any of the following campus organizations as an undergraduate?

    ____Diamondback             ____WMUC
    ____Argus                      ____SDX/SPJ
    ____Hakoach (Mitzpeh)     ____Ad Club
    ____Calvert                    ____PRSSA
    ____Black Explosion        ____Other journalism activity,
    ____Wheeler Times            excluding internships/employment    $\overline{45}\ \overline{46}$
                                       ____None

11. Did you participate in a journalism-related internship or were you employed in a journalism-related job while attending the University of Maryland?

    ____Yes                  ____No                               $\overline{47}$

12. Thinking of your own journalism classroom experiences, did you detect any way in which students were treated differently:

    a. On the basis of sex?     ____Yes     ____No     $\overline{48}$
    b. On the basis of age?     ____Yes     ____No     $\overline{49}$
    c. On the basis of race?     ____Yes     ____No     $\overline{50}$

13. Did you have a career or life goal while in college? IF YOU HAD NO CAREER/LIFE GOAL, SKIP TO 17.

    ____Yes                  ____No                               $\overline{51}$

14. Was there one person who influenced you in choosing your career/life goal? IF NOT, SKIP TO 17.

    ____Yes                  ____No                               $\overline{52}$

15. Was this person one of the following?

    ____Parent or relative        ____Media professional
    ____High school teacher     ____Peer your age
    ____College professor         ____Other adult (Specify)_____     $\overline{53}$
    ____Business professional                                    $\overline{54}$

16. Was this person male or female?

    ____Male                 ____Female                          $\overline{55}$

17. As you look back on your undergraduate education, how would you rate your overall experience with the College of Journalism?

    ____Extremely good        ____Somewhat good
    ____Very good                ____Not at all good              $\overline{56}$

Please explain:_____    $\overline{57}\ \overline{58}$

18. If you could do it over, would you major in journalism or in some other field?

    ____Journalism          ____Other field (Specify)_____    $\overline{59}\ \overline{60}$

Please Explain:_____    $\overline{61}\ \overline{62}$

19. If you could do it over, what learning experiences would you now seek to prepare yourself for your chosen career/life goal?

    ____The same           ____Other

Specify:_____    $\overline{63}\ \overline{64}$

150

20. What learning experiences should be included in our program that you didn't receive?
    Specify:_____ 65 66
    _____

**PART II. WORK EXPERIENCE**

THE FOLLOWING QUESTIONS CONCERN YOUR WORK HISTORY. MARK ONE ANSWER FOR EACH.

21. At any time since your graduation, have you been employed full or part-time and earned an income?
    ___Full-time          ___I have not been employed.        67
    ___Part-time

IF YOU HAVE NEVER WORKED AND ARE NOT SEEKING EMPLOYMENT, PLEASE SKIP THIS SECTION AND COMPLETE PART III.

22. How soon after graduation did you get your first income-producing job?
    ___Accepted job before grad.   ___6–10 years
    ___Less than 3 months          ___11–15 years
    ___4–6 months                  ___16 years
    ___7–12 months                 ___still looking
    ___1–2 years                   ___not looking
    ___3–5 years                                              68 69

23. Was this job full-time or part-time (less than 20 hours).
    ___Full-time          ___Part-time                        70

24. In your opinion how important was each of the following in helping you get your first job? IF YOU WERE SELF-EMPLOYED, SKIP TO 25.

| | Extremely Helpful | Very Helpful | Somewhat Helpful | Not at all Helpful | Does not Apply | |
|---|---|---|---|---|---|---|
| a. Personal interview | ___ | ___ | ___ | ___ | ___ | 71 |
| b. Clip Book | ___ | ___ | ___ | ___ | ___ | 72 |
| c. Letter of recommendation | ___ | ___ | ___ | ___ | ___ | 73 |
| d. Quality of resume | ___ | ___ | ___ | ___ | ___ | 74 |
| e. Academic record | ___ | ___ | ___ | ___ | ___ | 75 |
| f. Extracurricular activities | ___ | ___ | ___ | ___ | ___ | 76 |
| g. Pre-employment test | ___ | ___ | ___ | ___ | ___ | 77 |
| h. Professional contacts | ___ | ___ | ___ | ___ | ___ | 78 |
| i. Personal or family contacts | ___ | ___ | ___ | ___ | ___ | 79 |

25. For what type of firm or agency do you work? If you are unemployed, mark the appropriate box.

　　\_\_\_\_Corporation
　　\_\_\_\_Financial institution
　　\_\_\_\_Medical institution
　　\_\_\_\_Educational institution
　　\_\_\_\_P.R. or communication consulting firm
　　\_\_\_\_Government (federal)
　　\_\_\_\_Government (state, local)
　　\_\_\_\_Non-profit association
　　\_\_\_\_Advertising firm
　　\_\_\_\_Daily newspaper
　　\_\_\_\_Weekly/monthly newspaper
　　\_\_\_\_Radio/t.v. (news)
　　\_\_\_\_Radio/t.v. (production)
　　\_\_\_\_News services
　　\_\_\_\_Magazine/newsletter (other than public relations)
　　\_\_\_\_Other (Specify)_____
　　\_\_\_\_Unemployed, looking for journalism-related work
　　\_\_\_\_Unemployed, looking for other work

26. How many persons work for your firm or agency? IF YOU ARE UNEMPLOYED, SKIP TO 30.

　　\_\_\_\_1-10
　　\_\_\_\_11-25
　　\_\_\_\_26-50
　　\_\_\_\_51-150
　　\_\_\_\_151-300
　　\_\_\_\_301-500
　　\_\_\_\_More than 500

27. How satisfied are you with your present job?

　　\_\_\_\_Extremely satisfied
　　\_\_\_\_Very satisfied
　　\_\_\_\_Somewhat satisfied
　　\_\_\_\_Not at all satisfied

28. Are you satisfied with your earnings?

　　\_\_\_\_Extremely satisfied
　　\_\_\_\_Moderately satisfied
　　\_\_\_\_Somewhat satisfied
　　\_\_\_\_Not at all satisfied

29. In your opinion, what are your chances for career advancement in your line of work?

　　\_\_\_\_Extremely good
　　\_\_\_\_Moderately good
　　\_\_\_\_Somewhat good
　　\_\_\_\_Not at all good

30. To how many professional organizations related to your career do you belong?

　　\_\_\_\_None
　　\_\_\_\_1
　　\_\_\_\_2
　　\_\_\_\_3
　　\_\_\_\_4
　　\_\_\_\_5 or more

31. How often do you attend career-related professional seminars, luncheons or meetings?

　　\_\_\_\_Never
　　\_\_\_\_Less than one per year
　　\_\_\_\_Once per year
　　\_\_\_\_Twice per year
　　\_\_\_\_Every other month
　　\_\_\_\_Once per month
　　\_\_\_\_Twice per month
　　\_\_\_\_3 or more times per month

32. How often do you attend career-related continuing education workshops or classes?

　　\_\_\_\_Never
　　\_\_\_\_Seldom
　　\_\_\_\_Once each 3-5 years
　　\_\_\_\_Once each 1-2 years
　　\_\_\_\_Twice a year or more

33. Different people want different things from their jobs. How important is each of the following to you in deciding whether a job is satisfying?

|  | Extremely Important | Moderately Important | Somewhat Important | Not at all Important |  |
|---|---|---|---|---|---|
| a. Creative opportunity | ____ | ____ | ____ | ____ | 14 |
| b. Freedom/autonomy | ____ | ____ | ____ | ____ | 15 |
| c. Adequate salary | ____ | ____ | ____ | ____ | 16 |
| d. Career advancement | ____ | ____ | ____ | ____ | 17 |
| e. Managerial responsibility | ____ | ____ | ____ | ____ | 18 |
| f. Job security | ____ | ____ | ____ | ____ | 19 |
| g. Recognition of colleagues | ____ | ____ | ____ | ____ | 20 |
| h. Prestige | ____ | ____ | ____ | ____ | 21 |
| i. Potential for promotion | ____ | ____ | ____ | ____ | 22 |
| j. Value of job to society | ____ | ____ | ____ | ____ | 23 |
| k. Opportunity to apply specialized skills | ____ | ____ | ____ | ____ | 24 |
| l. Recognition of superiors in organization | ____ | ____ | ____ | ____ | 25 |

34. In thinking about your last three jobs or job titles, has your work been primarily that of a staff member or a staff director? If you worked in a journalism-related field, mark columns designated "A." Mark all answers applicable to you.

|  | Staff Member | | Staff Director | | Not applicable |  |
|---|---|---|---|---|---|---|
|  | (Jour-related) | (Not related) | (Jour-related) | (Not related) |  |  |
|  | A | B | A | B |  |  |
| a. Most recent | ____ | ____ | ____ | ____ | ____ | 26 |
| b. Next most recent | ____ | ____ | ____ | ____ | ____ | 27 |
| c. Third most recent | ____ | ____ | ____ | ____ | ____ | 28 |

35. In your most recent job, were you free to make work-related decisions on your own, or did you have to clear them with a supervisor?

____Free to make decisions     ____Had to clear decisions      29

36. If you were employed and earned an income at any time following your graduation, was your employment ever interrupted for any of the following reasons?

____Illness/injury              ____Additional education
____Military service            ____Layoff
____Childbearing                ____Other (Specify)_____
____Family responsibilities     ____My career was never interrupted     30 31

37. What was the longest period that you were without gainful employment? If you have always been employed, mark that.

____Less than 6 months          ____6–10 years
____7–12 months                 ____11–15 years
____1–2 years                   ____More than 15 years
____3–5 years                   ____I have always been employed     32

153

38. If you had a career interruption and resumed working sometime later, did you re-enter the same general field or change career paths altogether? IF YOU HAVE NEVER HAD A CAREER INTERRUPTION OR YOU ARE, FOR THE FIRST TIME, UNEMPLOYED, SKIP TO 40.

____Resumed same career        ____Had no interruption
____Started different career   ____Am now unemployed

$\overline{33}$

39. If you had a career interruption and resumed working, did you take a position at a higher level, the same level or a lower level in a firm or agency than before the interruption?

____Higher level   ____Same level   ____Lower level

$\overline{34}$

40. Do you plan a career change within the next two years?

____Yes                    ____No

If you answered yes, please explain: $\overline{35}$

_____ $\overline{36}\ \overline{37}$

_____

41. If you plan a career change, will you work in a journalism-related field?

____I plan a career change and it *will* be in a journalism-related field.
____I plan a career change and it *will not* be in a journalism-related field.
____I do not plan a career change.

$\overline{38}$

42. If your career develops as you hope, what will your job title be before you retire.
    (Title)_____

$\overline{39}\ \overline{40}\ \overline{41}$

**PART III. BASED ON YOUR PERSONAL EXPERIENCE OR OBSERVATION, DO YOU *AGREE* OR *DISAGREE* WITH EACH OF THE FOLLOWING STATEMENTS?**

|  | Agree | Disagree | No Experience |  |
|---|---|---|---|---|
| 43. Salaries of women doing journalism-related work are generally lower than salaries of men doing comparable work. | ____ | ____ | ____ | $\overline{42}$ |
| 44. Firms or agencies are more likely to hire a woman than a man for a communication staff position (writer, etc.) | ____ | ____ | ____ | $\overline{43}$ |
| 45. Men are promoted more quickly than women in most firms or agencies. | ____ | ____ | ____ | $\overline{44}$ |
| 46. Men are more apt to back down or seek compromises in office conflict situations than women are. | ____ | ____ | ____ | $\overline{45}$ |
| 47. If an equally capable woman and man applied for a job, the woman would probably be hired. | ____ | ____ | ____ | $\overline{46}$ |
| 48. If an equally capable woman and man had applied for a job ten years ago, the man would probably have been hired. | ____ | ____ | ____ | $\overline{47}$ |
| 49. The way to get into management-level positions is to earn a post-graduate degree. | ____ | ____ | ____ | $\overline{48}$ |
| 50. Women are often hired as a result of affirmative action policies. | ____ | ____ | ____ | $\overline{49}$ |

51. Men are more assertive than women in defining proposals and winning consent for decisions affecting the firm or agency.  ____ ____ ____

52. More men than women are hired as communication staff directors because they are better suited for management.  ____ ____ ____

53. Prior job experience counts more than education in getting journalism-related work.  ____ ____ ____

54. I would encourage my son (if I had one) to study journalism in college.  ____ ____ ____

55. I would encourage my daughter (if I had one) to study journalism in college.  ____ ____ ____

## PART IV: INTERVIEW

WE WOULD LIKE TO INTERVIEW SOME COLLEGE OF JOURNALISM ALUMNI BY TELEPHONE IN ORDER TO GET MORE COMPLETE INFORMATION ABOUT THE KINDS OF ISSUES WE HAVE RAISED IN THIS SURVEY. IF *YOU* WOULD BE WILLING TO HAVE AN INTERVIEWER CALL YOU, PLEASE WRITE YOUR NAME AND TELEPHONE NUMBERS HERE.

Name_____

Telephone_____ (day) _____ (evening) _____

## PART V. DEMOGRAPHIC INFORMATION: PLEASE COMPLETE THE FOLLOWING TO HELP US INTERPRET THE QUESTIONNAIRE.

56. What is your current marital status?

    ____Single    ____Married    ____Formerly married

57. Do you have any children?

    ____None      ____Three
    ____One       ____Four or more
    ____Two

58. What is your age?

    ____20–29     ____50–59
    ____30–39     ____60–69
    ____40–49     ____70+

59. What is your sex?

    ____Male      ____Female

60. To what racial group do you belong?

    ____Asian           ____American Indian
    ____Black           ____Caucasian
    ____Hispanic

61. Are you living in Maryland?

    ____Yes             ____No (Specify state) _____

62. Did you have to leave the state to find employment? (ANSWER *NO* IF YOU WANTED TO LEAVE THE STATE)

　　____Yes　　　　____No　　　　____I am not employed

63. What was your financial (personal) income last year, before taxes?

　　____I earned no income　　____$25,000-$34,999
　　____Under $4,999　　　　　____$35,000-$44,999
　　____$5,000-$9,999　　　　　____$45,000-$49,999
　　____$10,000-$14,999　　　　____$50,000 or more
　　____$15,000-$24,999

DO YOU HAVE ANY COMMENTS YOU WOULD LIKE TO ADD? (YOU MAY CONTINUE ON A SEPARATE SHEET)

THANK YOU VERY MUCH FOR TAKING TIME TO COMPLETE THIS QUESTIONNAIRE

# JOURNALISM STUDENT QUESTIONNAIRE

Questionnaire _____
Date _____

IN ORDER FOR THE COLLEGE OF JOURNALISM TO EVALUATE ITS CURRICULUM PLEASE COMPLETE THE QUESTIONNAIRE AT THIS TIME. IT WILL ONLY TAKE A FEW MINUTES. THEN MAIL IT TODAY IN THE PRE-PAID ENVELOPE ENCLOSED. *YOUR PARTICIPATION IS VERY IMPORTANT.* ALL ANSWERS ARE CONFIDENTIAL.

**PART I: EDUCATION**

THE FOLLOWING QUESTIONS CONCERN YOUR EDUCATIONAL HISTORY. MARK ONE ANSWER FOR EACH.

1. Did you attend any college and earn nine credits before entering the University of Maryland?
    ____Yes          ____No

2. If yes, how many credits had you earned when you transferred?
    ____I did not transfer    ____58–89 credits
    ____9–28 credits          ____90+ credits
    ____29–55 credits

3. How important was each of the following in choosing the University of Maryland rather than another college or university? Indicate whether each was extremely important, moderately important, somewhat important, or not at all important to you.

    |   | Extremely Important | Moderately Important | Somewhat Important | Not at all Important |
    |---|---|---|---|---|
    | a. Location | ____ | ____ | ____ | ____ |
    | b. Reputation of journalism program | ____ | ____ | ____ | ____ |
    | c. Cost of tuition/board | ____ | ____ | ____ | ____ |
    | d. Availability of financial aid | ____ | ____ | ____ | ____ |
    | e. Entrance requirements | ____ | ____ | ____ | ____ |
    | f. Recommendation of friends/peers | ____ | ____ | ____ | ____ |
    | g. Recommendation of alumni | ____ | ____ | ____ | ____ |
    | h. Recommendation of parents/relatives | ____ | ____ | ____ | ____ |
    | i. Recommendation of teacher/counselor | ____ | ____ | ____ | ____ |

4. As an undergraduate, what was your sequence within the journalism area?
    ____Advertising          ____Photojournalism
    ____Broadcast News       ____Public Relations
    ____Magazine             ____Science Communication
    ____News-Editorial       ____Other (Specify)_____

5. Did you ever have a major other than journalism? If so, what was it?
   \_\_\_\_No            \_\_\_\_Yes (Specify)_____   $\overline{21}\ \overline{22}$

6. How important was each of the following in influencing your decision to study journalism?

   |   | Extremely Important | Moderately Important | Somewhat Important | Not at all Important |   |
   |---|---|---|---|---|---|
   | a. Promise of money | \_\_\_\_ | \_\_\_\_ | \_\_\_\_ | \_\_\_\_ | $\overline{23}$ |
   | b. Promise of prestige | \_\_\_\_ | \_\_\_\_ | \_\_\_\_ | \_\_\_\_ | $\overline{24}$ |
   | c. Creative opportunity | \_\_\_\_ | \_\_\_\_ | \_\_\_\_ | \_\_\_\_ | $\overline{25}$ |
   | d. Value of job to society | \_\_\_\_ | \_\_\_\_ | \_\_\_\_ | \_\_\_\_ | $\overline{26}$ |
   | e. Seemed like easiest major | \_\_\_\_ | \_\_\_\_ | \_\_\_\_ | \_\_\_\_ | $\overline{27}$ |
   | f. Communication professional suggested it | \_\_\_\_ | \_\_\_\_ | \_\_\_\_ | \_\_\_\_ | $\overline{28}$ |
   | g. Peers/friends suggested it | \_\_\_\_ | \_\_\_\_ | \_\_\_\_ | \_\_\_\_ | $\overline{29}$ |
   | h. Parents/relatives suggested it | \_\_\_\_ | \_\_\_\_ | \_\_\_\_ | \_\_\_\_ | $\overline{30}$ |
   | i. Teachers/counselors suggested it | \_\_\_\_ | \_\_\_\_ | \_\_\_\_ | \_\_\_\_ | $\overline{31}$ |
   | j. Like to meet people | \_\_\_\_ | \_\_\_\_ | \_\_\_\_ | \_\_\_\_ | $\overline{32}$ |
   | k. Like to write | \_\_\_\_ | \_\_\_\_ | \_\_\_\_ | \_\_\_\_ | $\overline{33}$ |
   | l. Reputation of journalism program | \_\_\_\_ | \_\_\_\_ | \_\_\_\_ | \_\_\_\_ | $\overline{34}$ |

7. What was the most important *minor* field of study in which you earned 12 or more advanced credits? Mark one.

   \_\_\_\_Business, management, accounting
   \_\_\_\_Government
   \_\_\_\_History
   \_\_\_\_English
   \_\_\_\_Physical or biological Science
   \_\_\_\_Engineering or computer science
   \_\_\_\_Mathematics
   \_\_\_\_Psychology
   \_\_\_\_Sociology
   \_\_\_\_Foreign language
   \_\_\_\_Other (Specify)_____
   \_\_\_\_None                                  $\overline{35}\ \overline{36}$

8. Were you involved in any of the following campus organizations as an undergraduate?

   \_\_\_\_Diamondback
   \_\_\_\_Argus
   \_\_\_\_Hakoach (Mitzpeh)
   \_\_\_\_Calvert
   \_\_\_\_Black Explosion
   \_\_\_\_Wheeler Times
   \_\_\_\_WMUC
   \_\_\_\_SDX/SPJ
   \_\_\_\_Ad Club
   \_\_\_\_PRSSA
   \_\_\_\_Other journalism activity, excluding internships/employment   $\overline{37}\ \overline{38}$
   \_\_\_\_None

9. Have you participated in a journalism-related internship or have you been employed in a journalism-related job while attending the University of Maryland?
   \_\_\_\_Yes            \_\_\_\_No                          $\overline{39}$

10. Thinking of your own journalism classroom experiences, have you detected any way in which students were treated differently:
    a. On the basis of sex?      \_\_\_\_Yes      \_\_\_\_No      $\overline{40}$
    b. On the basis of age?      \_\_\_\_Yes      \_\_\_\_No      $\overline{41}$
    c. On the basis of race?     \_\_\_\_Yes      \_\_\_\_No      $\overline{42}$

11. Have you had a career or life goal while in college? IF YOU HAD NO CAREER/LIFE GOAL, SKIP TO 15.

    ____Yes            ____No
    
    If you answered Yes, what was it?_____
    
    _____
    
    $\overline{43}$
    
    $\overline{44}$ $\overline{45}$

12. Was there one person who influenced you in choosing your career/life goal? IF NOT, SKIP TO 15.

    ____Yes            ____No
    
    $\overline{47}$

13. Was this person one of the following?

    ____Parent or relative          ____Communication professional
    ____High school teacher/        ____Peer your age
         counselor                  ____Other adult (Specify)
    ____College professor/counselor  _____
    ____Business professional
    
    $\overline{48}$ $\overline{49}$

14. If one person influenced you, was this person male or female?

    ____Male           ____Female
    
    $\overline{50}$

15. As you look back on your undergraduate education, how would you rate your overall experience with the College of Journalism?

    ____Extremely good    ____Somewhat good
    ____Very good         ____Not at all good
    
    Please explain:_____
    
    _____
    
    $\overline{51}$
    
    $\overline{52}$ $\overline{53}$ $\overline{54}$

16. If you could do it over, would you major in journalism or in some other field?

    ____Journalism        ____Other field (Specify)_____
    
    Please Explain:_____
    
    _____
    
    $\overline{55}$
    
    $\overline{56}$ $\overline{57}$
    
    $\overline{58}$ $\overline{59}$ $\overline{60}$

17. If you could do it over, what learning experience would you now seek to prepare yourself for your preferred career/life goal? Name the goal and indicate appropriate courses.

    ____The same          ____Other
    
    Specify:_____
    
    _____
    
    $\overline{61}$
    
    $\overline{62}$ $\overline{63}$ $\overline{64}$

18. What learning experiences should be included in our program that you didn't receive?

    Specify:_____
    
    _____
    
    $\overline{65}$ $\overline{66}$ $\overline{67}$

19. Do you plan to go to graduate school after graduation? If yes, what area?

    $\overline{68}$
    
    ____No             ____Yes (Specify)_____
    
    $\overline{69}$ $\overline{70}$ $\overline{71}$

**PART II. CAREER PLANS**

THE FOLLOWING QUESTIONS CONCERN YOUR CAREER PLANS. MARK ONE ANSWER FOR EACH.

20. After your graduation, do you plan to work full-time or part-time (less than 20 hours) and earn an income?

    ____Full-time     ____I will not seek employment
    ____Part-time                                              $\overline{72}$

IF YOU DO NOT PLAN TO SEEK EMPLOYMENT, PLEASE SKIP THIS SECTION AND COMPLETE PART III.

21. For what type of firm or agency do you hope to work?

    ____Corporation              ____Advertising firm
    ____Financial institution    ____Daily newspaper
    ____Medical institution      ____Weekly/monthly newspaper
    ____Educational institution  ____Radio/t.v. (news)
    ____P.R. or communication    ____Radio/t.v. (production)
        consulting firm          ____News services
    ____Government (federal)     ____Magazine/newsletter (other than
    ____Government (state, local)    public relations)
    ____Non-profit association   ____Other (Specify)_____
                                                              $\overline{73}\ \overline{74}$

22. For how large a firm or agency do you hope to work?

    ____1-10          ____51-150
    ____11-25         ____151-300
    ____26-50         ____301-500
                      ____More than 500                        $\overline{75}$

23. Different people want different things from their jobs. How important is each of the following to you in deciding whether a job is satisfying?   $\frac{2}{1}$

|  | Extremely Important | Moderately Important | Somewhat Important | Not at all Important |  |
|---|---|---|---|---|---|
| a. Creative opportunity | ____ | ____ | ____ | ____ | $\overline{2}\ \overline{3}\ \overline{4}$ |
| b. Freedom/autonomy | ____ | ____ | ____ | ____ | $\overline{5}$ |
| c. Adequate salary | ____ | ____ | ____ | ____ | $\overline{6}$ |
| d. Career advancement | ____ | ____ | ____ | ____ | $\overline{7}$ |
| e. Managerical responsibility | ____ | ____ | ____ | ____ | $\overline{8}$ |
| f. Job security | ____ | ____ | ____ | ____ | $\overline{9}$ |
| g. Recognition of colleagues | ____ | ____ | ____ | ____ | $\overline{10}$ |
| h. Prestige | ____ | ____ | ____ | ____ | $\overline{11}$ |
| i. Potential for promotion | ____ | ____ | ____ | ____ | $\overline{12}$ |
| j. Value of job to society | ____ | ____ | ____ | ____ | $\overline{13}$ |
| k. Opportunity to apply specialized skills | ____ | ____ | ____ | ____ | $\overline{14}$ |
| l. Recognition of superiors in organization | ____ | ____ | ____ | ____ | $\overline{15}$ |
|  |  |  |  |  | $\overline{16}$ |

24. How important do you consider membership in professional organizations for your career advancement?

    ____Extremely important    ____Somewhat important
    ____Moderately important   ____Not at all important         $\overline{17}$

25. Are you more interested in being a staff member or a staff director of an organization?
    ____Staff member          ____Staff director
                                                                    $\overline{18}$

26. At some time in the future, do you expect your employment to be interrupted for any of the following reasons?
    ____Military service      ____Additional education
    ____Childbearing          ____Other (Specify)_____
    ____Family responsibilities                            $\overline{19}$ $\overline{20}$

27. Do you expect to change careers at any point in your working life?
    ____Yes                   ____No
                                                                    $\overline{21}$
    If you answered yes, please explain:_____
                                                              $\overline{22}$ $\overline{23}$

28. If you expect a career change, will you work in a journalism-related field?
    ____I plan a career change and it *will* be in a journalism-related field.
    ____I plan a career change and it *will not* be in a journalism-related field.
    ____I do not plan a career change.
                                                                    $\overline{24}$

29. If your career develops as you hope, what will your job title be before you retire.
    (Title)_____
                                                        $\overline{25}$ $\overline{26}$ $\overline{27}$

**PART III. BASED ON YOUR PERSONAL EXPERIENCE OR OBSERVATION, DO YOU *AGREE* OR *DISAGREE* WITH EACH OF THE FOLLOWING STATEMENTS?**

|  | Agree | Disagree | No Experience |  |
|---|---|---|---|---|
| 30. Salaries of women doing journalism-related work are generally lower than salaries of men doing comparable work. | ____ | ____ | ____ | $\overline{28}$ |
| 31. Firms or agencies are more likely to hire a woman than a man for a communication staff position (writer, etc.) | ____ | ____ | ____ | $\overline{29}$ |
| 32. Men are promoted more quickly than women in most firms or agencies. | ____ | ____ | ____ | $\overline{30}$ |
| 33. Men are more apt to back down or seek compromises in office conflict situations than women are. | ____ | ____ | ____ | $\overline{31}$ |
| 34. If an equally capable woman and man applied for a job, the woman would probably be hired. | ____ | ____ | ____ | $\overline{32}$ |
| 35. If an equally capable woman and man had applied for a job ten years ago, the man would probably have been hired. | ____ | ____ | ____ | $\overline{33}$ |
| 36. The way to get into management-level positions is to earn a post-graduate degree. | ____ | ____ | ____ | $\overline{34}$ |
| 37. Women are often hired as a result of affirmative action policies. | ____ | ____ | ____ | $\overline{35}$ |

38. Men are more assertive than women in defining proposals and winning consent for decisions affecting the firm or agency.  ___  ___  ___  $\overline{36}$

39. More men than women are hired as communication staff directors because they are better suited for management.  ___  ___  ___  $\overline{37}$

40. Prior job experience counts more than education in getting journalism-related work.  ___  ___  ___  $\overline{38}$

41. I would encourage my son (if I had one) to study journalism in college.  ___  ___  ___  $\overline{39}$

42. I would encourage my daughter (if I had one) to study journalism in college.  ___  ___  ___  $\overline{40}$

**PART IV. DEMOGRAPHIC INFORMATION:** PLEASE COMPLETE THE FOLLOWING TO HELP US INTERPRET THE QUESTIONNAIRE.

43. What is your current marital status?

   ___Single   ___Married   ___Formerly married   $\overline{41}$

44. Do you have any children?

   ___None   ___Three
   ___One   ___Four or more
   ___Two   $\overline{42}$

45. What is your age?

   ___20–29   ___50–59
   ___30–39   ___60–69
   ___40–49   ___70+   $\overline{43}$

46. What is your sex?

   ___Male   ___Female   $\overline{44}$

47. To what racial group do you belong?

   ___Asian   ___American Indian
   ___Black   ___Caucasian
   ___Hispanic

   $\overline{45}$

61. Are you a resident of Maryland?

   ___Yes   ___No (Specify state)   $\overline{46}$ $\overline{47}$
   _____

49. Do you hope to work in Maryland in the future?

   ___Yes   ___No   $\overline{48}$

DO YOU HAVE ANY COMMENTS YOU WOULD LIKE TO ADD? (YOU MAY CONTINUE ON A SEPARATE SHEET)

THANK YOU VERY MUCH FOR TAKING TIME TO COMPLETE THIS QUESTIONNAIRE

$\overline{49}$ $\overline{50}$ $\overline{51}$

# JOURNALISM EMPLOYER QUESTIONNAIRE

Questionnaire _____

Date _____

IN ORDER FOR THE COLLEGE OF JOURNALISM AT THE UNIVERSITY OF MARYLAND TO EVALUATE ITS CURRICULUM AND TO LEARN MORE ABOUT HOW ITS GRADUATES FARE IN THE WORKPLACE, WE ASK YOU TO COMPLETE THE FOLLOWING QUESTIONNAIRE. IT WILL ONLY TAKE A FEW MINUTES. THEN MAIL IT TODAY IN THE ENCLOSED PRE-PAID ENVELOPE. ALL ANSWERS ARE CONFIDENTIAL. *YOUR PARTICIPATION IS IMPORTANT!*

**PART I: THE WORKPLACE**

1. With what type of firm or agency are you working?
   ___Corporation
   ___Financial institution
   ___Medical institution
   ___Educational institution
   ___P.R. or communication consulting firm
   ___Government (federal)
   ___Government (state, local)
   ___Non-profit association
   ___Daily newspaper
   ___Weekly/monthly newspaper
   ___Radio/t.v. (news)
   ___Radio/t.v. (production)
   ___News services
   ___Magazine/newsletter (other than public relations)
   ___Other (Specify)_____

2. Approximately how many people doing communications or journalism-related work are now employed by your firm or agency?
   ___(Specify number)

3. How many of these are women?
   ___(Specify number)

4. If you know, approximately how many of your communications or journalism-related employees are graduates of the College of Journalism at the University of Maryland?
   ___(Specify number) ___None ___Don't know

5. If you employ graduates of the College of Journalism at the University of Maryland, how many of them are women?
   ___(Specify number) ___No University of Maryland
   ___None ___Don't know    Journalism graduates employed.

6. In the past five years, approximately how many graduates of the College of Journalism at the University of Maryland have you interviewed for communications/journalism-related positions in your firm or agency?
   ___(Specify number) ___Don't know
   ___None ___Haven't interviewed any University of Maryland College of Journalism graduates

7. In the past five years, approximately what percentage of males and females have you interviewed for communications/journalism-related positions in your firm or agency?

   MALE/FEMALE
   ___10/90 percent
   ___20/80 percent
   ___30/70 percent
   ___40/60 percent
   ___50/50 percent

   MALE/FEMALE
   ___60/40 percent
   ___70/30 percent
   ___80/20 percent
   ___90/10 percent
   ___100/0 percent

   $\overline{26}$ $\overline{27}$

8. Which college majors do you consider most useful for communications/journalism-related staff or management positions in your firms or agency? Check all that you consider particularly useful.

   ___Business, management, accounting
   ___Government
   ___History
   ___English
   ___Physical or biological Science
   ___Journalism
   ___Engineering or computer science
   ___Mathematics
   ___Sociology
   ___Psychology
   ___Foreign language
   ___Other (Specify)_____

   $\overline{28}$ $\overline{29}$

9. Considering the needs of your firm or agency, which of the following minor fields do you consider especially useful for journalism graduates? Check all that you consider especially useful.

   ___Business, management, accounting
   ___Government
   ___History
   ___English
   ___Physical or biological Science
   ___Engineering or computer science
   ___Mathematics
   ___Sociology
   ___Psychology
   ___Foreign language
   ___Other (Specify)_____

   $\overline{30}$ $\overline{31}$

10. Please indicate how important you consider each of the following in evaluating applicants for entry-level positions:

    |   | Very Impt. | Somewhat Impt. | Neither | Somewhat Unimpt. | Unimpt. |   |
    |---|---|---|---|---|---|---|
    | a. Personal interview | ___ | ___ | ___ | ___ | ___ | $\overline{32}$ |
    | b. Clip book/tapes | ___ | ___ | ___ | ___ | ___ | $\overline{33}$ |
    | c. Letter of recommendation | ___ | ___ | ___ | ___ | ___ | $\overline{34}$ |
    | d. Quality of resume | ___ | ___ | ___ | ___ | ___ | $\overline{35}$ |
    | e. Academic record | ___ | ___ | ___ | ___ | ___ | $\overline{36}$ |
    | f. Extracurricular activities | ___ | ___ | ___ | ___ | ___ | $\overline{37}$ |
    | g. Pre-employment test | ___ | ___ | ___ | ___ | ___ | $\overline{38}$ |
    | h. Professional contacts | ___ | ___ | ___ | ___ | ___ | $\overline{39}$ |
    | i. Personal or family contacts | ___ | ___ | ___ | ___ | ___ | $\overline{40}$ |
    | j. Other (Specify) _____ | ___ | ___ | ___ | ___ | ___ | $\overline{41}$ |

11. If you employ graduates of the University of Maryland College of Journalism and are familiar with their skills, please answer questions *11 and 12* for those graduates only. If you do not employ University of Maryland College of Journalism graduates, please answer questions *11 and 12* for journalism graduates in general. MARK THE APPROPRIATE BOX BELOW:

____I am answering Questions 11 and 12 for University of Maryland College of Journalism graduates specifically.

____I am answering Questions 11 and 12 for journalism graduates in general.

$\overline{43}$

12. How would you rate College of Journalism graduates (or journalism graduates in general) in the following communication skills?

|  | Extremely Good | | Moderately Good | | Not So Good | | Not At All Good | | |
|---|---|---|---|---|---|---|---|---|---|
|  | Male | Female | Male | Female | Male | Female | Male | Female | |
| Writing | ___ | ___ | ___ | ___ | ___ | ___ | ___ | ___ | $\overline{44}\ \overline{45}$ |
| Editing | ___ | ___ | ___ | ___ | ___ | ___ | ___ | ___ | $\overline{46}\ \overline{47}$ |
| Reporting | ___ | ___ | ___ | ___ | ___ | ___ | ___ | ___ | $\overline{48}\ \overline{49}$ |
| Public. Design | ___ | ___ | ___ | ___ | ___ | ___ | ___ | ___ | $\overline{50}\ \overline{51}$ |
| Photography | ___ | ___ | ___ | ___ | ___ | ___ | ___ | ___ | $\overline{52}\ \overline{53}$ |
| Media Relations | ___ | ___ | ___ | ___ | ___ | ___ | ___ | ___ | $\overline{54}\ \overline{55}$ |
| Events Planning | ___ | ___ | ___ | ___ | ___ | ___ | ___ | ___ | $\overline{56}\ \overline{57}$ |
| Speech Writing | ___ | ___ | ___ | ___ | ___ | ___ | ___ | ___ | $\overline{58}\ \overline{59}$ |
| Sales | ___ | ___ | ___ | ___ | ___ | ___ | ___ | ___ | $\overline{60}\ \overline{61}$ |
| Audio-Visual Production | ___ | ___ | ___ | ___ | ___ | ___ | ___ | ___ | $\overline{62}\ \overline{63}$ |
| Other (Specify) _____ | ___ | ___ | ___ | ___ | ___ | ___ | ___ | ___ | $\overline{64}\ \overline{65}$ |

13. How would College of Journalism graduates (or journalism graduates in general) compare in the following areas with non-journalism graduates you have hired?

|  | Extremely Well | | Moderately Well | | Not So Well | | Not At All Well | | |
|---|---|---|---|---|---|---|---|---|---|
|  | Male | Female | Male | Female | Male | Female | Male | Female | |
| Initiative | ___ | ___ | ___ | ___ | ___ | ___ | ___ | ___ | $\overline{66}\ \overline{67}$ |
| Creativity | ___ | ___ | ___ | ___ | ___ | ___ | ___ | ___ | $\overline{68}\ \overline{69}$ |
| Flexibility | ___ | ___ | ___ | ___ | ___ | ___ | ___ | ___ | $\overline{70}\ \overline{71}$ |
| Problem-solving | ___ | ___ | ___ | ___ | ___ | ___ | ___ | ___ | $\overline{72}\ \overline{73}$ |
| Responsibility | ___ | ___ | ___ | ___ | ___ | ___ | ___ | ___ | $\overline{74}\ \overline{75}$ |
| Work Ethics | ___ | ___ | ___ | ___ | ___ | ___ | ___ | ___ | $\overline{76}\ \overline{77}$ |

14. In your experience of hiring and supervising our graduates do you see anything that we should be teaching them—or teaching them better—than we are now? Anything that would help them be better employees for you?

____Yes (please specify)_____

_____

_____

$\overline{78}\ \overline{79}$

____No suggestions for improvement.

____No experience supervising College of Journalism graduates

**PART II. DO YOU *AGREE* OR *DISAGREE* WITH EACH OF THE FOLLOWING STATEMENTS?**

$\frac{2}{1}$

|  | Agree | Disagree | No Experience |  |
|---|---|---|---|---|
| 14. Salaries of women doing journalism-related work are generally lower than salaries of men doing comparable work. | ___ | ___ | ___ | $\overline{2}$ |
| 15. Firms or agencies are more likely to hire a woman than a man for a communication staff position (writer, etc.) | ___ | ___ | ___ | $\overline{3}$ |
| 16. Men are promoted more quickly than women in most firms or agencies. | ___ | ___ | ___ | $\overline{4}$ |
| 17. Men are more apt to back down or seek compromises in office conflict situations than women are. | ___ | ___ | ___ | $\overline{5}$ |
| 18. If an equally capable woman and man applied for a job, the woman would probably be hired. | ___ | ___ | ___ | $\overline{6}$ |
| 19. If an equally capable woman and man had applied for a job ten years ago, the man would probably have been hired. | ___ | ___ | ___ | $\overline{7}$ |
| 20. The way to get into management-level positions is to earn a post-graduate degree. | ___ | ___ | ___ | $\overline{8}$ |
| 21. Women are often hired as a result of affirmative action policies. | ___ | ___ | ___ | $\overline{9}$ |
| 22. Men are more assertive than women in defining proposals and winning consent for decisions affecting the firm or agency. | ___ | ___ | ___ | $\overline{10}$ |
| 23. More men than women are hired as communication staff directors because they are better suited for management. | ___ | ___ | ___ | $\overline{11}$ |
| 24. Prior job experience counts more than education in getting journalism-related work. | ___ | ___ | ___ | $\overline{12}$ |
| 25. I would encourage my son (if I had one) to study journalism in college. | ___ | ___ | ___ | $\overline{13}$ |
| 26. I would encourage my daughter (if I had one) to study journalism in college. | ___ | ___ | ___ | $\overline{14}$ |

**PART III: INTERVIEW**

WE WOULD LIKE TO INTERVIEW SOME EMPLOYERS IN ORDER TO GET MORE COMPLETE INFORMATION ABOUT THE KINDS OF ISSUES WE HAVE RAISED IN THIS SURVEY. IF *YOU* WOULD BE WILLING TO HAVE A FACULTY MEMBER CALL YOU, PLEASE WRITE YOUR NAME AND TELEPHONE NUMBERS HERE.

Name_____

Company Name_____

Telephone_____ (day) _____ (evening) _____

Best time to call_____

**PART IV. DEMOGRAPHIC INFORMATION**

27. What is your age?
    ____20–29          ____50–59
    ____30–39          ____60–69
    ____40–59          ____70+
                                                    $\overline{15}$
28. What is your sex?
    ____Male           ____Female
                                                    $\overline{16}$
29. To what racial group do you belong?
    ____Asian          ____American Indian
    ____Black          ____Caucasian
    ____Hispanic
                                                    $\overline{17}$
30. What is your job title?
    ____Editor or Managing Editor  ____Educator
    ____President or CEO           ____Officer
    ____Director of Personnel      ____Photographer
    ____News Director              ____Graphic Artist/Designer
    ____Account Executive          ____Specialist
    ____Director                   ____Coordinator
    ____General Manager            ____Editorial Assistant
    ____Supervisor                 ____Other (Specify)_____
    ____Manager
                                                    $\overline{18}$ $\overline{19}$
31. What is the total number of employees in your firm or agency?
    ____(Specify approximate number)
                                          $\overline{20}$ $\overline{21}$ $\overline{22}$ $\overline{23}$
32. What is the highest level of schooling you have completed?
    ____High School Graduate    ____Postgraduate Degree
    ____College Graduate        ____Professional Certification
    ____Postgraduate work           (APR, ABC, CAE, etc.)
                                                    $\overline{24}$
33. Is your firm or agency in Maryland or out of state?
    ____Maryland       ____Out of State
                                                    $\overline{25}$
34. What is the average weekly salary for entry-level employees in your firm or organization?
    ____$125–$150     ____$250–$275
    ____$151–$175     ____$276–$300
    ____$175–$200     ____More than $300
    ____$201–$225
    ____$226–$250
                                                    $\overline{26}$

# Selected Bibliography

# Selected Bibliography

## Books and Published Reports

American Society of Newspaper Editors. *Newsroom Management Handbook*. Washington, DC.: ASNE Foundation, 1985.

Baker, Richard T. *A History of the Graduate School of Journalism, Columbia University*. New York: Columbia University Press, 1954.

Beasley, Maurine H., ed. *The White House Press Conferences of Eleanor Roosevelt* . New York: Garland, 1983.

_____ and Sheila Gibbons. *Women in Media: A Documentary Sourcebook*. Washington, D.C.: Women's Institute for Freedom of the Press, 1977.

Boughner, Genevieve Jackson. *Women In Journalism: A Guide to the Opportunities and a Manual of the Technique of Women's Work for Newspapers and Magazines*. New York: D. Appleton & Co., 1926.

Brazelton, Ethel M. Colson. *Writing and Editing for Women: A Bird's Eye View of the Widening Opportunities for Women in Newspaper, Magazine & Other Writing Work*. New York: Funk & Wagnalls, 1927.

Chafe, William H. *The American Woman: Her Changing Social, Economic, and Political Roles, 1920–1970*. New York: Oxford, 1972.

Clayton, Charles C. *Fifty Years for Freedom 1908-1959: The Story of Sigma Delta Chi's Service to American Journalism*. Carbondale Ill.: Southern Illinois University Press, 1959.

Deckard, Barbara Sinclair. *The Women's Movement: Political, Socioeconomic and Psychological Issues*. New York: Harper & Row, 1983.

Densmore, Dana, ed. *Syllabus Sourcebook on Media and Women*. Washington, D.C.: Women's Institute for Freedom of the Press, 1980.

Epstein, Laurily Keir, ed. *Women and the News*. New York: Hastings House, 1978.

Gelfman, Judith. *Women in Television News*. New York: Columbia University Press, 1976.

Hartmann, Susan M. *The Home Front and Beyond: American Women in the 1940s*. Boston: Twayne, 1982.

Hudson, Frederic. *Journalism in America*. New York: Harper, 1873.

International Association of Business Communicators. *Profile '79* and *Profile '83: A Survey of Business Communications and Business Communicators.* Syracuse, N.Y.: Syracuse University, 1979, 1983.

Logie, Iona Robertson. *Careers for Women in Journalism: A Composite Picture of 881 Salaried Women Writers at Work in Journalism, Advertising, Publicity and Promotion.* Scranton, Pa.: International Textbook Co., 1938.

Marzolf, Marion. *Up From the Footnote: A History of Women Journalists.* New York: Hasting House, 1977.

Matthaei, Julie A. *An Economic History of Women in America: Women's Work, the Sexual Division of Labor, and the Development of Capitalism.* New York: Schocken, 1982.

"New Directions for News." Washington, D.C.: Women Studies Program and Policy Center, George Washington University, 1983.

O'Dell, De Forest. *The History of Journalism Education in the United States.* New York: Columbia University Teachers College, 1935.

Porter, Philip W. and Norval N. Luxon. *The Reporter and the News.* New York: D. Appleton-Century Co., 1935.

Project on the Status and Education of Women. "The Classroom Climate: A Chilly One for Women?" Washington, D.C.: Association of American Colleges, 1982.

Report on 1983 Conference for Professional Support of Journalism Education. Reston, Va.: American Newspaper Publishers Association Foundation, 1983.

Ross, Ishbel. *Ladies of the Press.* New York: Harper's, 1936.

Scherman, William H. *How to Get the Right Job in Publishing.* Chicago: Contemporary, 1983.

Shuler, Marjorie, Ruth A. Knight and Muriel Fuller. *Lady Editor.* New York: Dutton, 1941.

Smith, Ralph E., ed. *The Subtle Revolution.* Washington, D.C.: Urban Institute, 1979.

Sutton, Albert A. *Education for Journalism in the United States From Its Beginning to 1940.* Evanston, Ill: Northwestern University, 1945.

"The Wage Gap: Myths and Facts." Washington, D.C.: National Committee on Pay Equity, 1983.

Ware, Susan. *Holding Their Own: American Women In the 1930s.* Boston: Twayne, 1982.

Williams, Sara Lockwood. *Twenty Year of Education for Journalism.* Columbia, Mo: Stephens Publishing Co., 1929.

_____, ed. "Written by Students in Journalism: Selected Articles Written by Students in the School of Journalism, University of

Missouri as a Part of Their Class Work During 1926–1927." University of Missouri Bulletin No. 26, 1927.

"Women and the Newspaper." University of Missouri Bulletin, Journalism Series No. 30, 1924.

## Periodicals

Allen, Betty Conrad. "Queen Smith, Dean of Society Editors," *The Matrix* 41 (Oct. Nov. 1955) 4–5.

Amrine, Abbie A. "This Is Our Day," *The Matrix* 27 (Oct. 1941) 15, 19.

Angelo, Betty. "Career: Metropolitan vs. Community Newspaper," *The Matrix* 39 (Oct.–Nov. 1953) 14.

Applegate, Roberta. "Fran Harris: Pioneer Newscaster," *The Matrix* 28 (Aug. 1943) 6–7.

_____ "Women as Journalism Educators," *The Matrix* 50 (June 1965) 4–5.

Bagdikian, Ben H. "Woodstein U.: Notes on the Mass Production and Questionable Education of Journalists," *Atlantic* 239 (March 1977) 80–92.

Berkman, Dave. "Student Quality Fall Affects J-Schools," *Journalism Educator* 39 (Winter 1985) 33–37.

Bowers, Thomas A. "Student Attitudes Toward Journalism as a Career," *Journalism Quarterly* 31 (Summer 1974) 265–270.

Bradshaw, James S. "Mrs. Rayne's School of Journalism," *Journalism Quarterly* 60 (Fall 1983) 513–517.

"College Walk." *Columbia* 10 (Nov. 1984) 49.

Covert, Catherine L. "Journalism History and Women's Experience: A Problem in Conceptual Change," *Journalism History* 8 (Spring 1981) 2–6.

Crumley, Wilma, Joye Patterson and Patricia Sailor. "Journalism Career Patterns of Women Are Changing," *Journalism Educator* 31 (Oct. 1977) 50–53, 75.

Daly, Ann. "Journalism Faculty Women," *The Matrix* 58 (Winter 1972–73) 20–21.

"Dr. Carol Oukrop Survey Brings Women's Rape Reporting Concerns Together With Editors' Viewpoints," *Media Report to Women* 12 (Sept.–Oct. 1984), pp. 12–13.

Dorfman, Ron. "The Median Is the Message," *The Quill,* Feb. 1985, pp. 24–26.

Duncan, Charles T. "Again Too Few Graduates to Go Around; Salaries Up," *Journalism Quarterly* 34 (Fall 1957) 493–95.

"Employers' Symposium," *The Matrix* 26 (Oct. 1940) 7–8.

"Enough Women on the Faculty?" *PW* (Press Woman) 46 (Feb. 1983) 1.

Fedler, Fred and Philip Taylor. "Two-Year Analysis Discloses Effects and Problems of Required Grammar Tests," *Journalism Educator* 37 (Summer 1982) 20–22, 56.

Frank, Stanley and Paul Sann. "Paper Dolls," *Saturday Evening Post,* May 20, 1944, pp. 20, 93–96.

Genovese, Margaret. "J-Schools Try to Keep Up With Change," *Presstime,* Sept. 1980, pp. 4–8.

Green, Laura. "Job Market for J-Grads Stable," *The Quill,* Feb. 1985, pp. 8–11.

Grunig, James E. "Hard Thinking on Education," *Public Relations Journal,* April 1985, p. 30.

Harvey, Ken and Ronald E. Smith. "News Execs Urge Major Overhaul of Journalism Training Program," *Editor & Publisher,* March 6, 1982, pp. 10, 30.

Hage, Jerald and Michael Aiken. "Relationship of Centralization to Other Organizational Properties," *Administrative Science Quarterly* 12 (1967) 72–92.

Hecker, Anne. "WICI Survives the Challengers of Time," *Pro/Comm* 4 (April 1984) 2, 6.

Hyde, Grant M. "The Next Steps in Schools of Journalism," *Journalism Quarterly* 14 (Winter 1937) 35–41.

"J-Schools Continue to Grow," *The Matrix* 53 (Feb. 1968) 8.

Johnson, Mrs. Lyndon B. "Woman's Tomorrow Is Here," *The Matrix* 50 (April 1965) 3.

Jones, Adelaide H. "Women Journalism Graduates in the 1941–51 Decade," *Journalism Quarterly* 30 (Winter 1953) 49–50.

Jones, Rosamond Risser. "The Campus Beat," *The Matrix* 29 (April 1944) 16.

_____ "The Campus Beat," *The Matrix* 31 (Feb. 1946) 30.

"Journalism Faculties—Where Do We Stand," *The Matrix* 58 (Fall 1972) 20–21.

Jurney, Dorothy, "Percentage of Women Editors Creeps Upward to 11.7—But Other Fields Continue to Progress Faster," *ASNE Bulletin,* Jan. 1986, pp. 8–9.

Keyserling, Mary D. "Women Journalists and Today's World," *The Matrix* 50 (April 1965) 4–5, 12.

Kleinhenz, L.E.R. "'30' to Thirty Years," *The Matrix* 30 (Aug. 1945) 9.

Lantz, Helen Ross. "Seven Sisters With Vision," *The Matrix* 29 (Aug. 1944) 5–6, 13.

Lewin, Ellen and Joseph Damrell. "Female Identity and Career Pathways," *Sociology of Work and Occupations* 5 (Feb. 1978) 31–54.

McLaughlin, Steven D. "Sex Differences in the Determinants of Occupational Status," *Sociology of Work and Occupations* 5 (Feb. 1978) 5–30.

Marzolf, Marion, Ramona R. Rush and Darlene Stern. "The Literature of Women in Journalism," *Journalism History* I (Winter 1975–75) 117–128.

"Matrix Final" column, *The Matrix* 28 (Dec. 1942) 3.

Meyer, Josephine Caldwell. "A B C for Jobs," *The Matrix* 25 (Aug. 1940) 10–11.

Murray, J. Edward. "Quality News Versus Junk News," *Nieman Reports,* Summer 1984, pp. 14–19.

Ott, Louise. "Child Care Issue Gains Momentum," *Pro/Comm* 5 (Jan.–Feb. 1985) 1, 10.

Quinn, Doris. "Are We Going for a Discount Price?" *The Matrix* 56 (Summer 1971) 14–15.

Peterson, Paul V. "Enrollment Surges Again, Increases 7 Percent to 70,601," *Journalism Educator* 34 (Jan. 1979), 3.

_____. "J-School Enrollments Reach Record 71,594," *Journalism Educator* 34 (Jan. 1980), 3–9.

_____. "1984 Survey: No Change in Mass Communication Enrollment," *Journalism Educator* 40 (Spring 1985) 3–9.

_____. "Survey Indicates No Change in '83 Journalism Enrollment," *Journalism Educator* 39 (Spring 1984) 3–10.

"Recruiting Young Journalists," *The Matrix* 44 (Sept.–Oct. 1959), 10.

"Recruiting Young People for Communications Careers," *The Matrix* 46 (Sept.–Oct. 1961) 26.

Sherwood, Midge W. "No Such Thing as Part-time Mother," *The Matrix* 39 (Oct. 1951) 9–10.

Smith, Henry Ladd. "The Beauteous Jennie June: Pioneer Woman Journalist," *Journalism Quarterly* 40 (Spring 1963) 160–174.

Smith, Joy. "Field of Promise for Women," *The Matrix* 31 (Feb. 1946) 8, 12.

Sohn, Ardyth B. "Goals and Achievement Orientations of Women Newspaper Managers," *Journalism Quarterly* 61 (Autumn 1984) 600–605.

Stilley, Joy T. "Unathletic Sports Editor," *The Matrix* 30 (Oct. 1944), 3.

Talevich, Tim. "Liberal Arts Tradition Backed at J-Education 'Summit,'" *Presstime,* Feb. 1984, pp 38–39.

Wilensky, Harold J. "The Professionalization of Everyone?" *American Journal of Sociology* 70 (1964) 142–146.

Willett, Millie. "Career Vs. the Home and Family," *The Matrix* 44 (June–July, 1956) 3, 22.

Williams, Sara Lockwood. "The Editor's Rib," *The Matrix* 27 (Dec. 1941 and Feb. 1942) 10, 14.

Wilson, Jean Gaddy. "Are Newswomen Changing the News?" *Ms.,* Dec. 1984, pp. 45–50, 124–128.

Winn, Bernell. "It's Ladies Day," *The Matrix* 28 (April 1943) 6–7.

Wolseley, R.E. "Deadline for Women," *The Matrix* 24 (Feb. 1939) 9–10.

## Newspapers

Donovan, Judy. "Wisconsin Author Recalls Colorful Journalism Career," *Tucson* (Ariz.) *Star,* Jan. 11, 1961, as reported in Marzolf, *Up From the Footnote,* p. 253.

Friendly, Jonathan. "Journalism Educators Debate Strategies, Technology and Ties to the Media," *New York Times,* Jan. 23, 1984, A15.

Langley, Monica. "Office Marriages Win More Firms' Blessings, But Problems Crop Up," *Wall Street Journal,* Oct. 16, 1984, p. A1.

Lupo, Caryl Rivers. "If You Ask Me: Superwoman's a Myth...," as reprinted in *Washington Post,* June 20, 1984, B5.

Mann, Judy Luce. "Choosing the Best College," *Washington Post,* April 10, 1985, p. C3.

_____. "Working," *Washington Post,* June 29, 1983, C1.

Mansfield, Stephanie. "Hittin' It Big & Kissin' It Goodbye: No Kids, No Job: Women at Home Just for Themselves," *Washington Post,* Feb 26, 1985, C1.

Sandler, Bernice R. "The Quiet Revolution on Campus: How Sex Discrimination Has Changed," *Chronicle of Higher Education,* Feb. 29, 1984, p. 72.

Thomas, Barbara. "Parenthood and Career Overtax Rising, Productivity Declining; Loyalty Sometimes Shifts," *Wall Street Journal,* Sept. 7, 1983. Al.

## Manuscript Collections, Unpublished Theses, Papers and Speeches

Carl W. Ackerman papers, Manuscript Division, Library of Congress.

Allen, Donna. Text of speech on "Shifting Priorities in Mass Communication Education." Plenary session, Association for Education in Journalism and Mass Communication convention, Gainesville, Fla., Aug. 8, 1984.

Buck, Elizabeth, Christine L. Ogan and Ramona R. Rush. "Women and the Communications Revolution: Can We Get There From Here?" English translation of paper in *Chasqui,* publication of the Centro Internacional de Estudios Superiores del la Communicacion para America Latina, Quito, Ecuador, July–September, 1982.

Diner, Hasia R. "Service and Scholarship: Seventy-five Years of the School of Social Service Administration of the University of Chicago, 1908-1983." Unpublished paper completed in Dec. 1984.

Dow Jones Newspaper Fund/Gallup Survey. Final tabulation of data on 1983 journalism graduates. Dow Jones Newspaper Fund, Princeton, N.J., 1984.

Dozier, David. M., Sharon Chapo and Brad Sullivan. "Sex and the Bottom Line: Income Differences Among Women and Men in Public Relations." Paper presented to the Public Relations Division, Association for Education in Journalism and Mass Communications convention, Corvallis, Ore., Aug. 7, 1983.

Keeshen, Kathleen K. "Journalism's Pulitzer Penwomen." Paper prepared as part of Ph.D. coursework in American studies, University of Maryland, 1978.

McAdams, Katherine C. "Some Effects of Sex-Role Socialization on Women Entering Journalism Careers." Unpublished master's thesis, University of North Carolina, 1981. Also draft of unpublished follow-up report, June 1984.

Ida Aldrich Minter scrapbook in possession of Maurine H. Beasley, Bethesda, Md.

Rush, Ramona R. "Women in Academe: Journalism Education Viewed From the Literature and Other Memorabilia." Paper presented at the Association for Education in Journalism convention at Ft. Collins, Colo., Aug. 1973.

VanSlyke, Judy K. "Women in Educational Communications: Profile of Case Members, 1982." Paper presented to the Committee on the Status of Women, Association for Education in Journalism convention, Athens, Ohio, July, 1982.

Wood, Janice Ruth. "The Foundation Years of American Journalism Education, 1908–1930." Master's thesis in journalism, University of South Carolina, 1981.

# INDEX

Advice. *See also* Counsel
  for editors' wives, 9
  from male instructors, 17
  in book on careers, 28
  on admitting women, 12
  to women, 7, 9, 16–17, 23–25, 33
Affirmative action
  called for, 40
  women hired, 70, 74, 78
Aggressiveness
  in women, 92
  versus assertiveness, 105–106
Aspirations
  and sexism, 119
  of young women, 124
  women and high, 133–134
Attitude scales. *See* UM survey
Ayers, Bonnie Joe (roundtable), 88, 98, 102, 106

"Barbie dolls," phenomenon 100–101
Barkdull, Clovis (roundtable), 107, 109, 113–114
Beasley, Maurine (roundtable), 87, 89–90, 93, 97–98, 100, 102, 104, 106
Bias. *See also* Discrimination; UM survey
  gender, in education, 54
  sexual, in employment, 69, 77

Career. *See also* UM survey
  and family life, 131
  goal, difficulty articulating, 129
  life goal, 63–64, 72
  interruption, 73, 133
  planning, 54
Carroll, Melanie (roundtable), 107, 109–111, 113, 115
Caudell, Robin (roundtable), 107, 109, 114–115
Census. *See also* U.S. Census
  women editors and reporters, 13, 25
  working women, 17
Cleghorn, Cheree (roundtable), 87, 94, 96, 99, 102, 104
Cleghorn, Reese (roundtable), 87–88, 92, 107, 112–113, 115
Cochrane, Elizabeth. *See* "Nellie Bly"
College, pay off of, 26
Communications era, women in, 136
Counsel for women, 7, 17, 34, 107. *See also* Advice
Course goals, 120

Courses
  for women, 22–25
  in journalism (1893–94), 8
  on media and women, 120–122 (*see also* Schools)
  stereotyping issues added to, 125
  women's studies, 42
Croly, Jane Cunningham. *See* "Jennie June"

Demographics. *See* UM survey
Departments of journalism (1910), 10
Dickman, Sharon (roundtable), 87, 97, 106
Differences. *See also* Discrimination; UM survey
  by age, 65
  by sex, 65, 68
  between employers, 79
  in communication, 106
  in salary, 127
  in selecting news, 121
Discrimination. *See also* Differences; UM survey
  against women, 33
  among male managers, 127
  charged, 41
  classroom, 63, 72, 126
  help women cope with, 42
  illegal, 38
  in defense of, 17
  in 1920s, 14–16
  in pay, 27, 42, 97, 125, 128–130
  sex, 27, 44, 46

Educational history. *See* UM survey
Electronic information, 101–102
  processing, 99
Employment history. *See* UM survey

Family situation, 112–113. *See also* Career Factors
  in getting a job, 64–65, 76
  in job satisfaction, 66
  in study of journalism, 62, 72
Female
  career planning, 54
  fields, 24, 140 (*see also* Occupational segregation; "Pink collar" ghetto)
  labor force (1948), 29–30
  staff, 67
Forbes, Mary Lou (roundtable), 87, 90, 92, 95, 99, 107

Gender. *See also* Bias; Differences; Discrimination;
  bias in education, 54
  differences in the field, 104
Gianfagna, Jean (roundtable), 87, 94–95, 97–98, 100, 107
Greene, Marcia Slacum (roundtable), 87, 91, 93, 102

Hamorsky, Sandra (roundtable), 107–108, 112–114
Harvey, Chris (roundtable), 107, 109–114
Haskin, Lynn M. (roundtable), 87, 93–94, 103–104
Heneberry, Connie (roundtable), 107, 109–110, 112, 114
Hoxie, Carol (roundtable), 107, 109–110, 112–115

Information processing, 99. *See also* Electronic information
Interviewing experience, 102. *See also* Negotiating; Networking

Jackson, Beverly (roundtable), 87, 89, 93, 95, 97, 99–101, 104
"Jennie June," (Jane Cunningham Croly), 7
Jones, Laurie (roundtable), 107, 109, 111, 113–114
Journalism
  academic training proposed, 6
  alumnae quoted (1938), 26 (*see also* Advice)
  courses (1893–94), 8
  enrollment, 42, 47
  history of, 6–11
  majors, 64, 116
  and marriage, 27–28
  professionals, recommendations for, 141–142
  sex stereotyped, 97
  and traditional occupations, 28
Journalism education
  different approach to, 12
  encouraging news for, 134
  established, 8
  few women accepted, 25
  flooding the market, 43
  and gender bias, 54 (*see also* Bias)
  hostile to women, 5
  male dominance in, 38–41
  new directions in, 47
  and prejudice against women, 38–41
  preparation given women, 128
  ramifications of, 88
  remedial education, 117
  suggestions to improve, 77
  vital issues in, 53
  and women, 18, 38, 47
Journalism educators
  fear women, 21
  ignore women's questions, 122
  and labor market, 54
  recommendations for, 124–125, 136
Journalism instruction
  available to women, 12
  established, 8
Journalism school, first, 6–8
Journalism schools
  accept women, 12
  employers displeased with, 116
  not informing students, 102
  recommendations for, 95–96, 104, 118–119
Journalists
  child care and women, 135
  first formal study on women, 39–40
  1938 study on women, 26
  opportunities for women, 28–31

Katz, Tonnie (roundtable), 88, 90, 91–92, 106

Marriage. *See also* Career; Family situation
  and journalism, 27–28
  prime aim in 1950s, 33
Material aimed at women, 7
Monaghan, Nancy (roundtable), 87, 92–93, 101
Mentors. *See* Role models
Musgrave, Carol (roundtable), 87, 91, 93, 100, 105

Negotiating
  to enhance benefits, 98
  journalism schools should teach, 104
  workshops to teach, 114
  women not, 110–111
  re-entry before leaving, 113
"Nellie Bly," (Elizabeth Cochrane), 7
Networking, 99–100, 103, 111
"New majority"
  basic questions about, 87
  implications of the, 141

Occupational segregation, 125–126. *See also* Female fields; "Pink collar" ghetto
Organizations. *See* Professional/student organizations

"Pink collar" ghetto. *See also* Female; Occupational segregation
  journalism may become, 5, 45, 140
  occupations, 98-99
  why should men enter a, 127
Poussaint, Renee (roundtable), 88, 92, 95-96, 99-101, 103, 105, 106, 108
Power and communications, 97, 99-101
Prejudice, 22, 25. *See also* Bias; Discrimination
Professional
  conduct, 106
  organizations, 111
  success, aiding women in, 121
  world, facilitate entrance to, 91-92
Professional/student organizations, 8, 72
  Advertising Club, 7
  American Society of Newspaper Editors, 102
  Association for Education in Journalism, 38-40
  Public Relations Student Society of America, 72
  Sigma Delta Chi (Society of Professional Journalists), 10, 40, 63, 72
  Theta Sigma Phi (Women in Communications), 6, 10, 40, 42
Professions, lower income, 140. *See also* Female; Occupational segregation; "Pink collar" ghetto
Prospects in journalism, 140
Pulitzer, Joseph
  boosts prestige of journalism, 11
  establishes school, 11-12
  and women students, 8

Quota, unspoken system, 103

Rayne, Martha Louise, 6-7
Recruit males into communications, 97, 113
Renshaw, Anne M. (roundtable), 87, 91, 98, 103
Role models
  drew women (1930s), 25
  finding suitable, 119-125
  lack of, 40, 111, 124
  mothers not positive, 108
  needed on faculties, 45, 91, 94
  visible, 134
  for Women in Communications, 103
Roundtable
  excerpts, 88-115
  participants, 87-88
Roosevelt, Eleanor
  helps women, 24
  and press conferences, 25-26

Schools
  first journalism, 6, 8
  with courses on women and the media, 120-121
Sex discrimination. *See* Bias; Discrimination; Prejudice
Sexism and career aspirations, 119
"Sob sisters," 13-14, 117
Socialization, 128-129
Study
  of newspapers (1943), 28
  of women journalists, 26, 39-40, 42
Survey. *See also* UM survey
  American Society of Newspaper Editors, 102
  employment patterns (1984), 45
  enrollment in journalism schools (1948), 33
  enrollments of students (1983), 43
  of graduating classes (1939), 22
  of newspapers (1944), 30
  on sex and salary discrimination, 27-28
  on women, 25-28, 32-33, 40, 43-44, 129-130
  on women journalists (1938), 25-28

Theus, Kathryn (roundtable), 107-110, 113-114
Townsend, Claudia (roundtable), 87, 90, 98
Transition
  from school to work, 90-92
  problem for females, 110

University of Maryland majors, 53
UM (University of Maryland) survey, 53-86
  attitude scales, 69-70, 74-75, 77-78
  demographics, 70-71, 75, 78-79
  discrimination in classroom, 63, 72
  educational history, 61-64, 71-74
  employment history, 64-69
  methodology, 54-55
  organizational history, 75-77
  sexual bias in the workplace, 77-78
  survey details, 60-79
  survey highlights, 55-59
U.S. Census. *See also* Census
  average earnings (1982), 46
  women editors and reporters (1960), 34
  women journalists (1870-90), 7

Variables in study of journalism, 72. *See* Factors

Waters, Karen (roundtable), 107–108, 110, 115
Williams, Cristal (roundtable), 107, 109–110, 113
Women. *See also* Census; Study; U.S. Census
  accepted in journalism schools, 12
  dedicated workers, 129–130
  demoted after war, 30–31
  faculty, 38, 120, 122
  graduates, options for, 22, 24
  journalism teachers, (1920s), 14–16
  in lower ranks, 122
  material aimed at, 7
  more qualified than men, 92
  motherhood and labor force, 88–90
  reporters (early), 7
  and self-esteem, 124 (*see also* Aspirations)
  settle for less, 93–94, 130
  students, not encouraged, 21
  workers, facts on, 132

Women's
  clubs, 7
  colleges, fostered self-confidence, 124
  communication patterns, 130
  issues and news, 121–122
  liberation movement, 34, 38, 41
  studies course, 42
Work ethic, 107
World War I, II
  opportunities for women, 12–13, 28–32, 34
  women demoted after, 30–31
Writing
  ability, 95–96
  acquiring skills, 116–118

PN 4888 .W65 B4 1988

| | DATE DUE | | |
|---|---|---|---|
| JUN 15 1990 | | | |
| | | | |
| | | | |
| | | | |
| | | | |
| | | | |
| | | | |
| | | | |
| | | | |